Teach Living Poets

NCTE Editorial Board

Teach Living Poets

Lindsay Illich
Curry College
Milton, Massachusetts

Melissa Alter Smith
Lake Norman Charter High School
Huntersville, North Carolina

NCTE
National Council of Teachers of English
340 N. Neil St., Suite #104, Champaign, Illinois 61820
www.ncte.org

Staff Editor: Bonny Graham
Interior Design: Jenny Jensen Greenleaf
Cover Design: Pat Mayer
Cover Photo: Melissa Alter Smith

NCTE Stock Number: 52614; eStock Number: 52621
ISBN 978-0-8141-5261-4; eISBN 978-0-8141-5262-1

It is the policy of NCTE in its journals and other publications to provide a forum for the open discussion of ideas concerning the content and the teaching of English and the language arts. Publicity accorded to any particular point of view does not imply endorsement by the Executive Committee, the Board of Directors, or the membership at large, except in announcements of policy, where such endorsement is clearly specified.

NCTE provides equal employment opportunity to all staff members and applicants for employment without regard to race, color, religion, sex, national origin, age, physical, mental or perceived handicap/disability, sexual orientation including gender identity or expression, ancestry, genetic information, marital status, military status, unfavorable discharge from military service, pregnancy, citizenship status, personal appearance, matriculation or political affiliation, or any other protected status under applicable federal, state, and local laws.

Every effort has been made to provide current URLs and email addresses, but, because of the rapidly changing nature of the web, some sites and addresses may no longer be accessible.

Library of Congress Cataloging-in-Publication Data

Names: Illich, Lindsay, 1977- author. | Smith, Melissa Alter, 1980- author.
Title: Teach living poets / Lindsay Illich, Curry College; Melissa Alter Smith, Lake Norman Charter High School.
Description: Champaign : National Council of Teachers of English, 2021 | Includes bibliographical references and index. | Summary: "Opens up the flourishing world of contemporary poetry to secondary teachers, giving advice on discovering new, diverse poets and reading contemporary poetry, as well as sharing sample lessons, writing prompts, and ways to become an engaged member of a professional learning community"—Provided by publisher.
Identifiers: LCCN 2020038154 (print) | LCCN 2020038155 (ebook) | ISBN 9780814152614 (trade paperback) | ISBN 9780814152621 (adobe pdf)
Subjects: LCSH: Poetry, Modern—20th century—Study and teaching (Secondary) | Poetry, Modern—21st century—Study and teaching (Secondary)
Classification: LCC PN1101.I45 2020 (print) | LCC PN1101 (ebook) | DDC 808.1/0712—dc23
LC record available at https://lccn.loc.gov/2020038154
LC ebook record available at https://lccn.loc.gov/2020038155

Accept the place the divine providence has found for you, the society of your contemporaries.
—Ralph Waldo Emerson, "Self-Reliance"

Look at all the diamonds.
—Kaveh Akbar, "Portrait of the Alcoholic Floating in Space with Severed Umbilicus"

Contents

Acknowledgments

First, we would like to thank the poets featured in this book for their double generosity: first for writing poems for the world, and second, for giving us permission to share them in this volume. Special thanks to Kaveh Akbar, whose work profoundly impacts and inspires us. And to Janais Phillips, thank you for sharing your story.

We also would like to thank NCTE, the NCTE Twitter community, and the teachers who have allowed us to share their ideas in this book: Susan Barber, Scott Bayer, Matt Brisbin, Amber Buckley, Ann Cox, Kristin Dreyer, Tricia Ebarvia, Jen Flisinger, Joel Garza, Monet Hardison, Kelly Herrera, Karla Hilliard, Jori Krulder, Nikki Lehman, Angela Massingale, Carrie Mattern, Tia Miller, Adrian Nester, Valerie Person, Noel Poynter, Kristin Runyon, Tolly Salz, Roy Smith, Sarah Soper, Brian Sztabnik, Nicole F. Tong, Melissa Tucker, Donna Vorreyer, and Jay Ward.

Lindsay would like to thank Curry College for its institutional support during this project, especially for the sabbatical in the spring of 2017, during which the original post for the *Literacy & NCTE* blog spurred this book; the Curry College faculty creative writing group: Melissa Anyiwo, Pebble Brooks, Heather Falconer, Dorothy Fleming, Don Gervich, David Miller, Rebecca Paynich, Kara Provost, and Patricia Stevens; mentors, friends, and colleagues: Amanda Crabb, Kristen Getchell, Crystal Goodman, Julie Groesch, Esther Guenat, Jimmie Killingsworth, Tom Martin, Janet McCann, and Nancy Young; my coauthor, Melissa Smith, who agreed to write a book with a stranger and made me a better teacher; my family, who have pulled me into the future: Wilma Lewis, who dared to disturb the universe; my parents, who wouldn't let up; Lauren Brisbin, for being my ever-fixéd mark; Dee and Pop, and our Nebraska crew; and, of course, most of all my dear loves Dobie, Hazel, and Craig, with whom I dwell in possibility.

Melissa would like to thank the educators and poets who support #TeachLivingPoets; the #aplitchat squad, who make me a better teacher—your support and friendship is a gift; RA Villanueva, for his mentorship and generosity; Clint

Smith and José Olivarez; Jamie Lord, for her encouragement and help; coauthor Lindsay Illich, for her guidance and camaraderie through this project; my parents, Don and Carol; my husband, Craig, and my children, Payson and Chase—I love you more than the universe.

Finally, we thank our students, who inspire us daily.

Introduction: Why Teach Living Poets?

Portrait of the Alcoholic Floating in Space with Severed Umbilicus

in Fort Wayne I *drank the seniors*   Old Milwaukee
Old Crow   in Indianapolis I stopped   now I regret
every drink I never took   all around   coffee grounds
and eggshells   this sweating   a mouthful
of lime   as a boy I stole a mint green bra
from a laundromat   I took it home to try on
while my parents slept   filled its cups with the smallest
turnips in our pantry   the underwire grew
into me like a strangler fig   my blood roiled then
as now   back on earth frogspit is dripping
down wild aloe spikes   salmon are bullying
their way upstream   there is a pond I leapt into once
with a lonely blonde boy   when we scampered out one of us
was in love   I could not be held responsible
for desire   he could not be held at all   I wonder
where he is now   if he looked up he might see
me   sparkling   I always hoped that when I died
I would know why   my brother will be so sad   he will tell
his daughter I was better than I was   he will leave out
my crueldrunk nights   the wet mattresses my driving alone
into cornfields unsure whether I'd drive out   I wish
he were here now   he could be here   this cave
is big enough for everyone   look at all the diamonds

—*Kaveh Akbar*

Why teach living poets? Let's begin with Janais's words. Janais, who uses *they/them* pronouns, is reflecting on the experience of having the poet Kaveh Akbar visit their class:

> That poet visit meant everything to me. I got to analyze Kaveh Akbar's poem ["Portrait of an Alcoholic Floating in Space with Severed Umbilicus"] for my poetry project. I spent about a month just looking at the same poem. And I learned so much from it that I didn't think I would be able to learn because when I read it at first, I was like, "Okay, I don't understand this." And then once I started understanding it, it was like something new every single day. I was learning something new about that poem every single day. And even after I presented my project, I was still like, "Oh man, I just figured out something else about this poem that I wished I could've talked about in my presentation.
>
> Kaveh's reading was a spiritual experience in all honesty. The way he read his own poetry was completely raw. Every poem that was supposed to make me uncomfortable did so tenfold in person. Every poem that was as powerful as a punch on paper knocked me out in person. Raw is exactly the word to use here—the entire classroom was laden with emotional vulnerability as soon as he spoke the first word of each poem. This was, without a doubt, the pinnacle of my day. I was sitting in the audience pretty much trying not to cry. Hearing him read my favorite work of art in-person is an invaluable experience.
>
> And finally getting to meet him and talk to him was amazing because, before him, I didn't have a favorite author, and he's my favorite author now. He's created my favorite work of art, and I think that's a really valuable thing. Getting to present the man who made me sort of fall in love with poetry—that is something that I am never ever ever going to forget. Getting to read his poetry and analyze the inner workings of it was a little spot of brightness in this year because it has been hard for me. You know, I haven't really been super happy all year, and his poetry makes me really really happy. I'm immediately in a good mood when I'm reading his poetry. I needed that.
>
> I am signed up for a poetry class in college. My first semester is going to have a poetry class, and I definitely would not have signed up for that if not for reading a ton of poetry in class this year and getting to meet some of my favorite poets. That completely influenced my decision, and I'm really excited to have that experience.

Janais, a junior Honors English student, had been struggling with mental health and the sudden loss of a parent, which they note in their reflection. We start with Janais's words because they amplify what we think is the most compelling reason for teaching the work of living poets: students are moved by the poems written by contemporary poets. Relevant and timely in their subject matter and ways of using words, poems by contemporary poets connect with students and offer new ways of understanding the world, like Akbar's "Portrait of an Alcoholic Floating in Space with Severed Umbilicus," which implores readers to "look at all the diamonds," even when faced with death, as the speaker of the poem was.

Supporting ELA and SEL Outcomes

Aside from the meaningful connections students make with contemporary poems and the powerful ways that students identify with the speakers of these poems, we find that contemporary poems support learning outcomes in the English language arts curriculum. Specifically, the #TeachLivingPoets approach that we have developed supports outcomes related to rhetorical and genre knowledge, the writing process, and social-emotional learning.

When we talk about **rhetorical knowledge**, we're referring to how texts respond to specific contexts, audiences, and purposes. For example, in Akbar's "Portrait of an Alcoholic," the evocations of embodiment, the metaphors of the body, to express experience are similar to rhetorical appeals used by environmental writers when they talk about global warming as the Earth having a fever. In this figuration, we understand the Earth as having a body and global warming as a fever, a symptom of a deeper sickness (in this case, climate change). Appeals to the body are powerful to humans because that's the way we experience the world—through our body's senses—and when it is used as a metaphor, our bodily experience (the poetic vehicle) gets transferred to the thing being explained in terms of the body (the poetic tenor). When Janais analyzed Akbar's poem, for example, they considered the speaker's comparison of the universe all around him as he was dying to a cave with diamonds on the wall, which might be interpreted as stars. In Chapter 2, we go into more detail about embodied metaphors. You can also read more about modern appeals in Killingsworth's *Appeals in Modern Rhetoric: An Ordinary-Language Approach*.

Reading contemporary poetry also builds students' abilities to analyze poems, which leads to **genre knowledge**. Asking questions about the purposes and audiences being addressed in a piece of writing and having the ability to recognize patterns across an array of poems constitutes the kind of textual problem solving that will help students become more critical readers of texts and also better prepared to analyze genres they will be asked to produce in academic settings. In traditional literature courses that include poetry as a genre, analyzing poems is sometimes treated as an issue of identifying literary devices, and while contemporary poems do sometimes employ literary devices such as metaphor or polysyndeton, contemporary poets have also developed a repertoire of *moves*, a word John Swales uses to describe these patterns or textual features, that extend beyond more superficial ideas of literary devices (we discuss the moves of contemporary poems in detail in Chapter 3). As students are introduced to other genres and analyze them in ways they have learned to do with contemporary poems, they are more likely to be able to read with higher levels of comprehension and learn to write in those genres when there is a reason to do so. In other words, when students are introduced to unfamiliar genres, this way of analyzing genre can be transferred to new situations and genres.

Returning to Janais's analysis of "Portrait of the Alcoholic Floating in Space with Severed Umbilicus," their growing genre knowledge helped them understand Akbar's use of caesura, the pauses occurring in the lines of the poem, as the ragged dying breaths of the speaker. Rather than employing conventional punctuation marks or end-stopped lines, Akbar punctuated the poem with caesuras. By comparing what they know about poems from analyzing other poems, Janais was able to determine that the caesura, a structural element, served to emphasize the drama of the dying speaker.

Genre awareness that is fostered by such activities—recognizing textual features and patterns that distinguish different genres particular to specific audiences and purposes for writing—leads to genre knowledge, knowledge that's more likely to transfer across contexts in other writing situations and beyond, ultimately preparing students to meet the demands of college writing (Reiff and Bawarshi).

In addition to rhetorical and genre knowledge, contemporary poems help students understand and practice the **writing process**. Often, contemporary poems and their commentary (e.g., online interviews like the ones on Divedapper or craft criticism by writers on the *Ploughshares* blog and elsewhere) highlight the social aspect of invention in ways that aren't obvious in older texts. Invention, one of the five areas or "departments" of rhetoric defined by Aristotle, addresses how texts come to be, where ideas come from, or what in everyday language we call "inspiration." Often, outside education circles, when people think about where writers get their ideas, they picture the solitary genius writing from his (almost always his) singular vision, a culturally influenced image we've inherited from the Romantic tradition. But writing teachers and scholars recognize that this model not only isn't helpful for student writers, but it also doesn't reflect the reality of writing processes. Ideas spark other ideas. Scholars such as Kristopher M. Lotier who study theories of the mind have described the highly social nature of invention—the writing process—as having more to do with our curatorial function, which, like the work of a museum curator, is our way of sorting or filtering ideas we're getting from what we see, read, watch, and experience. In *this* theory of the writing process, writing starts with finding and selecting, seeing what goes together, and adding to it. For students and teachers, this theory of the writing process, sometimes called "externalized theories of invention," offers a starting point for thinking about where ideas come from, easing the burden of "coming up" with ideas.

We see evidence of externalized theories of invention in poems that show traces of other poems, either explicitly, as in the following example, or in other less obvious borrowings or evocations. For example, let's trace the genealogy of Ocean Vuong's poem "Someday I'll Love Ocean Vuong." The poem's epigraph reads "After Frank O'Hara / After Roger Reeves." It's a poem about family history and what that means for Vuong, and the poem is addressed to himself, a kind of self-talk. Ultimately, it looks forward to a future: "The most beautiful part of your body / is where it's headed." The poem's title is a riff on Roger Reeves's poem "Someday I'll Love Roger Reeves," which is acknowledged in the epigraph, along with the parentage of Reeves's poem, a line from Frank O'Hara's "Katy":

> They say I mope too much
> but really I'm loudly dancing.
> I eat paper. It's good for my bones.
> I play the piano pedal. I dance,
> I am never quiet, I mean silent.
> Some day, I'll love Frank O'Hara.
> I think I'll be alone for a little while.

At the time of this writing, we have identified at least two more iterations of this "family line" of poems: Claire Schwartz's "Someday I'll Love Claire Schwartz" in *Waxwing* and Elaine Olund's "Someday I'll Love (Your Name Here)" at Medium. Sharing the iterations of "Someday I'll Love" with students invites them to write their own versions, prompts discussions of creativity and composing as acts of connection, and encourages an understanding of writing as contributing to ideas—as a social act.

In addition to what contemporary poems offer students in terms of understanding how language works to affect readers and how to employ those techniques in their own writing, studying contemporary poems supports outcomes related to **social-emotional learning (SEL)**. Studies have found that SEL benefits students by raising self-awareness and improving relationships, the ability to make good decisions, and academic performance, such as improved test scores (Payton 3). Reading contemporary poems supports social-emotional learning by helping readers identify emotions, both the poet's in the poem and the reader's emotional response. Those who research emotional intelligence suggest that the recognition of emotion, in ourselves and in others, is often the first step toward strengthening emotional intelligence. When students read words that name their struggles, grief, and stress, they find some relief in the recognition of the emotion and in its expression. If your students are like ours, they probably share with you their troubles and issues. Poetry can be equipment for life, an antidote to stress, or as Wallace Stevens puts it, "the imagination pressing back against the pressure of reality" (36). Sharing words—reading and writing—uniquely helps us cope with the world when it's awful. For instance, Adam Zagajewski's "Try to Praise the Mutilated World" is a poem that asks readers to remember the moments during which we felt the most alive—perhaps with a loved one, being moved by beautiful music, or being immersed in an autumn landscape—even when the world seemed hopeless. This quality of poetry to evoke emotion is felt acutely at times of collective grief and tragedy, like 9/11. In the *New York Times*, reflecting on 9/11 a year after the attack, the writer Mary Karr said, "I probably faxed more copies of poems—and received more faxes from other devoted readers—in the following weeks than I had in years, and with a diverse audience of readers." Lyric poetry offered the relief of connection with other humans.

When students *write* poems, they enjoy the benefits of self-expression, for which they have fewer and fewer opportunities, at least in academic settings. In a national study that analyzed writing assignments across the curriculum, Dan Melzer found that of the 2,101 assignments he collected, only 3 percent were expressive in nature, and less than 1 percent were poetic in purpose (22). Even though Melzer's study was limited to colleges and universities, previous studies have documented that British public schools require fewer writing assignments for expressive purposes as students progress through the system (Britton), with similar findings in US schools in the 1980s (Applebee and Langer). Writing for the self, for a purpose and audience beyond what is sometimes called the "teacher-as-examiner" mode, students can exercise their creativity, process emotion, and give voice to personal experiences.

Expanding the Canon

Author Pankaj Mishra, recognizing the need for a dynamic approach to the literary canon, argues for an expansive approach to the texts we include in our classes: "Our experience of the world grows ever more complex; any syllabus, whether of history or literature, has to engage with that complexity." This approach doesn't mean that we should close the door on the canon, but instead, open it wider to usher more voices into the classroom.

Reflecting the complexity of the world means not only complexity of theme but also the range of voices in the world, which should be reflected in the choices we make about the texts we bring into the classroom. In her blog post "Disrupting Texts as a Restorative Practice," educator Tricia Ebarvia urges teachers to look at our curriculum and the texts we offer to our students and to ask ourselves:

> Are any of these texts absolutely essential, especially ones that continue to reinforce the same voices? And if so, why? Consider the themes or essential questions explored in the curriculum and ask: whose voices, what points-of-view are not reflected in our study? Which voices are marginalized or absent?

By including poems by living poets in the curriculum, we not only hear more voices, but we invite students to see themselves in the texts they read.

This approach doesn't foreclose the use or value of the canon. Reading a poem like Rudy Francisco's "To the Girl Who Works at Starbucks, Down the Street from My House on Del Mar Heights Road, I Swear to God I'm Not a Stalker," which he performed on Jimmy Fallon's *The Tonight Show*, doesn't mean teachers should abandon Byron's "She Walks in Beauty." What this approach does offer is a reconsideration of what might work in our classes and empowerment for teachers to choose the texts they want to teach to satisfy curricular needs. Perhaps Francisco's poem could be paired with Byron's, students' facility with the first poem opening the second to them in ways that were inaccessible to them without the pairing.

Joining the #TeachLivingPoets Community

The #TeachLivingPoets movement began online, in Twitter feeds, NCTE litchats, and blogs, and this is where you'll find a rich community to support your efforts to innovate your language arts curriculum with the work of contemporary poets. Teachers involved in the movement are dedicated to teaching and advocating for the voices of contemporary poets to be heard in schools. In fact, that's how the coauthors of this book met: Lindsay Illich wrote a blog post for NCTE on why teachers should include poems by contemporary poets, and Melissa Smith retweeted the link with the hashtag #TeachLivingPoets. We followed each other, and within months realized our mutual interest and shared goal of supporting the work of teachers who would like to implement this approach in their classrooms. Like we did, in joining the social media conversation around #TeachLivingPoets you will find teachers who share your tastes in contemporary poetry and poets, and from them you'll learn about new poems and books, as well as get real answers to questions from practicing teachers, and sometimes even from the poets themselves.

Since we've been teaching living poets, we've witnessed a significant improvement in students' feelings about reading and understanding poetry. Janais's experience is a testament to the power of a single poem, written in language they understood about ideas and situations with which they are familiar. Another student, Charanya, included an excerpt from Clint Smith's poem "Meteor Shower," from his book *Counting Descent*, in her valedictorian speech at Melissa's school:

> Today is a day of gratitude. A day to thank those who helped us get here. To thank every teacher, every parent, and every friend who stood by our side and cheered us on. Today is the first day of the rest of your life. The moment we leave this building, we enter the real world, but we will always hold a piece of this school with us. One example of how this school has shaped me was last summer when Mrs. Smith had us read a Clint Smith poetry collection for class. And there was something about the poem "Meteor Shower" that really stuck with me for the rest of the year. He says, "Even when we enter a new atmosphere, become subsumed in flames, turn to dust, lose ourselves in the wind . . . we bring a part of where we are from to every place we go."
>
> The most important thing I discovered during my time at [this school] is the beauty of different backgrounds and cultures. But, unfortunately, sometimes these are things that tend to be overlooked or even sneered at. We, as a society, don't always acknowledge that our differences are what truly unites us. But I really believe that each of our unique backgrounds is what truly contributed to the success of this graduating class. It was through our teamwork, collaboration, but most importantly through our attitude that we all are here today. And in that way, we leave an impact on this school and it will forever be a part of who we are. I hope that you'll remember this and embrace your differences because it's truly what makes us human and unites us. We must take all that we have learned these

past four years and apply it to the world we are about to enter. This is only the beginning of something great.

Janais and Charanya are only two examples of the profound impact teaching living poets can have on our students.

This book was written to help teachers introduce students to the work of contemporary poets, from discovering the work of contemporary poets and reading the poems, to providing strategies for teaching poems and creating assignments to help engage students, to using contemporary poetry as a way to help students grow as readers and writers. We also wanted to offer suggestions for becoming engaged literary citizens by joining the online teaching community and for how to help you plan classroom visits with poets.

To quote Kaveh Akbar, we are living in "a golden age of poetry" ("The Rumpus"). We hope this book helps open up the world of contemporary poetry and renews your passion for language and literature, which is so vital to engaged teaching. Indeed, in our own writing and teaching lives, reading and engaging with this world has opened us to a flood of generosity from writers and other educators, invaluable gifts that led us to write this book. We hope it will lead you to your own projects that will be gifts to others.

1

Discovering Contemporary Poetry

The book was in her lap; she had read no further. The power to change one's life comes from a paragraph, a lone remark. The lines that penetrate us are slender, like the flukes that live in river water and enter the bodies of swimmers. She was excited, filled with strength. The polished sentences had arrived, it seemed, like so many other things, at just the right time.

—*James Salter,* Light Years

Before We Begin

In Chapter 3, we discuss strategies for reading contemporary poems, but in this first chapter, as you're getting to know the landscape and getting a feel for your own poetic tastes, we discuss concepts that will help you think about your engagement with poetry as one that is renewed by recognizing your own *contingencies of reception*, by your generosity in reading work that is unfamiliar or strange and thus developing *comfort with ambiguity*, and, on the practical side, by keeping track of poems you like by *creating a system for cataloging poems*. Then we discuss some resources for discovering contemporary poetry on your own.

Contingencies of Reception

In the epigraph at the beginning of this chapter, James Salter's character in *Light Years* is changed by something she reads, words that are like "flukes," the narrator tells us, a masterful word choice because it conveys the metaphor of the fish while also connoting our conversational usage of *fluke*—"an accident." The character stumbles on this book, and not only that, but she stumbles on it "at just the right time" (351). This sense of contingency—both that she is reading that particular book and that she is moved by the words, not just because of the words but because she's reading them at that particular moment in her life—is relevant as we begin discussing how to discover poems and poets that you love and want to share with your students.

The epigraph reflects a truth that we know as readers: at different times in our lives, we receive words differently because we change—our needs are different, the circumstances of our lives are different, our tastes evolve, our understanding of the world enlarges. We probably know this instinctively, but it strikes us most powerfully when we read something we read years ago, and suddenly we realize its message has changed—because we have changed. We start with this acknowledgment of our fluid affinities and ways of reading because discovering poems and poets you love isn't a one-time event. As long as you continue reading, you will continue to discover new meanings in the texts you've read. Also, this approach, teaching living poets, will inspire you to switch things up by continually bringing new work into the classroom. As coauthors, we've discussed how making choices about which poems to include in this book was highly contingent on circumstance, and we admit that in ten years' time, it's highly likely we would choose other poems—in fact, we hope that is the case because it would mean that we are continuing to grow as readers.

Circumstances and taste also mean that others may find things to admire in a poem that hasn't opened up for you, and that's fine. As you explore, love the poems that you love when you love them, and let others do the same. In poetry, the tent is wide enough to include all of us and all of our evolving tastes, needs, and desires.

Comfort with Ambiguity

As you're exploring and discovering new poems and new poets, give yourself the freedom to appreciate poems that may not immediately be open to your understanding, especially after only one reading. In Chapter 3, we discuss some habits of mind that are developed by reading poetry, one of which is *comfort with ambiguity*, a willingness to read along without a firm foothold of understanding. For now, as you're exploring, center this habit of mind. In our experience, sometimes a work is compelling before we can actually describe what it's expressing. Some quality, maybe the texture of the language, a striking image, or musicality, is interesting. Remember that we forgive songs for nonsensical lyrics because we like the way the song makes us feel: think Queen's "Bohemian

Rhapsody," Nirvana's "Smells Like Teen Spirit," or the Barenaked Ladies' "One Week." Don't let the strangeness of a poem stand in the way of bookmarking it to come back to later, or of finding more poems from the author to read. At this point, as you're discovering what speaks to you, what opens up for you (notice here the metaphors for recognizing the beautiful: a voice you can hear, a door or a window opening), don't limit yourself by making instant accessibility a criterion for liking a poem.

Here's a strange and beautiful poem by Heather Christle (pronounced like *crystal*) that we think is a good example of the kind of poem that would have been intimidating to us as teachers before we started incorporating more contemporary poetry:

People Are a Living Structure Like a Coral Reef

People love to clean their ears and I love people
very much They are everywhere! Every single
thing I love I love for windows only and if
one window reflects another then friends
for me it's all over And in the windows are trees
and in the windows are people What are they even doing
with their hunger and in their new shirts They are
taking care of themselves and they are taking each other out
for lunch Oh even the rain has to love them People
are just too attractive! and the rain places itself
on the window in order to be closer to the people
the ones who are eating The ones who are
busting out vigor Oh people You have to love
people They are so much like ourselves

A few things may trip up novice readers of contemporary poetry: (1) unlike most canonical poetry, this poem isn't end-stopped; rather, the lines run to the next line without a pause (this is called an *enjambed* line or *enjambment*); and (2) unlike most canonical poetry, this poem doesn't observe the conventions of written discourse like punctuation (except for the exclamation points!). But you feel the speaker's ebullience(!), a person struck by the idea of being part of humanity, a "structure" so beautiful that even droplets of rain stick to windows to be closer to people. The oral, uncrafted quality of the language conveys the immediacy of the emotions, the feeling of being part of a larger thing.

But this isn't to say you won't find some of the same elements in contemporary poetry that you find in canonical poetry. Take this life-imbued and life-buoying poem by Ross Gay:

Sorrow Is Not My Name
—after Gwendolyn Brooks

No matter the pull toward brink. No
matter the florid, deep sleep awaits.
There is a time for everything. Look,
just this morning a vulture
nodded his red, grizzled head at me,
and I looked at him, admiring
the sickle of his beak.
Then the wind kicked up, and,
after arranging that good suit of feathers
he up and took off.
Just like that. And to boot,
there are, on this planet alone, something like two
million naturally occurring sweet things,
some with names so generous as to kick
the steel from my knees: agave, persimmon,
stick ball, the purple okra I bought for two bucks
at the market. Think of that. The long night,
the skeleton in the mirror, the man behind me
on the bus taking notes, yeah, yeah.
But look; my niece is running through a field
calling my name. My neighbor sings like an angel
and at the end of my block is a basketball court.
I remember. My color's green. I'm spring.

—for Walter Aikens

We recognize that the emotional freight of this poem is loaded into images and colors—the vulture and his sickle beak evoking the grim reaper, the double meaning of *sleep* and *death*, and then the things that ground the speaker: the sweet bounty of the Earth, the simple but deep pleasures of children who love you, the human voice singing, and basketball. And the final line, connecting this poem to Gwendolyn Brooks's poem "To the Young Who Want to Die," which concludes with the lines: "Graves grow no green that you can use. / Remember, green's your color. You are Spring."

Gay's echo of Brooks's "Spring" is life-affirming, transforming his poem into a response in the call-and-response tradition. Worth noting, however, is that the same life-affirming sense is conveyed even without connecting his poem to the early Brooks poem. Gay's poem doesn't depend on the Brooks poem, but a reader's appreciation is deepened by knowing the connection. We return to Gay's poem in Chapter 7 as a mentor poem for a poetry prompt that helps students write original poems. We also discuss comfort with ambiguity further in Chapter 2 as a mindset for readers to develop as they become more familiar with contemporary poetry.

Planning Your Archive

One last word of advice before we discuss resources for discovering new poetry: plan in advance how you will archive all the poems you find. My (Lindsay's) grandmother taught composition and literature courses at a community college, and she was a prolific newspaper clipper. She subscribed to home delivery for the small local newspaper and the nearest metro newspaper, and she began most days by reading both while drinking coffee and cutting out stories that she thought might be relevant for her classes. After she died, the family found file cabinets worth of clippings, photocopied pages, and handouts she had meticulously created for her students. She retired in 1991, three years before her campus had its first internet-connected student computer lab.

If she were teaching today, I think her system of curating material for the classroom, especially poems, would probably be some combination of print and digital archive. The landscape of contemporary poetry is a world of both print and digital culture, and having a system—a folder in the cloud, a bookmarking app, a file with links to URLs—will help you keep track of all the treasures you find (there will be many!). I take lots of pictures of poems from books on my phone and use a scanner app to convert them to PDFs, and then I save them to a file labeled, generically, "Poems for Class."

Complicating the Canon, Escaping the Echo Chamber

As the media landscape has changed, so has the dissemination of texts. When print culture was dominant, the canon was bolstered not only by critics and teachers but also by the publishing industry. Unless you lived in or near a city with access to cultural arts, teachers had limited access to new poetry depending on what they could find at a local library, bookstore (if one existed), and whatever educational publishers were producing for teachers in the form of textbooks, workbooks, unit bundles, and classroom sets. In a strange way, even the writers of educational policy and test writers became gatekeepers of the literary canon because of the widespread dissemination of classroom resources and text exemplars published for curriculum development and instruction.

Because social media facilitates the circulation of content, texts gain rhetorical velocity, and as social networks grow, our access grows as a product of our connectedness. Suddenly, making new work visible and new voices heard is easier. Even in the case of books, the standard of print culture, the internet has allowed us to share our ideas about them, to share pages of books, and even to connect with publishers. In the case of poetry, one of the most portable arts to begin with given the average size of poems and books of poetry, the internet has played a part in its recent flourishing. The following list includes both virtual and print resources, but we begin with social media because we think that it has the most potential for you to connect with others and learn about the works people are reading and teaching in their classes (many poets are teachers too!).

Social Media

A few days after the Pulse Nightclub shooting in 2016, the online literary journal *Waxwing* published Maggie Smith's poem "Good Bones," and the poem went viral. It was shared thousands of times, providing a communal salve for our grief. We mentioned in the introduction that the writer Mary Karr shared poems with friends using her fax machine after the Twin Towers fell on 9/11. In the age of social media, Maggie Smith didn't need a fax number to share a poem with us; if someone we follow shared it (or even liked it), then it showed up in our Twitter feeds. The same thing happens even on days when we aren't in the aftermath of something awful. I found my way to one of my favorite writers, Heather Christle, from a tweet written by Paige Lewis, a poet I follow whose work I very much admire. Here's the tweet:

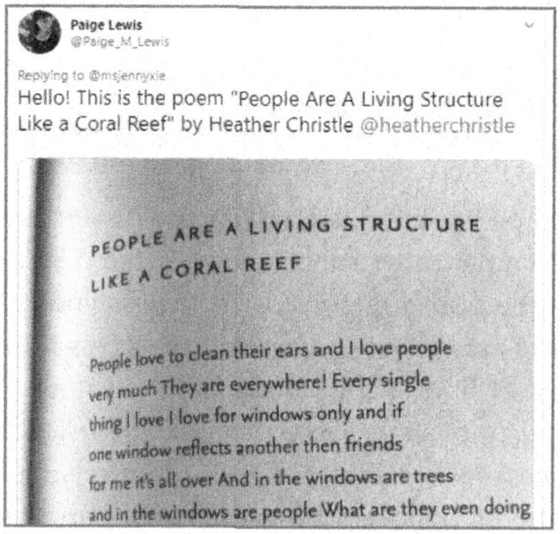

When a poem is shared that you connect to, find other poems by that poet. After reading this post, I found that Heather Christle has published multiple books of poetry (*The Trees the Trees*, *The Difficult Farm*, *Heliopause*, *What Is Amazing*) and a book of nonfiction, *The Crying Book*. The tweet led me to order *What Is Amazing*; at the end of the book, I found a list of literary journals where the poems were originally published, providing further sources to explore for editorial tastes I can appreciate (journals or sites such as The Awl, *Columbia Poetry Review*, *Everyday Genius*, *Front Porch*, and *Harpur Palate*). From one poem shared online, a trove of new poetry.

In addition to showcasing writers and educators who share poems, Twitter has become a platform for real-time conversations through the use of hashtags. Hashtags are keywords added to a tweet using the pound sign (#). Melissa created the hashtag #TeachLivingPoets, but many ELA educators have generated others, such as #NCTEvillage, #DisruptTexts, #APLitChat, #THEBOOKCHAT, to create online communities and real-time (synchronous) and slow (asynchronous) chats. Hashtags connect you to others interested in the same topics and issues you're interested in. These online communities of educators and grassroots curricular discussions have proved to be rich ground for innovation, idea sharing, and community building.

Some poets use Instagram as a platform for their poetry, quiply called "Instapoets." A quick Google search for "Instapoets" will reveal lots of mixed opinions about the quality of the work you'll find there. When my students ask about Instapoets, I share a quote from Ariana Reines:

> I think an essential lever for the great shift in consciousness that is required of each of us at this stage on the planet is the writing of poetry, and the more people who begin practicing this art with curiosity, love and attention, the better. (Tamás)

They may find much to admire in the mix of text and image on the Instapoet threads, a way into the art they might not otherwise have found, and for this reason, we see value there. Similarly, when Dean Young responded to the haters about how many poetry graduate programs there are, an issue ancillary to some Instapoetry complaints, he wrote: "All of it is a great sign of health, that the imaginative life is thriving and important, and worthy of time and attention, worthy of conditions in which it is honored and encouraged to wildly grow" (5). You might also use the critical backlash to Instapoets as an occasion to discuss with your students the politics of canon formation, who decides who is in and who is out. As Anna Leszkiewicz notes, the term *Instapoets* itself has become an unhelpful gatekeeping term by those who may not appreciate the new voices and new medium.

BOOKS 6 MARCH 2019

Why are we so worried about "Instapoetry"?

The legitimacy of "Instapoetry" has long been fiercely debated: but the rise of the term has sparked a fragmented critical conversation.

BY ANNA LESZKIEWICZ Follow @annaleszkie

YouTube also offers a rich library of content related to contemporary poetry, including channels dedicated to showcasing the work of contemporary poets, like Ours Poetica, produced in collaboration with the Poetry Foundation, Complexly, and Paige Lewis. On this channel, writers, artists, or celebrities read poems, with each poem as it appears on the page shown on screen as it is read. The videos capture both the oral and the written, elements of the poetic that are generally separated when poems are performed (the audience doesn't have access to the print version) or, alternatively, read silently by a single reader (where the reader, depending on their fluencies with the kind of poem they're reading, may feel detached from the aural/oral qualities of the poem).

Button Poetry is another YouTube channel that features contemporary poetry. In these videos, poets perform their own work. Students find the work featured on this channel compelling and appreciate hearing poems performed in the original poet's voice. Button Poetry provides a category of "Classroom-Friendly Poems," those that are "appropriate (content and language) for youth classroom settings." We realize that appropriateness is largely context-specific; you know your students and cultural climate best. As teachers, we continue to negotiate these constraints and make decisions with our students in mind.

A final note on YouTube: aside from Google, YouTube has the most-used search engine on the internet. Many poetry readings and craft talks (poets talking about the writing process) are archived there.

Online Collections of Poetry and Email Subscriptions

Nonprofit organizations that support poetry and the literary community, such as Poets.org, which is sponsored by the Academy of American Poets, and the Poetry Foundation, publishers of *Poetry* magazine, have extensive and evolving online collections of poems by contemporary writers. Poets.org provides subscriptions to its Academy newsletter, a newsletter especially for educators, a Poem-a-Day daily email, and the weekly Teach This Poem series, along with printables, information about local poetry events, and lesson plans. The Poetry Foundation includes Poem Guides for teaching specific poems and articles about effective strategies for teaching poetry. In September 2019, in collaboration with Paige Lewis, they launched Ours Poetica, a video series in which guests share a poem that's been important to them.

Smaller organizations are building online collections and resources as well. Verse Daily, which offers a daily email subscription, is produced by J. P. Dancing Bear. Split This Rock has a poetry database called "The Quarry: A Social Justice Poetry Database" that is searchable by poet, theme, geography, poet identity, language, format, and prize winners. Split This Rock also makes available a Poem of the Week subscription. Other websites with many resources include Cave Canem: A Home for Black Poetry and PennSound, which offers thousands of recordings and a free Modern & Contemporary American Poetry ten-week course through Coursera.

Literary Magazines and Book Reviews

Many print and online literary magazines are published monthly or quarterly every year in the United States. The lit mags with the largest circulation are the most recognizable of these magazines—*The Paris Review*, *Poetry*, *Prairie Schooner*, *Tin House*, *Gulf Coast*, *Kenyon Review*, and *American Poetry Review* (to name only a few)—but many more of excellent quality exist, such as *32 Poems*, *Waxwing*, *Glass*, *Beloit Poetry Journal*, *AGNI*, *Crazyhorse*, *Ploughshares*, among others. Both *Poets & Writers* and NewPages.com maintain databases of literary magazines, good places to start exploring the many avenues for reading and publishing poetry.

Some literary journals also publish book reviews of poetry collections. Book reviews of contemporary poetry not only give you glimpses into the collection through direct quotations (sometimes extensive quotation), but they also provide the experience of an ideal reader (arguably the function of criticism). Book reviews can also be found in *Publishers Weekly*, *The New York Times Book Review*, *Los Angeles Review of Books* (*LARB*), and *The Times Literary Supplement*. One online magazine, *The Review Review*, is devoted entirely to reviews of books and other literary magazines.

Finally, widely circulated periodicals such as *The New Yorker*, *Boston Review*, and *The Nation* publish poems and keep archives that often include audio versions.

Independent Booksellers and Small Presses

The decline of independent bookstores has meant less access to titles of single volume collections of poetry for customers who rely on buyers at their local bookstores to introduce them to new voices. For more on bookstores and literary points of interest by city, explore Poets & Writers (pw.org) City Guides, which include not only the best bookstores but also the literary haunts and reading series information.

A good source to find booksellers and small publishers is Small Press Distribution (SPD), the nonprofit distributor of independently published books in the United States dedicated to supporting diversity in the publishing community. Their website (spdbooks.org) includes up-to-date bestseller lists, information about new releases, and staff picks and also offers a weekly newsletter with book recommendations and local events. For teachers, they offer free desk copies of books adopted for classroom use and teaching guides.

Best American Poetry Series and Pushcart Awards

The Best American Poetry anthology is part of the larger Best American series that includes *The Best American Short Stories*, *The Best American Essays*, and *The Best American Nonrequired Reading*, among others. It's published annually, with a different editor each year making the selections from poems published in literary magazines during the previous year. Year after year in September, I await the publication date for *Best American Poetry*, and when it arrives, I allow myself to read it only in titrated drips of time, letting each poem work its magic. If you enjoy holding books when you read, this may be the best entree into the world of contemporary American poetry. Series Editor David Lehman always writes a foreword that gives an overview of that year's selections and highlights some poems and themes, and the volume editor for that year writes an introduction, always insightful but varying widely in perspective from year to year.

The Pushcart Prize anthology is also published annually, with texts chosen from nominations by small presses and literary magazines that include poems, essays, fiction, and experimental work. Because it includes genres other than poetry, it does have a smaller selection of poems compared to the Best American Poetry (BAP) series. In addition to BAP and the Pushcart Prize anthology, annual honors such as the PEN America Literary Awards and the Pulitzer Prize for Poetry are a good source for finding new, critically acclaimed work by contemporary poets because both publish longlists of finalists that include the most critically acclaimed poetry books each year.

Podcasts

As of this writing, podcasts are gaining in popularity, and audiences interested in poetry haven't been ignored. Rachel Zucker's podcast, *Commonplace: Conversations with Poets (and Other People)*, offers episodes with extended format interviews with contemporary poets. If you don't have that kind of time, Tracy K. Smith's *The Slowdown*, produced in partnership with the Poetry Foundation, discusses one poem in each weekday five-minute episode. *Poetry* magazine now offers *The* Poetry *Magazine Podcast* featuring a discussion of one of the poems from the most current issue. Other podcasts that stand out for their excellent content include *VS*, hosted by Danez Smith and Franny Choi, and *The Poet Salon*, hosted by Gabrielle Bates, Luther Hughes, and Dujie Tahat.

Literary Festivals and Conferences

If you're lucky enough to live close to a city that hosts literary or poetry festivals, take advantage of the programming. Some big annual festivals include the Dodge Poetry Festival in Newark, New Jersey, which offers a specialized educator resource guide to the festival; Split This Rock, held in Washington, DC; the Massachusetts Poetry Festival, held annually during the month of April in Salem; the O, Miami Poetry Festival, sponsored by the Knight Foundation and held in Miami during the month of April; and the New York Poetry Festival, held in the summer on Governors Island in New York Harbor. In Texas, Poetry at Round Top is held annually in April. In late March, the Tennessee Williams/New Orleans Literary Festival is held in New Orleans. These are only a few of the many poetry and literary festivals held annually with vibrant programming featuring poets reading and discussing their work.

Another opportunity to see many poets in one place is the Association of Writers & Writing Programs annual conference, which is held in a different city every year. Poets give readings as part of the conference and also give readings offsite for nonconference attendees. The conference also has a fabulous book fair with hundreds of vendors, and on the last day of the conference, publishers sell books at deep discounts.

Anthologies

Even though anthologies sometimes get a bad rap for decontextualizing poems, there are some really good themed poetry anthologies out there that introduce readers to new voices. In essence, the editor of an anthology is acting as a curator for their readers: here, reader, are some poems I love, that I think you'll also love. Some anthologies that have helped us discover new voices include *Isn't It Romantic* (Wave Books), *Poets against the War* (Nation Books), *Bullets into Bells: Poets and Citizens Respond to Gun Violence* (Beacon Press), *Come as You Are* (Anomalous Press), *New Poets of Native Nations* (Graywolf), *The Art of Losing: Poems of Grief and Healing* (Bloomsbury), and Volumes 1–4 of The BreakBeat Poets series (Haymarket Books): *The BreakBeat Poets: New American Poetry in the Age of Hip-Hop*, *Black Girl Magic*, *Halal If You Hear Me*, and *LatiNext*.

Teacher as Anthologist

The classroom is the publishing world in microcosm, with the teacher acting as a skilled anthologist, culling poems from everywhere for the small audience they know best, their students. As mentioned at the beginning of this chapter, I maintain a digital folder of poems (the current count is forty-six, and for whatever reason I have kept that number steady by rotating poems in and out). I've also found that this set of poems has become a source of inspiration for my own writing and the writing of poetry prompts, which we discuss in more detail in Chapter 7. When I have discussed the folder of poems in other contexts, I've called it a *spellbook*, for what I think are the magical qualities of the language in the poems. Finally, the folder has been the basis for an assignment that asks students to curate their own anthologies, complete with a short foreword in which they describe their own editorial process, i.e., how they chose the poems they included in their anthology.

One last word: sometimes your own tastes, as they grow and become more explicit, can become blinders to poems that will be important to you. A poet I follow on Twitter, Julian David Randall, reminds us that we should learn something from poems we don't enjoy. This is a good reminder for the end of this chapter about discovering new poetry: sometimes connecting with new work requires work on our part, work that will be rewarded with wisdom we would have missed if we had stopped reading the poem prematurely.

2

Reading Contemporary Poetry

In this chapter, we begin with a discussion of the difference between knowing about poetry generally and the practice of reading poems, each representing a specific kind of knowledge—declarative knowledge and procedural knowledge, respectively. Then we describe three habits of mind that we think are essential to reading contemporary poetry. Finally, we share a reading protocol you can use in your classroom to support your own and your students' development as engaged readers of contemporary poetry.

The Difference between Knowing and Doing

Claudia Rankine's *Citizen: An American Lyric* was published in 2014 to resounding acclaim: a National Book Award finalist and winner of a National Book Critics Circle Award in *two* categories, poetry and criticism. A mix of text and images, prose-ish poems alongside line-breaked poems written in a sometimes sparse, reportorial style, this book about microaggressions and what it means to be a citizen was widely read, discussed, taught, and, yes, used as a vehicle for protest at political rallies. A Boston arts college organized reading groups around *Citizen* to discuss the book as a way to facilitate conversations about race, and more than 1,300 people signed up.

When I (Lindsay) assigned the book in a creative writing class, I admitted to being anxious, because I didn't know how students would respond to it. Not only does *Citizen* challenge ideas about genre, but more important, Rankine addresses what she refers to elsewhere as the "internalized dominance" of whiteness and how it functions in American culture.

I should not have been anxious. My students were ready to talk. It was one of those moments we are gifted as teachers when we can sit back and let the students take the lead. For a fleeting moment, I wanted to stop the conversation and point out to them that *they were getting it.*

I wanted to interject because their energy and responses upended the commonly held belief among many teachers and students alike that *poetry is hard*. In an interview, Rankine describes this belief about poetry as an illusion, saying the "illusion of complexity" results from not having "a habit of reading poetry" (Zucker). In other words, the notion that poetry is difficult doesn't reflect an essential quality of the genre but instead reflects an unfamiliarity generally with the domain of poetry. We could say it another way: the habit of reading poetry dispels the illusion of difficulty.

When we talk about learning, the **domain** is the thing or content being studied. For the sake of illustration, let's say that we're studying ballroom dancing—the domain. Within every domain, there are two kinds of knowledge: **declarative knowledge** and **procedural knowledge**. In our ballroom dancing example, declarative knowledge would be all the stuff you might know about ballroom dancing: its history, the scoring of competitive ballroom dancing, traditions of costuming, popular dances. It may be helpful to think of declarative knowledge as the kind of knowledge you might be quizzed on or knowledge that might show up in a trivia game. Procedural knowledge would be demonstrated by, well, dancing. That is, demonstrating the moves. Procedural knowledge can be applied to a task.

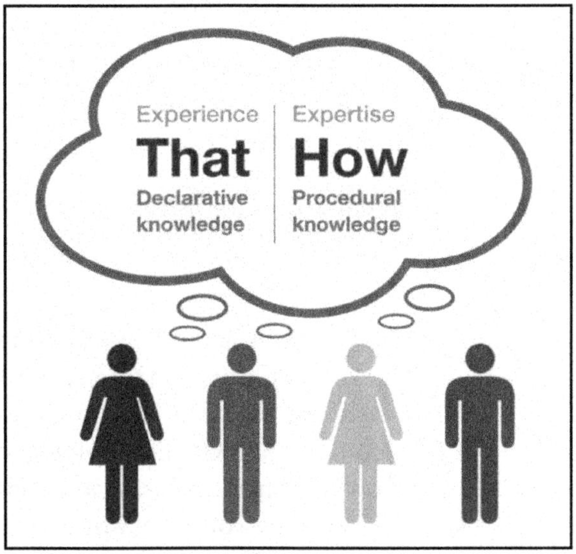

What researchers notice when they study the differences between novices and experts in a domain is related to procedural knowledge. First, there's agreement among researchers that an enormous amount of domain or content knowledge is necessary to reach expert status within a domain. But the real difference between the novices and experts shows up when faced with a task. In one study, for example, groups of novice and expert teachers were shown videotaped classroom sessions and asked to comment on what was going on in the video (see Figure 2.1). It probably won't surprise you to learn that the expert teachers were able to analyze and draw conclusions about the level of engagement in the classroom, make assessments about students' familiarity with the concepts being taught, and make good assumptions about the nature of the class (in this case, an accelerated class).

Expert 6: "On the left monitor, the students' note taking indicates that they have seen sheets like this and have had presentations like this before; it's fairly efficient at this point because they're used to the format they are using."

Expert 7: "I don't understand why the students can't be finding out this information on their own rather than listening to someone tell them because if you watch the faces of most of them, they start out for about the first 2 or 3 minutes sort of paying attention to what's going on and then just drift off."

Expert 2: "I haven't heard a bell, but the students are already at their desks and seem to be doing purposeful activity, and this is about the time that I decide they must be an accelerated group because they came into the room and started something rather than just sitting down and socializing."

Novice 1: "I can't tell what they are doing. They're getting ready for class, but I can't tell what they're doing."

Novice 3: "She's trying to communicate with them here about something, but I sure couldn't tell what it was."

Another novice: "It's a lot to watch."

FIGURE 2.1. What expert and novice teachers notice. (From Bransford et al., p. 62, reprinted with permission.)

If we think about how all of this relates to Rankine's conclusion that the "illusion of complexity" about poetry exists because we don't have a habit of reading poetry, we then can start thinking about *reading poetry* as a demonstration of procedural knowledge, applying knowledge to a task. This is a different kind of knowledge from knowing about poetry generally, i.e., declarative knowledge.

Rankine's comment also highlights another idea about poetry that doesn't serve us well when we're learning about it or how to read it, that is, that the abstract concept of poetry can act as a kind of stand-in for actual, particular poems. We can easily fall into the trap of focusing on generalizations about the entire genre without paying attention to specific poems. When we're saying more about *poetry* than we are about specific poems, it may mean that the illusion of difficulty is about received notions, misconceptions, or even ahistorical ideas about poetry in general. When Rankine suggests that a habit of reading poetry will help dispel the illusion of complexity, we think she is making an argument for letting go of the generalities that exist about the art form and getting to know poems in particular, individually, through the act of reading.

Ben Lerner in *The Hatred of Poetry* illustrates this point using Marianne Moore's famous Modernist poem "Poetry." He points out that the first line gets quoted and anthologized often—"I, too, dislike it: there are things that are important beyond this fiddle"—but not the rest of the stanza that clarifies her meaning. After that first line, the poem goes on to read:

> Reading it, however, with a perfect contempt for it, one
>   discovers that there is in
> it after all, a place for the genuine.
>   Hands that can grasp, eyes
>   that can dilate, hair that can rise
>   if it must, these things are important

We get the humanizing effect of poetry only at the level of the particular, from actual poems, not from theorizing about them generally. It's the particular body parts of this poem that illustrate this idea: grasping hands, dilating eyes, raised hair.

Habits of Mind for Reading Contemporary Poetry

In addition to reading more poems to become an experienced reader of contemporary poetry, it's helpful to develop a few key habits of mind. Habits of mind, or dispositions, are described in the *Framework for Success in Postsecondary Writing* as "ways of approaching learning that are both intellectual and practical" (Council of Writing Program Administrators et al. 4). The Framework identifies eight habits of mind fostered and reinforced by writing, habits such as curiosity, openness, engagement, creativity. We think the habits of mind can be extended to reading and would like to add the following habits of mind that are drawn on, fostered, and developed by reading poetry: (1) comfort with ambiguity, (2) attention, and (3) gratitude, or the sense of the poem as a gift.

Comfort with Ambiguity

The first habit of mind that is drawn on and developed by reading contemporary poetry is being comfortable with not knowing what to make of a poem: being okay with liminality, being on the threshold of understanding. The impulse to message-hunt is strong, but poetry offers something more. Liminal space is space that's primed for revelation, which may be why Terrance Hayes says he loves the "moment of 'not-knowing' more that the moment of 'knowing' in a poem" (Introduction xxv). Like vulnerability, being comfortable with not-knowing opens readers to *bewilderment*, a term that poet Emilia Phillips describes in "The Poetics of Bewilderment" as "a kind of sublime state, one of intense awe that allows for the ineffable and unanswerable." In the same essay, she goes on to quote poet Kaveh Akbar on the idea of bewilderment as central to the goals of poetry, one that he associates with another term, *wonder,* which is accessed by permeability:

> I really do sincerely feel that bewilderment is at the core of every great poem, and in order to be bewildered, you have to be able to wonder. You absolutely have to be permeable to wonder. Maintaining an orientation towards wonder in a time where the government is conspiring against it, in a time where black people are being murdered at the hands of the state, in a time when the Earth is very much trying to warn us about what we're doing to it, maintaining an orientation towards wonder becomes really difficult. It's the work that I have to do every day, the work of trying to find sources of wonder, even in our sadness and loneliness, or even in our anger.

Attention

Giving a poem our full attention is a habit of mind that Matthew Zapruder might call the habit of mind that helps us access "the poetic state of mind," that is, the sense that something important is being said and therefore listening. Attention is also a demonstration of care, and in this way, attending to poems is the demonstration of relational obligation, an ethic of care. Profound attention is marked by attunement, an all-ears listening that is agendaless, granting the object of attention our full presence. Especially in this historical and cultural moment when so much is competing for our attention, giving poems our attention is a way of holding space for other voices, the concept of holding space that we think Hanif Abdurraqib means when he says, "I know nothing except that this grief is a river carrying us to another new grief, and along the way, let us hold a space for a bad joke or a good memory" (*They Can't Kill Us* 285). It's another way, he says in his acknowledgments as he thanks his readers, of "sharing a small corner of this brief and sometimes fantastic life with me" (285). The attention we give poems as readers is the attention we give to its writer: shared time, an antidote to disruption and distraction.

Gratitude: The Poem as Gift

Poetry—the way it is published, circulated, supported, read, and written—operates as a gift economy, meaning that it exists in networks of generosity and creative abundance (Hyde). Approaching the reading of poems from this habit of mind and treating the poem as a gift helps us remember that someone created the poem. It has a maker. For many teachers and scholars, this is a habit of mind that was undermined by the long-lasting effects of New Criticism, which instructed readers of literature to separate the work of art from the artist who created it, even though poetry is uniquely suited to help us "imagine someone else's interior life, almost as if it were or could have been ours," as Stephanie Burt writes in *The Poem Is You*. Burt goes on to say that poems "project a voice and embody a compelling or attractive individual consciousness, which we can then hear, or speak, or sing, or try on or try out, as if it were our own" (10). The result of receiving this gift is identification with a larger collectivity, an unbounding of ego that results from receiving the gift of the poem.

Approaching the reading of poetry as gift reception also attunes us to the creative spirit of the work of art and a key principle in gift economies: gifts compel us to share them. As teachers, we know this intimately because the creative spirit of teaching was a gift we received from other teachers before we chose to become teachers ourselves. The same is true with works of art; they move us to create.

Strategies for Reading Contemporary Poetry

Unlike genres that have clear rhetorical purposes, like this book, the purpose of which is to inform and persuade an audience of secondary teachers about the various ways teaching living poets will support students' literacy and engagement with the world, poems can be in service to multiple and varied rhetorical purposes. Yes, the aim is literary, but the arguments that specific poems make can be as varied as the kinds of arguments made in any text. It may be helpful for you and your students to think of the argument of the poem as the poem's thesis. Again, this won't always be unambiguous or unilateral, but having a protocol when reading new poems based on principles of rhetorical reading will help.

Before You Read

Before you read, find out more about who wrote the poem. Most actively publishing writers try to cultivate an online presence through an author webpage and/or social media. A simple search might yield important information for a reader, providing you and your students a sense of the poet as a person who has real and important motivations as a writer. If any video or audio is available online, watch or listen. Having the voice of the writer in your head sometimes helps you hear the rhythms of their lines. A word of caution: while biographical information sometimes lends insight into individual poems, biography shouldn't drive interpretation. Always remember that many poets distinguish between themselves and the speakers of their poems in some way.

Next, consider where the poem was first published. Was it published in an anthology of poems around a theme or a themed issue of a literary journal? Was it published in a full-length collection of poetry by the poet? Knowing the context of the poem's publication will help you orient to the original intended audience's motivations and expectations as you read the poem. Last, take a moment to read the title and look at how the poem appears on the page. Can you make some predictions about the poem based on the title or its shape?

First Read

For the first full read of the poem, read for impressions, first responses, and hunches. Remember that a poem is an event that you experience. Think of the first reading as the emotive read rather than an analytical one.

It may be helpful at this point to take the poem's temperature: is this an up or a down poem? This may sound like a simplistic way to begin reading a poem, but the **up-down metaphor** offers a rich basis of understanding given how we use spatial orientation metaphors to describe a range of things: emotional well-being (where up is happy and sad is low), positive and negative experiences (highs and lows), and physical wellness (he's up and at 'em). For a first read, applying the up-down metaphor allows the reader to do some provisional thinking, to identify some points, however tenuous, that further the reader's understanding—some preliminary fingerholds or purchase on the poem. For example, in the poem that opens the introduction to this book, Kaveh Akbar's "Portrait of the Alcoholic Floating in Space with Severed Umbilicus," taking an up-down approach focuses the reader's attention on the many negatives and potential sources for negative emotion: an astronaut's air supply has been severed, and we get the impression that the speaker's life is imperiled. There's frog-spit and spikes, salmon "bully" upstream. Even though we don't have a full grasp of the poem, the up-down approach is a starting point. The idea is to help readers find ways into the text, and this is a first step for a first read.

At this point, readers can also locate **hotspots** in the poem. We're using the term in a geologically metaphoric sense, a hotspot being a place where volcanoes are most likely to erupt. In poetry, the hotspots are the moments in the poem that seem to be the maximum tension points, points that may offer opportunities for greater understanding. The National Oceanic and Atmospheric Administration website illustrates hotspots as the places where the Earth's mantle gets pushed up and new land is formed, as in Hawaii. In reading, we like to think of this new land as the meaning-making that results from the hotspots. The hotspots could be intense language, striking imagery, unexpected juxtapositions, even disruptive line breaks (more on this in the next section).

After getting the first read impressions of the poem, it might be good to let it rest. There's good reason to walk away, do something else, and return to the poem after a little time. In the classroom, sometimes this is a good time to suggest coming back to the poem at the next class meeting. That way, the music of the poem and some of the phraseology has time to work on readers.

Second and Subsequent Reads

When you return to the poem, read it from beginning to end. After this reading, consider the scene and central images of the poem: Who is speaking and to whom? Where and when is the poem? One way for students to think about this step in the reading process is as ***mise-en-scène***, a French term from film criticism meaning "everything in the scene and the overall effect of it." As you consider the scene of the poem, locate what you think is the dominant image or images. Images powerfully activate imagination and convey emotion through association. The Modernist poet T. S. Eliot referred to the central images or system of images as the "objective correlative," which functions as the emotional center of the poem.

This is also the point at which you should look up any unfamiliar words or references. As teachers we do a good job of teaching students how to draw conclusions about the meanings of words from context because on high-stakes standardized tests, students don't have access to reference materials. But students often internalize this inference process and bypass looking up unfamiliar terms even when they have access to reference material, in print or online. Even when I (Lindsay) am sure I know a word, I look it up anyway to see if there are definitions that didn't immediately occur to me or histories of the word that will add to the texture of the poem. (If your library doesn't have a subscription to the *Oxford English Dictionary* online, try to find a public library that does, if only for this purpose.)

Next, consider individual sentences. Even some of our most fragmentary and elusive contemporary poetry, by poets like Jean Valentine, employs sentences as the basic units of discourse in poetry (even when conventional punctuation is missing, as in Ellen Bryant Voigt's poems in *Headwaters*). Finding the subjects and verbs of sentences will help readers make sense of who is doing what, and to whom. It will also help reattach modifiers to their antecedents, which might be separated by line breaks, stanza breaks, or disruptions in the sentence such as appositives, parentheticals, absolute phrases, or asides. This is also a good time to consider the effects of **line breaks**. Line breaks are either **end-stopped**, which means that the end of the line comes at the end of a phrase, or **enjambed,** lines that don't stop naturally at the end of the line. End-stopped lines are sometimes marked with punctuation like a comma or a period, but they might not be. Sometimes the effect is to keep the reader moving along to the next line; other times, the enjambment thwarts and thus disrupts the through-movement to the next line.

In "Learning the Poetic Line: How Line Breaks Shape Meaning," Rebecca Hazelton analyzes the enjambed line breaks of the first few lines of Geoffrey Brock's "Homeland Security":

> The four AM cries
> of my son worm
> through the double
> foam of earplugs
>
> and diazepam.

She says, "Brock's use of enjambment allows him to dole out information bit by bit, heightening readers' curiosity and the drama hidden inside an otherwise common domestic scene." Then she asks readers to consider the same lines if they were end-stopped:

> The four AM cries of my son worm through
> the double foam of earplugs and diazepam.

Compared to Brock's original line poem, the lack of line breaks in this rendering makes the scene almost boring. Hazelton notes, "Without the odd tones and questions the original enjambed lines produced, this scene seems ordinary and dull."

Now it's time to think about the poem's **volta**. The volta, or "turn," has been called many things to describe the variety of intensities (or voltages) at which the turn operates: *fulcrum, modulation, torque, swerve, veer*. What these terms have in common is the field of physics, the vocabulary of force upon an object to cause it to move. The volta is where things change. We start in one place at the beginning of a poem and we end somewhere else. Where in the poem did that happen? That's the volta. Ellen Bryant Voigt, writing in *The Art of Syntax,* says the volta has become "an inherent expectation for most short lyric poems."

Identifying the volta is helpful only if it enhances the reading of the poem. Sometimes we get caught up in the finding of a thing (the volta) rather than allowing the thing to be an instrument that facilitates understanding. More important, we think, than identifying the volta is to ask, what is being troubled by this poem? How is this poem disturbing the received notions we have about the subjects of the poem? What's different at the end of the poem?

The Mutability of Poems

What poems say to us may change according to mood, age, experience, time of day. Be prepared for this mutability. Like photographs, poems are memento mori not only for their writers but also for their readers, for each reading records a specific response to the poem tied to who you are—were—in the moment you read it, which of course is momentary. That mutability is also the reason we return to the poems we love, continually grafting them onto us, or being grafted by them.

On this note, it's important to consider ways we can share authority with students regarding the meanings of poems. Because poems are experienced differently depending on the reader, we teachers need to let go of being the arbiter of the meaning of poems. That doesn't mean giving up our role as pointers, at shining the spotlight on poems that move us and change the way we see the world, but it does mean giving up on the other illusion—not the illusion of complexity, but the illusion of the single-meaning, univocal poem. It means giving up some power, but the shared authority that comes when we read poems together with our students means that we are ceding our power in order to empower their own readings and connections to language and meaning. We believe that this shared authority in the reading of contemporary poems is the reason students respond so powerfully to poems being written in our current historical moment and the reason we feel so strongly about sharing this approach with other teachers.

Poem Reading Protocol

Before you read

- Who wrote this?
- Where was it published?
- What predictions can you make from the title and physical shape?

First read

- First impressions, responses, and hunches
- Up-down temperature
- Locate hotspots

Second and subsequent reads

- Consider the scene of the poem: Who is speaking? Where and when is this happening?
- Locate the central image(s) of the poem. What effect(s) is created by the imagery?
- Look up all unfamiliar words and references.
- Locate modifiers and antecedents, which will help with difficult or fragmented syntax.
- Consider the effects of line breaks.
- Consider the volta, or ask, what has changed?

3

Recognizing Common Moves in Poetry

In fiction, messages are conveyed through stories, or narrative. So dominant a mode of meaning-making is narrative that when the story is missing or hazy—as is the case in lyric poetry—readers sometimes lose their footing, and meaning-making feels slippery. But what if this seeming deficiency is a *strength* of poetry?

In the last chapter, we discussed being comfortable with ambiguity as a habit of mind to develop as readers of poetry. Comfort with ambiguity—the struggle with meaning-making that we may feel as readers—begins with changing the way we think about poetry. Rather than a deficit, the complexity we find in poetry is its superpower: in this compact art of language in the miniature are coiled layers of meaning, evocativeness that leaps, that lights up the dark carapaces of readers' minds. Stephanie Burt, poet and professor of English at Harvard University, articulates this aspect of poetry best:

> This absence of story, or vagueness of story, is for lyric poems a feature, not a bug; lyric poetry can present states of mind, ways to be alive, without having to say how we got there or what happens next. (*Don't Read Poetry* 28)

In other words, the decentering of story in poetry creates possibilities for characterizing experience, for capturing moods, feelings, and mental states. In resisting closure, poetry opens new ways of thinking.

How do these moods, feelings, and mental states get conveyed in poetry? One way to think about how poems work is to consider the kinds of moves that poets make in poems, *move* meaning something like the moves that a dancer makes, or, as Elisa Gabbert describes them in "The Moves: Common Maneuvers in Contemporary Poetry," like the moves a chess player makes on a chessboard. The term *rhetorical move* comes from genre analysis, which describes moves as patterns of usage or strategies that writers use in specific genres. For example, John Swales, a linguist and pioneer in the field of genre analysis, analyzed patterns of usage in academic journal article introductions and discovered that writers typically make three moves: establishing a territory, establishing a niche, and occupying that niche. For students, knowing these moves helps support active reading in nonfiction texts and helps them know what to include when writing introductions themselves (this model is called the "Creating a Research Space" or CARS model for introductions). Another source that uses moves to help students understand and write is Gerald Graff and Cathy Birkenstein's *They Say/I Say: The Moves That Matter in Academic Writing*.

In this chapter, we discuss some common moves in contemporary poetry. The inspiration for this chapter is Gabbert's essay "The Moves: Common Maneuvers in Contemporary Poetry," an essay intended for graduate students and experts in the field of poetics. Our goal here is to provide readers examples of common moves that are likely to show up in the kinds of poems teachers share with students in middle and high school classrooms. Recognizing moves helps readers see patterns within the genre, see how writers treat subjects differently (and how they're in conversation with each other), and see units of meaning above the level of literary devices. Recognizing moves also helps readers think about how a poem is shaping meaning and achieving effects. In this way, thinking about "moves" is connected to what poems do: they move us.

A word of caution, though. Just as it's tempting to present literary devices as a list of vocabulary to master, it may be tempting to focus on these moves by hunting for them the way students hunt for symbols in literature to the detriment of connecting with the text. Instead, let these moves be a starting point for thinking about moves. When John Swales developed the CARS mode of analysis, he started with reading research articles and began seeing patterns, such as the way writers introduced direct quotes or framed a question in the introduction. He didn't start with a particular move and then go hunting for examples. Approaching the moves in poems with an open mind will also help you see trends in the craft of poetry that will elucidate the dynamic and historical nature of poetical moves. For example, the moves we discuss in this chapter would be different if our source poems were written by British Romantic poets.

Further, thinking about poems through the lens of moves shouldn't be used as a reductive means of rendering a poem down to a closed interpretation. Literary devices are tempting lures because they let readers feel confident in their identifications. But poetry isn't so easily hemmable; it's meant to be undone. Instead, the moves may be a tool for perceiving patterns in the way poets see the world and understand our place in the world, which again is rooted in situatedness—*where* we are and *when* we are in the world.

Also, please note that almost all of the poems listed in this chapter can be found online.

"And I Think to Myself, What a Wonderful World," or, Staying Alive

There's a move poets do (as they do, the saying goes) that's maybe my (Lindsay's) favorite thing: for a hot blinding and brief second, they manage to capture the hum of life, that electric, motes-floating shimmer of being alive and being so in love with life. I suspect that the pull of heightened sensitivity poets feel about the world operates on a spectrum: on one end, a heaviness, the world-weariness of despair, and on the other end, the sublime, the ecstatic, the feeling akin to Whitman's "I Sing the Body Electric." Or like the emotions in Gabrielle Calvocoressi's "Hammond B3 Organ Cistern," which describes days when "All the people / in the streets waiting for their high fives / and leaping, I mean *leaping,* / when they see me" (lines 2–5). The speaker ends the poem with an ebullient "Hallelujah!" When these moments happen in poems or in our lives, poets remind us that the moments are precious gifts that should be celebrated, as when the speaker in Hieu Minh Nguyen's "Heavy" sees the river and affirms: "I am alive. I know this. Alive now / to see the world, to see the river / rupture everything with its light." Or in "The Conditional," when the speaker in Ada Limón's poem imagines the end of the world and taking heart in the moment, holding hands with her beloved, feeling lucky to be alive.

In the following poem by Donika Kelly, "The moon rose over the bay. I had a lot of feelings," a similar sentiment is expressed. The speaker is experiencing embodiment, identifying with the dead squid that were "startled to find themselves in the sun." The singularity of the moment—the eighteen seagulls, the ditch lily, the Jeep—all heighten the speaker's ultimate refrain: "I am in love."

> The moon rose over the bay. I had a lot of feelings.
> I am taken with the hot animal
> of my skin, grateful to swing my limbs
> and have them move as I intend, though
> my knee, though my shoulder, though something
> is torn or tearing. Today, a dozen squid, dead
> on the harbor beach: one mostly buried,
> one with skin empty as a shell and hollow
> feeling, and, though the tentacles look soft,
> I do not touch them. I imagine they
> were startled to find themselves in the sun.
> I imagine the tide simply went out
> without them. I imagine they cannot

feel the black flies charting the raised hills
of their eyes. I write my name in the sand:
Donika Kelly. I watch eighteen seagulls
skim the sandbar and lift low in the sky.
I pick up a pebble that looks like a green egg.
To the ditch lily I say I am in love.
To the Jeep parked haphazardly on the narrow
street I am in love. To the roses, white
petals rimmed brown, to the yellow lined
pavement, to the house trimmed in gold I am
in love. I shout with the rough calculus
of walking. Just let me find my way back,
let me move like a tide come in.

Poems your students might enjoy about transcendent emotion include the following:

"Advent" by Heather Christle

"The Conditional" by Ada Limón

"Hammond B3 Organ Cistern" by Gabrielle Calvocoressi

"Heavy" by Hieu Minh Nguyen

"Love" by Alex Dimitrov

"Pathetic Fallacy" by Emilia Phillips

Addressing an Unnamed "You" and Epistolary Poems

When the speaker of a poem employs second-person address, "you," an intimate space opens. Think of the kinds of phrases that *you* is used for: "I love you," "I need you," "I forgive you." Using *you* invokes a relationship, a kind of speech act that calls into being an I-Thou dynamic. Remember also that in some languages, like Spanish, the second-person pronoun has formal and informal variations, the informal reserved for usage among people with whom you are friendly or intimate. This convention probably arose partly because speakers are aware of the power of *you*. (It's also the reason we ask students to refrain from using *you* in academic writing; it might be off-putting to some readers or too informal for some kinds of academic audiences.)

Another way of thinking about the *you* in poems is by considering that the poet may be addressing themself, employing self-talk, like someone saying affirmations in a mirror or processing some problem they're facing, as in Mary Oliver's "Wild Geese." In this poem, which is widely available online, the speaker of the poem uses direct address to encourage the self/reader to stop trying to be what they're not and to accept human desires.

Epistolary poems are addressed to a specific person, as writers do in letters or email, and as Victoria Chang does in "Dear P." We know from Poets.org that Chang wrote "Dear P." as part of a series of poems to her children, this one about love, "the only thing that is not an argument." In epistolary poems, readers overhear what was intended for another, resulting in an emotional transference, as if the reader were the intended audience.

Dear P.

Someone will love you many will love
you many will brother you some of these
loves will bother you some will leave you
one might haunt you hunt you in your
sleep make you weep the tearless kind of
weep the kind of weep that drowns your
organs slowly there are little oars in your body
little boats grab onto them and row and row
someone will tell you no but you won't know
he is right until you have already wrung your
own heart dry your hands dripping knives until
you have already reached your hands into his
body and put them through his heart love is
the only thing that is not an argument

Unnamed "you" and epistolary poems your students might enjoy include the following:

"Inappropriate Dreams" by Brenda Shaughnessy

"Kite" by Stephanie Burt

"Love Song (Smelt)" by Dan Chiasson

"Wild Geese" by Mary Oliver

After Poems and Intertextuality

In the *Ion,* Plato explains poetic inspiration by comparing it to the way metal becomes magnetized: an unmagnetized piece of metal becomes magnetized when it comes in contact with a piece of metal that *is* magnetized. In Plato's telling, the metal rings form chains or networks of inspiration that continue to be formed as readers read works that inspire them to create new works. Lewis Hyde's *The Gift: Creativity and the Artist in the Modern World* makes a similar claim about inspiration and creativity—that art exists in a gift culture in which works of art circulate, gain value, and precipitate further imaginative works of art. Both Plato's and Hyde's theorizing of inspiration captures the social currency of poems and is reflected in the many poems written in conversation with other poems, poems that take up similar questions, and poems that become a branch of a family tree of similar poems. *After poems* often reference the original poet or poem in a subtitle as a clear acknowledgment of the new poem's provenance.

A recent example of the currency of poetry that results in After poems is Ocean Vuong's "Someday I'll Love Ocean Vuong." When this poem was published in the *New Yorker,* it had an epigram after the title that read "After Frank O'Hara / After Roger Reeves." Here, the word *after* conveys that the poet has borrowed or will be riffing on some aspect or specific lines from these two poets. In this case, that line is "Someday I'll Love ______." Here is Roger Reeves discussing his poem "Someday I'll Love Roger Reeves":

> It's a poem that I kind of wrote to myself. It's a love poem, again. . . . Frank O'Hara is a guy I always turn to. He had this one line in his poem—I can't find the poem again because you know Frank O'Hara has a lot of poems—and it's a poem where he says "someday I'll love Frank O'Hara." I thought, that is the best thing to say in the middle of a poem—someday you'll love yourself. So I said, I'm going to title a poem "Someday I'll love Roger Reeves." (qtd. in Epstein)

Here is the original Frank O'Hara poem, "Katy":

Katy

They say I mope too much
but really I'm loudly dancing.
I eat paper. It's good for my bones.
I play the piano pedal. I dance.
I am never quiet. I mean silent.
Some day I'll love Frank O'Hara.
I think I'll be alone for a little while.

Even though in this poem it doesn't seem as though the poet is talking about himself but instead being talked about, perhaps by a little girl, Roger Reeves picked up on the line, using it as a title for a poem aimed at self-acceptance. Enter Ocean Vuong's poem "Someday I'll Love Ocean Vuong." It's a poem about family history and what that means for him, and it's addressed to himself, a kind of self-talk. And ultimately, it looks forward to a future: "The most beautiful part of your body / is where it's headed." Since Vuong's poem was published, more "Someday I'll Love" poems are appearing, such as Claire Schwartz's "Someday I'll Love Claire Schwartz."

If you are interested in exploring these poems and having your students write them, you may want to use them as an opportunity to explore issues around plagiarism, poetic appropriation, and the ethics of writing about others' traumas. Susan Sontag's *Regarding the Pain of Others* would be a good resource for exploring these questions regarding representation and responsibility.

After poem pairings your students might enjoy include the following:

"Dear White America" by Danez Smith and "Dear Hearing World" by Raymond Antrobus

"Squall" by Stanley Moss and "Red Squall" by Wanda Coleman

"There Are Birds Here" by Jamaal May, "There Is a Lake Here" by Clint Smith, and "There Are Trans People Here" by H. Melt

"To the Young Who Want to Die" by Gwendolyn Brooks and "Sorrow Is Not My Name" by Ross Gay

"Try to Praise the Mutilated World" by Adam Zagajewski and "Prayer for the Mutilated World" by Sam Sax

The Protest Poem

From poems addressing the shooting deaths of unarmed Black people to the scourge of mass shootings in schools and other public arenas, poems highlighting injustice are sadly necessary and showing up everywhere, poems such as Ross Gay's "A Small Needful Fact," about Eric Garner's work as a gardener, and Devorah Major's "Newtown interview," in which a reporter tells a seven-year-old "it's over now," but the girl "knows / in a corner of her belly / that has never hurt like this before / that it is not over." Other poems memorialize, bear witness to violence, or even transform, as Jericho Brown does in "The Tradition," which transforms the lives of John Crawford, Eric Garner, and Michael Brown into flowers, cut down in a color-saturated apocalypse.

The way this move sometimes plays out in poems attempting to center marginalized subjects is by approaching the subject from an unconventional perspective. For example, Roger Reeves's "The Mare of Money," a poem that centers the lynching death of Emmitt Till, is written from the perspective of a dead horse in the shallow water where Till's body was dumped—in other words, by indirection, or, as Emily Dickinson puts it, "Tell all the Truth but tell it slant." For an essay-length treatment of this topic, read Camille T. Dungy's "Tell It Slant: How to Write a Wise Poem" on the Poetry Foundation website.

And sometimes the poem protests division. In the following poem, Ada Limón imagines a new version of the national anthem that unites Americans, "a song that says my bones / are your bones, and your bones are my bones":

A New National Anthem

The truth is, I've never cared for the National
Anthem. If you think about it, it's not a good
song. Too high for most of us with "the rockets
red glare" and then there are the bombs.
(Always, always, there is war and bombs.)
Once, I sang it at homecoming and threw
even the tenacious high school band off key.
But the song didn't mean anything, just a call
to the field, something to get through before
the pummeling of youth. And what of the stanzas
we never sing, the third that mentions "no refuge
could save the hireling and the slave"? Perhaps,
the truth is, every song of this country
has an unsung third stanza, something brutal
snaking underneath us as we blindly sing
the high notes with a beer sloshing in the stands
hoping our team wins. Don't get me wrong, I do
like the flag, how it undulates in the wind
like water, elemental, and best when it's humbled,
brought to its knees, clung to by someone who
has lost everything, when it's not a weapon,
when it flickers, when it folds up so perfectly
you can keep it until it's needed, until you can
love it again, until the song in your mouth feels

like sustenance, a song where the notes are sung
by even the ageless woods, the short-grass plains,
the Red River Gorge, the fistful of land left
unpoisoned, that song that's our birthright,
that's sung in silence when it's too hard to go on,
that sounds like someone's rough fingers weaving
into another's, that sounds like a match being lit
in an endless cave, the song that says my bones
are your bones, and your bones are my bones,
and isn't that enough?

Protest poems your students might enjoy include the following:

"Gate A-4" by Naomi Shihab Nye

"I saw Emmett Till this week at the grocery store" by Eve L. Ewing

"It won't be a bullet" by Danez Smith

"The Mare of Money" by Roger Reeves

"Newtown interview" by devorah major

"A Small Needful Fact" by Ross Gay

"The Tradition" by Jericho Brown

Extended Metaphors

Though John Donne's "A Valediction Forbidding Mourning" contains two metaphors for the estranged lovers in the poem—gold that is stretched but never separated and the legs of a compass—it is often the poem used as the exemplar for extended metaphor. Another popular poem that gets anthologized and taught to highlight this move is Donne's "The Flea." Extended metaphors continue to be used by poets writing today in innovative ways.

A contemporary example of extended metaphor is Ada Limón's "Lashed to the Helm, All Stiff and Stark," the title of which is borrowed from a Longfellow poem, "The Wreck of the Hesperus." The poem's central metaphor is the shipwrecked marriage, the final fight coinciding with an actual ice storm. The speaker is "as cold as I have ever been," as she thinks about "the wreck that was the two of us." She imagines herself as the boat, "a lost sea-tossed daughter," with the wreck's debris—unread books, unwashed dishes, unfed dog—all around her. Another poem that employs extended metaphor to dazzling effect is Leila Chatti's "MRI Song," in which the MRI machine receives her body "like a pill on your cold / white tongue. You hum / me cradled in your mouth / like a song" (12–15).

Extended metaphor poems your students might enjoy include the following:

"Clarinet" by Terrance Hayes

"Ear Muffs" by Andrea Gibson

"Lashed to the Helm, All Stiff and Stark" by Ada Limón

"MRI Song" by Leila Chatti

"Song of Smoke" by Kevin Young

"Topography" by Sharon Olds

"Trophic Cascade" by Camille T. Dungy

Meta-Moments: Poems about Poems, Reading, and Writing

The opening lines of Ruth Stone's "Always on the Train" explains the compulsiveness of writing poems about writing: "Writing poems about writing poems / is like rolling bales of hay in Texas. / Nothing but the horizon to stop you." Sometimes these poems are more narrowly about *why* poets write, called *ars poetica* poems, but more generally the meta-moment as a move reveals the inner workings of reading and writing. A variation of this move dramatizes the connection between writer and reader, as with the speaker in Walt Whitman's "Crossing Brooklyn Ferry," who imagines the poem connecting poet and reader across generations, continuously, as the (always) present participle in the title suggests.

Riffing on William Carlos Williams's adage that a poem "is a machine of words," Cynthia Cruz's speaker in "Fragment" says she "would like this poem / to be a machine," the kind of machine that keeps memories, and by the end, identifies a source of poetry: "in that static, in the rip, / the mar, the error / between, is where, / when it begins, it will / begin."

Fragment

I would like this poem
to be a machine.
Concise, metallic,
a counting apparatus.
A means to keep each moment
contained and fixed, akin
to a series of Polaroids,
photographed and fixed
to cardboard or some other
paper-panel backing.
Then photographed and affixed
with Scotch tape to the wall.
Or, a vitrine, a glass case,
within which to gather and collect
each moment, each object
representing each moment.
A bundle, assemblage, or archive
constructed of letters and notes,
diary entries and fragments,
articles and photographs
torn from books.
A machine that measures
the space between
the body and the mind,
the dissonance that exists
inside that moment. And there,
in that static, in the rip,
the mar, the error
between, is where,
when it begins, it will
begin.

The following poem, "Reading," by Denise Duhamel recounts the experience of unfocused reading, which many of my students relate to, the feeling of looking up from reading and not being able to say what you just read, and then the speaker turns to the experience of writing, wondering why writers bother at all, before arriving at her answer: connecting people.

Reading

Sometimes I read pages of books without retaining anything.
I am thinking about my own drama and caesura
until I come across a word like *creosote,* which seems familiar
but I have to look up. When I go to the dictionary, I realize
I am wondering who will bury me and where,
going over the time I was almost hit by a car on A1A.
It was dark, and he'd left me in the parking garage
saying, "I'll go ahead and get us a table." He meant
inside of Le Tub where there was always a long wait.
I stood in front of the Master Meter with my fistful of coins.
"Ok," I said. What if that had been the end, that flattened smack, of me?
He would have looked up from the menu to the sirens—
that wila and red pulsing light—and it might have taken him
a moment to realize I was the one on the ground.
The thing about reading is that your mind might wander
to imagine the author sitting long enough
and silent enough to recall such a moment, so intimate
she never even mentioned it to her date.
The driver who almost hit me had forgotten
to turn on his headlights. And what about the intimacy
of writing itself? Each finger pad on a key, or the pen's whisper
into paper. What makes us do it, relive instead of live, go back
and forward in time? It's like dancing
to empty chairs in an empty room of a closed bar,
your shimmery ghost there long after you've left.
Only a few people will come to the dive
where you once danced, or turn to the page
where you left some marks, look at the words you wrote.
Fewer still will read them. Then a mixture
of vanity and humility of a stranger understands.
Or looks up a word she'd forgotten she knew.

Meta-moment poems your students might enjoy include the following:

"Always on the Train" by Ruth Stone

"American Sonnet for My Past and Future Assassin" by Terrance Hayes

"Are All the Break-Ups in Your Poems Real?" by Aimee Nezhukumatathil

"Ars Poetica (cocoons)" by Dana Levin

"Eating Poetry" by Mark Strand

"Miracles" by Brenda Shaughnessy

"Scarecrow on Fire" by Dean Young

"to the notebook kid" by Eve. L. Ewing

"Vocabulary of Dearness" by Naomi Shihab Nye

"You, Reader" by Billy Collins

The Obvious and Ordinary as Transcendent

American philosopher John J. McDermott, in *Streams of Experience,* writes: "Our affective presence converts the ordinary to the extraordinary" (140). Though McDermott wasn't a poet, his words resonate with me as a poet who considers writing poetry a practice of noticing what may not be noticed without my attention. This approach to writing, shared by many poets, elevates consciousness, and some see this function of poetry as one that makes it necessary for the world.

In Jessica Greenbaum's "I Love You More Than All the Windows in New York City," the speaker of the poem finds a corollary to her frenetic mind in the pulse of the city and its ordinary urbanity: buildings and trucks, pigeons and streetlights, a busy street corner and a paper bag from which she pulls this poem, a gift for her beloved.

Examples your students might enjoy of poems that elevate the ordinary include the following:

"Bildungsroman" by Meg Freitag

"Double Dutch" by Gregory Pardlo

"I Love You More Than All the Windows in New York City" by Jessica Greenbaum

"My Heart Belongs to Qdoba" by Laurin Macios

"Poem with the Smell of Coffee Inside" by Devin Kelly

"Sono" by Suji Kwock Kim

Prayers

Of the relationship between prayer and poetry, Jericho Brown says, "The work of prayer and the work of poetry are the same in that they both ask us to broaden our awareness, to become more conscious of that which we've avoided or ignored" ("Jericho Brown"). Like poems about identity and love, addressing the divine, reaching out to communicate with God in whatever form the poet imagines, is a common move in contemporary poetry, a move that seems related to poems addressed to an unnamed "you." Addressing another is a way of establishing spiritual connection, and that's what we find happening in these poems, even (especially) in the presence of doubt and spiritual darkness, as in Marie Howe's "Prayer." In other prayer poems, addressing God becomes an opportunity to reimagine or recast the image of God.

Examples of prayer poems your students might enjoy include the following:

"Despite My Efforts Even My Prayers Have Turned into Threats" by Kaveh Akbar

"God Says Yes to Me" by Kaylin Haught

"Prayer" by Marie Howe

"Prayer for the Mutilated World" by Sam Sax

"6. the eternal dice" by Tom Sleigh (from "House of Fact, House of Ruin")

Self-Fashioning and Persona Poems

Very few topics are more widely explored in contemporary American poetry than questions about origins, belonging, alienation, self-fashioning, sexual orientation, gender identity, body image, home literacies, and more. In American poetry, self-fashioning is part of our poetic tradition, from Whitman ("Song of Myself") to the confessional poets (think Sylvia Plath, Amy Lowell, Anne Sexton). Some contemporary poets enact this move when they write self-portrait poems (for exemplars of this mode, see the section on self-portrait poems in Chapter 7: "Writing Poems from Prompts"). But many other poems beyond self-portrait pieces make the self-fashioning move. For example, Tiana Clark's speaker in "Bear Witness" considers her sense of self as she engages with an image from artist Carrie Mae Weems's Roaming series, staring at "a long black dress I called *Woman*." There's a doubleness in this search for meaning through representation since Weems's photography interrogates self-representation and what it means to bear witness; "Bear Witness" is also an example of ekphrasis, poetry engaging with a work of art.

Another move related to self-fashioning is writing from the perspective of another person, also called *persona* poems. Another Tiana Clark piece, "Conversation with Phillis Wheatley #1," illustrates the reciprocal self-fashioning typical of persona poems: the poet is speaking on behalf of another and by extension grafts some of that persona onto themself, the trace result of the act of embodying another. In this poem, the poet imagines a slave ship as a hyphen on the sea, the hyphen between "African-American."

Conversation with Phillis Wheatley #1

Don't you hate your name?

–

I was named like all things are named:
after the things that carry them. Blacked
out belly of my slave ship, the pitching

womb of the ocean slapped against splint-
ered and swollen wood. My only mother
was born-again darkness slated with sun

and moonlight. There is no mercy before
this one. How do you cry for a continent
that you cannot smell? I had no ears or nose

before the stench of damp and sour bodies
chained with moaning, calling out in different
tongues to different gods—all midnight babel.

Small and unchained, I slipped through feverish
thighs like a small, soft egg floating inside
the scorching center of this moving hyphen—

African-American: dash exposing the break.

Self-fashioning poems your students might enjoy include the following:

"Bear Witness" by Tiana Clark

"Families" by Fatimah Asghar

"Heavy" by Hieu Minh Nguyen

"Martha Anne Dae" by Amber Tamblyn

"Someday I'll Love Ocean Vuong" by Ocean Vuong

"Testimony" by Hafizah Geter

"what the cicada said to the black boy" by Clint Smith

Conclusion

In the next chapters, we move from discovering and reading contemporary poetry to practical strategies for bringing contemporary poems into your classroom using activities that will help students interpret poems, write poems, and complete poetry projects.

4

Teaching Poems

This chapter provides examples of lesson plans for teaching individual poems, including discussion questions, activities, and assignments that support students for whom text complexity presents a challenge for their reading proficiencies. We also share lesson plans based on poem pairings or groups that address outcomes related to rhetorical and genre knowledge.

The lessons in this chapter were designed for a fifty-minute class period, though they can all be adapted to different time lengths depending on your schedule. We have laid out scaffolded, organized lessons focused on identifying tone and other poetic elements, as well as lessons for interpreting poems. We've included several interactive and thought-provoking activities and lessons you can do in your classroom with *any* poem that you think your students will enjoy and most relate to. We also offer some activities for specific poems we have found to be successful, but even these activities can be modified for any poem of your choosing to fit your students' needs. We hope that the ideas in this chapter will help inspire your students to engage with poetry in new ways.

Introduction to Poetry Lessons: What Is Poetry?

Day 1

The majority of my (Melissa's) students have developed an aversion to poetry somewhere along their educational way. All the wonder and fun has been sucked out of it, and I'm faced with a roomful of groans and students slouching so far down in their desks they're almost on the floor when I first tell them we're going to start a poetry unit. My first job is to unteach. I have to help them reset their understanding of poetry by working through their initial definitions and opinions. Forget about iambic pentameter and ABABCBCB rhyme scheme; we need to consider how students view poetry as an art form and challenge them to see it in new, and perhaps unexpected, ways.

Materials needed:

- Play-Doh
- Colorful paper
- Markers
- Devices for using Flipgrid app or website

Melissa's Creative Writing students exploring their definitions of poetry *using Play-Doh.*

This lesson asks students to use Flipgrid, a free social learning platform that allows students to record short videos. You set up a "grid" to which students can upload videos, which are then viewable by other members of the grid (i.e., a class). Members can also comment on one another's videos. To begin the lesson, directions are displayed on the board as follows:

To begin our poetry adventures together, I would like for you to consider your personal definition of poetry.

1. With a partner, brainstorm a list of different ways you define poetry.
2. Create a Play-Doh sculpture that physically illustrates your perception of poetry.
3. Set your sculpture on a sheet of colored paper. Write individual words and phrases around the paper that sum up your definition.
4. Using Flipgrid, record a 90-second video together that:
    a. Shares your definition
    b. Explains how your sculpture encapsulates your definition
    c. Explains the words around your paper

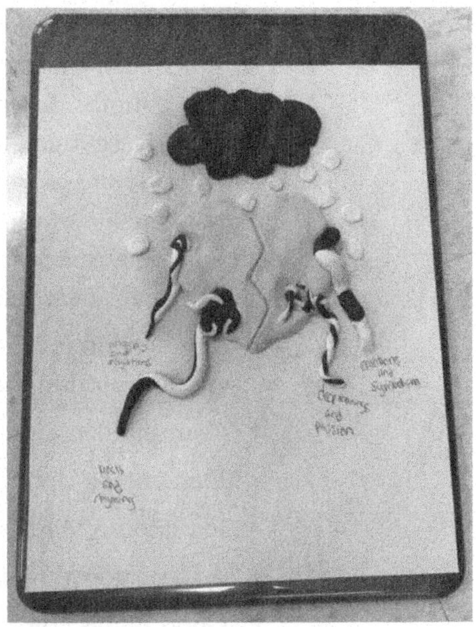

A final product with definitions including "deep meaning and passion" and "imagery and rhythms."

This hands-on activity allows students to work together, discuss, and ultimately come up with their own definitions of poetry. As expected, common words students use are *emotional*, *creative*, *expressive*, *musical*, and *personal*. While those serve as a basic foundation, I want students to dig a little deeper.

Days 2 and 3

The next step is for students to reflect on, add on to, and hopefully gain some new perceptions of what poetry is and what it can accomplish. Over the course of two fifty-minute class periods, I show them a playlist of poems. Some are personal favorites, and all will be used in some way later in the semester as part of a poetry prompt (see Chapter 7 for more about writing poems from prompts).

> Directions:
> We will watch a string of poems. After each video, write down your thoughts in regard to these questions:
>
> - What do you think the poem is about?
> - How does the poem make you feel, or what does it make you think?
> - What words or phrases stood out to you in the poem and why?
> - What are your overall thoughts on the poem/reading/performance/video?
> - If you had to assign a COLOR to the poem, which color would it be and why? (Note: this question leads into the Color Poem prompt described in Chapter 7.)

In between each video, I set a three-minute timer for students to freewrite their thoughts using these questions as a guide. They can't stop writing. If they get stuck and have a writer's block moment, they can simply copy down the questions. The point is to keep the pencil moving, which tends to keep the thoughts flowing. After each freewrite, I ask for a quick show of hands. Well, thumbs, actually. Thumbs up if they like the poem, sideways thumb for "It's okay," and thumbs down if they don't like it. This is mostly to satisfy my own curiosity and to gauge their likes and dislikes when it comes to poetry, and perhaps to modify the list for the next year.

Here is the list of videos I show my students, all of which are easily found with a quick internet search. Please revise the list accordingly for poems you feel will speak to your students:

- "Application for the Position of Abdelhalim Hafez's Girl" by Safia Elhillo (video at motionpoems.org)
- "Counting Descent" by Clint Smith
- "Elementary" by Savon Bartley
- "Explaining My Depression to My Mother" by Sabrina Benaim
- "A Genealogy" by Hanif Abdurraqib
- "Good Bones" by Maggie Smith (video at motionpoems.org)
- "Paper People" by Harry Baker
- "Tamara's Opus" by Joshua Bennett

After the last freewrite, students find a partner or two and discuss the following questions:

- After watching these videos and hearing these poems, what new ideas would you add to how you define poetry?
- Are these poems like other poems you have read before? Which ones? Explain similarities and/or differences to poems you have read before.
- What did you learn about poetry from watching these?
- What words would you add to your definitions from yesterday?
- Which poem stood out the most to you and why? Favorite and least favorite poem?

As a culmination, we come together as a whole class to discuss our opinions, thoughts, and any new perceptions about poetry. By now, students are confident enough to share their ideas about each poem, voicing their varying thoughts and opinions. They are developing a shared language for discussing the genre.

Introduction to Poetry: Blind Dating

This lesson was originally written as a post on teachlivingpoets.com by Kristin Dreyer and Nikki Lehman, co-teachers at Chantilly High School in Chantilly, Virginia. It was inspired by an idea executed by teacher Monet Hardison and documented by researcher Amy Rottmann that they termed Blind Date Poetry. *Classrooms were arranged to look like a café or restaurant to set the mood, including tablecloths, faux candles, and centerpieces.*

Materials needed:

- Classroom transformation: tablecloths, flowers, electric candles, etc. to create a café atmosphere
- Envelopes with poems inside, key words written on the outside
- Music to play softly in the background (optional)

This lesson entices students to try out poetry by "dating" unknown poems, choosing them based only on a few key words offered on the front of an envelope. To hook them, the poems we present have to say something to our kids about the lives they lead and what is important to them. Some of the poems include the following:

- "Are All the Break-Ups in Your Poems Real?" by Aimee Nezhukumatathil
- "Belief in Magic" by Dean Young
- "Consider the Hands That Write This Letter" by Aracelis Girmay
- "Deer Hit" by Jon Loomis
- "Epistemology" by Catherine Barnett
- "How to Triumph Like a Girl" by Ada Limón
- "My Father's Song" by Simon F. Ortiz
- "Ode to Pork" by Kevin Young
- "Pass On" by Michael Lee
- "Playground Elegy" by Clint Smith
- "A Sad Child" by Margaret Atwood
- "Scary Movies" by Kim Addonizio
- "A Small Needful Fact" by Ross Gay

Place a group of envelopes on each of the students' tables with poems inside and the key words written on the outside, facing up. Students then "date" at least five poems, spending time reading and attempting to connect with each one. If they find one that doesn't fit, they put it back in the hopes that maybe one of their peers will find their match.

Some students immediately connect with poems and others are more resistant. Some students need additional scaffolding or support throughout the dating process, so we [Kristin and Nikki] created the response checklist in Figure 4.1. What we found occurring naturally: students were chatting about the poems they found interesting and even recommending them to their friends. As we circulated the room, we felt like nervous best friends waiting to find out how a blind date went. We hoped the kids would choose their best matches and were rewarded when one of our students found the first poem she ever liked, telling us, "I finally 'get' a poem." This activity was a nonthreatening way to get students to read a poem without any preconceived notions; since the poems were hidden inside envelopes, students weren't intimidated by their language or length.

Once our students found a poem they wanted to "spend more time with," we asked them to read it again, paying attention to the emotions it conjured within them—the ways in which they found connections to their lives. As a culmination to the activity, students wrote a paragraph reflection on their favorite

Blind Date with a Poem

Based on the words listed on the outside of the envelope, choose a poem from your table that interests you. Then "rate your date" using the columns below.

Poem #	So . . . how was your date? (circle one)	2nd date? Why or why not?	Rate your date (1 = hated it, 7 = loved it)
1: #____	We have lots of chemistry! We're better off friends. Don't text me . . . ever.		1 2 3 4 5 6 7
2: #____	We have lots of chemistry! We're better off friends. Don't text me . . . ever.		1 2 3 4 5 6 7
3: #____	We have lots of chemistry! We're better off friends. Don't text me . . . ever.		1 2 3 4 5 6 7
4: #____	We have lots of chemistry! We're better off friends. Don't text me . . . ever.		1 2 3 4 5 6 7

FIGURE 4.1. Blind Date with a Poem response checklist.

poem. According to Amy Rottmann's study, Blind Date Poetry "allowed students to connect to various poems in an enjoyable, high-speed, interactive way. . . . [S]tudents enjoyed Blind Date Poetry because it provided them autonomy, which motivated them to continue reading the poem they were able to choose" (5).

Breaking Down Line Breaks

Parts of this lesson were shared with me by Nicole F. Tong, a professor of English and author of How to Prove a Theory.

Students need to realize the impact a line break can have in order to truly appreciate the structure of a poem. They need to learn the difference between end-stopped and enjambed lines, as well as the potentialities of poetic line structure. We start with reading the beginning of poet Rebecca Hazelton's essay "Learning the Poetic Line: How Line Breaks Shape Meaning," stopping where she shifts into sound. Hazelton's essay does a fantastic job of explaining the various effects specific enjambments have, and then how those effects would change if the line breaks were placed differently.

Next, I give students a handout with Gwendolyn Brooks's poem "We Real Cool" written in paragraph form without the line breaks—just a continuous line across the page, punctuation included. With a partner, students rewrite it as a poem and attempt to re-create the poem the way they think Brooks wrote it. They discuss where she would break lines, most guessing after the periods.

After a few minutes of discussion, as students are in the throes of end-stopped lines, I play the audio of Brooks reading her poem (available on poets.org). Once students hear her read, there are a lot of "Ooooohhhs" and side-cocked heads as they start to reconsider their previous choices. As students reevaluate, they discuss how the meaning changes when lines break after *We*. Now the focus gets placed on *We*, which creates a sense of community and identity. We chat about this for a bit, and then I show them the actual poem.

From there, we read the explanation of the "golden shovel" form written by Don Share for the Poetry Foundation, and we read the bio for Terrance Hayes, who invented the form. When teaching living poets, it's important for students to learn a little bit about who they are reading, which is why I always include poet bios. It helps to give them a sense of personal relevance if they can "meet" the individual who wrote the poem.

Next, I give students the text of Hayes's poem "The Golden Shovel" and ask them to consider the line breaks as we read it out loud. Some students will catch on fairly quickly, but for some it takes a revisit of the poem after listening to it. Once they realize that the last word in each line of Hayes's poem is each individual word Brooks uses in hers, the room buzzes with "Woooah, that's so cool!" This moment, as students make their discovery, is effective in empowering students to form their own insights about poetry. Once the realization has been made, we discuss how the enjambment progresses throughout the poem, and how by the end of it, Hayes is breaking lines in the middle of words. This poem most certainly gives my students a new appreciation for the poetic line. Students might also enjoy Poet Laureate Joy Harjo's golden shovel poem, "An American Sunrise," included in her book of the same title.

To conclude the lesson, we return to the idea of line breaks and move into a read-aloud of "In His Mouth" by Tyree Daye from his collection *River Hymns*.

A student volunteer reads it once and then a different student reads it again. I believe in reading every poem at least twice. The first time through we just get a feel for what it's about; the second time around we can possibly derive some thoughts on meaning and how that meaning is created. The more times we read it, the better.

In His Mouth

I am my daddy's scored hands
each line something that began and ended
he let go of my useless fingers
I am his poked mouth saying I love you
I am a tongue
        behind in his teeth
my mother saw me
        drowning in his mouth
laid down under him
saw me closer   they kissed
I entered   an idea
said *I love you*
I was given a name

Discussion ensues about Daye's enjambment choices and the effects they have on the poem, and how we as readers place emphasis on certain words. Ask students to consider why they think he forgoes punctuation, which I've found offers some impressive student insights.

This lesson could be followed up by a prompt to write a golden shovel poem. Or students could go back to a previous poem they've read and try to change its meaning simply by changing its line breaks. Can they create new emphasis on certain words? What happens to lines when they are longer versus shorter? Enjambed versus end-stopped? Seeing all the different variations and explanations could offer interesting discussion.

Teaching Tone

Students may feel confused or lost when trying to identify a speaker's attitude in a poem. To help teach students how to grapple with tone, I start with a poem that has a clear and easily recognizable tone, followed by scaffolded poems with tones that are more subtle and complex.

In Elizabeth Acevedo's award-winning novel in verse, *The Poet X*, Acevedo explores the complex relationship between the teenage protagonist and her mother. How many students might be able to relate to having strife with their parents? Or that their mothers just don't understand them? Whether their parental problems are monumental or superficial, most students will be able to relate to Acevedo's poem in some way. Since the following poem is taken out of context from the novel, students should be informed that the "you" of the poem is the speaker's mother.

In Translation

My mouth cannot write you a white flag.
It will never be a Bible verse.
My mouth cannot be shaped into the apology
you say both you and God deserve.

And you want to make it seem
it's my mouth's entire fault.
Because it was hungry,
and silent, but what about your mouth:

how your lips are staples
that pierce me quick and hard.

And the words I never say
are better left on my tongue
since they would only have slammed
against the closed door of your back.

Your silence furnishes a dark house.
But even at the risk of burning
the moth always seeks the light.

Even students who tend to struggle with reading tone in poetry can recognize the frustration Acevedo's speaker feels toward her mother. Students can successfully support their tone insights by picking out connotative words and heavily charged phrases, as well as the metaphors of the staples, door, and moth.

Next, we read "The Raincoat" by Ada Limón from her book *The Carrying*, which allows students to experience a very different tone toward a mother. Students compare and contrast the diction in each poem to understand how each poet achieves her desired tone. Finally, we read Patrick Rosal's "If All My Relationships Fail and I Have No Children Do I Even Know What Love Is," which has a more subtle and complex tone. When asked to identify the tone, students' first inclination is to focus on the way the father in the poem feels about his daughter: loving, caring, protective. They explore that for a bit and identify phrases or lines as textual support. But here's where the complexity comes in—because the father is not the speaker. I direct students back to the title, which includes information about the speaker with "I have no children." I ask them:

"Who is the speaker of the poem? Is it the father?"

"No."

"Okay, then, who is it?"

"Some guy watching the father and daughter."

"Right. So how does he feel about watching this moment happen in the café?"

With some guiding questions, students will start to pick up on the poem's tonal complexities.

This lesson starts off by building students' confidence in identifying tone using Acevedo's poem, provides a contrasting tone with Limón's piece, and then stretches students' abilities to infer with Rosal's poem. Students also find the topic of parent-child relationships relevant to their own lives and are able to bring experiences and opinions of their own to the poem based on their individual familial relationships and backgrounds.

More poems by living poets about parent-child relationships include the following:

- "Barbie Chang's Father Paid" and "Barbie Chang's Father Calls" by Victoria Chang
- "Boy and the Belt" and "My Mom Puts on Makeup" by José Olivarez
- "c'mon" by Ross Gay
- "Counterfactual" and "a lineage" by Clint Smith
- "Fish Heads" by R. A. Villanueva
- "for Carol, who is no one" by Rachel McKibbens
- "Icarus Does the Dishes" by Tommye Blount
- "Learning to Pray" by Kaveh Akbar
- "Mother" by Tarfia Faizullah

Tone Bottles

This activity was originally written as a post on teachlivingpoets.com by Valerie A. Person, a teacher at Currituck County High School in North Carolina.

One of the tenets of ELA instruction is helping students recognize, understand, and explain complexity in literature. The following activity offers scaffolding for students to do more work with abstraction and provides a concrete, hands-on approach to teaching tone.

Inspired by an inservice professional development event hosted by arts and career and technical education teachers, in which a teacher of parent and child development demonstrated how to make calming bottles, Valerie's English-teacher brain's wheels started turning around how she could incorporate them into her class. This is Valerie's account of transforming a calming, therapeutic tool into a product that enhances students' understanding of tone in poetry—a tone bottle.

Materials needed:

- Bottles with caps (students can provide their own, but I always keep a few extra for those who forget)
- A variety of glitters
- Extra floaters such as beads and large sequins (optional)
- Clear craft glue (such as Elmer's)
- Food coloring (optional)
- Mineral oil
- Clear soap
- Chopsticks
- Index cards

Students choose one poem by a living poet that speaks to them. Once they select a poem they like, they type it out into a Google Doc. There is value in typing out a poem, paying attention to the lines, the spacing, the punctuation, the perhaps unconventional spelling, and more. Copying a poem gives a student more time to hear the words and fall in love with the essence of the poem, observing more acutely the nuances.

Once they copy the poem and share it with me [Valerie], they mark the places where the tone shifts and provide a written explanation of why they see shifts where they do. Next, students need a plastic bottle with a cap (see the directions in Figure 4.2). Smooth, tall, and slender bottles are perfect for gazing at the finished products. Students fill their bottles three-fourths full with very warm or hot water. They then add three or four globs of clear craft glue, about two tablespoons, and give it a good shake to combine. (Make sure you get actual

Tone Bottle Directions

- Fill bottle ¾ full with hot water
- Add two big globs of clear glue; *SHAKE*
- GLITTER! Funnel in using a piece of paper:
    - One of two fine-grain glitters to represent one tone; *SHAKE*
    - One big chunky glitter to represent second tone; *SHAKE*
- Food coloring—2 drops to represent overall meaning of poem; *SHAKE*
- Add beads and/or sequins to represent a chosen image/phrase/line; *SHAKE*
- Fill bottle with 1 tbsp mineral oil, and the rest with clear hand soap; *SHAKE*
- Glue the cap shut
- Fill out index card with your name and explanation of your choice
- Tape card to bottle

FIGURE 4.2. Directions for creating a tone bottle.

clear glue, not just *dries clear.*) Using paper to funnel the glitter, students then add colors of glitter to correspond with their poem tones. One becomes the primary glitter, so they add a bit more of it. I provide a wide variety of color and grade of glitter from very fine to big and food coloring to change the color of the water. Additionally, students can place sequins, beads, and other floaters in the bottles

Melissa's students add sequins and beads to their tone bottles to represent images or specific lines from their chosen poems.

Monique's tone bottle explanations for Clint Smith's poem "Something You Should Know," the first poem in his collection Counting Descent. *Refer to Chapter 5 for teaching ideas and resources for* Counting Descent.

to symbolize details in the poem. They add mineral oil, more water, and clear soap to their bottles, playing around with the amounts, to get a good texture and viscosity. Finally, they shake, shake, shake it. Having some chopsticks on hand helps too, because it breaks up any glitter clumps.

Once their bottles are complete, students write a paragraph on an index card for a gallery walk to explain why the tone bottle represents their poem. Students can also share them in small groups or present them to the whole class.

Poems That Rhyme

While rhyming isn't typically the norm with poets nowadays, it certainly comes up frequently with canonical poems. And I often find myself pairing contemporary with canonical poems that have similar topics or forms. Knowing how to sophisticatedly analyze for rhyme in a poem is a skill that requires practice. How many times have you heard superficial reasoning from your students that rhyming "helps to make the poem flow" or "it creates a singsong effect"? Or maybe students avoid rhyme completely because they don't know where to start thinking about it from an academic viewpoint. In a poetry workshop, poet and professor Alan Michael Parker shared an inventive strategy for discussing the effects of rhyme (more information about that workshop can be found in Chapter 10). Parker's solution offers remarkable improvement in students' ability to effectively analyze rhyme. It's an equation, actually. Just tell them to think:

$$1 + 1 = 3$$

The formula works by taking the two individual words that rhyme (the 1 and the 1) and creating a new meaning (the 3) by merging the two words into a new idea. Let me show you some examples from my student Julia, who used the formula to examine rhyme in William Blake's "Introduction to *Songs of Innocence*," a poem that appears simple, but with this formula, can evoke insightful analysis.

Introduction to *Songs of Innocence*

Piping down the valleys wild
Piping songs of pleasant glee
On a cloud I saw a child.
And he laughing said to me.

Pipe a song about a Lamb;
So I piped with merry cheer,
Piper, pipe that song again—
So I piped: he wept to hear.

Drop thy pipe, thy happy pipe
Sing thy songs of happy cheer,
So I sung the same again
While he wept with joy to hear

Piper sit thee down and write
In a book that all may read—
So he vanished from my sight.
And I plucked a hollow reed.

And I made a rural pen,
And I stained the water clear,
And I wrote my happy songs
Every child may joy to hear

Structurally overall, Julia notices that the stanzas are separated by the various actions of the piper and by the different requests of the child on the cloud. (Fun fact about Blake: he claimed to have spiritual visions of angels and God.) Here's what happens in the poem:

> *Stanza 1:* piper encounters a child on a cloud. *Stanza 2:* child requests a particular song for piper to play. *Stanza 3:* child requests the piper to sing a song. *Stanza 4:* child requests piper to write his songs in a book. *Stanza 5:* piper writes the songs with the purpose of sharing them with other children. Based on these simplified stanza summaries, Julia takes a closer look at how rhyme enhances each.
>
> The rhyming words *wild* and *child* in stanza 1 emphasize the playful and carefree nature of children in a peaceful world—and the cloud child sure is a happy kid. Not to mention, a little demanding. The child is oscillating between laughing and crying tears of joy, certainly "wild" in his joyful emotions.
>
> Also in stanza 1, *glee* and *me* combine to mimic the child's happiness that is infecting and bringing delight to the speaker. The cloud child is gleeful, wanting to share his glee with the piper.
>
> In stanzas 2 and 3, *cheer* and *hear* double-time and join forces to reiterate that hearing the piper's song makes the little cloud dweller feel all the feels.
>
> *Write* and *sight* in stanza 4 can be interpreted two ways. Perhaps the piper needed to see this divine vision in order to be inspired to write his joyful songs for others. And the child serves as his muse. Or perhaps the child urges the piper to "write" the songs down so that all the world may see them and receive the same joy the child is feeling.
>
> Also in stanza 4, there's *read* and *reed*" which aren't just rhyming words but also the exact same sound. So what do we make of that? Added importance? Julia thinks so. As a Romantic poet, Blake certainly found inspiration in nature. This pairing of words shows us the connection between nature and art. The speaker is using a piece of nature, a reed, to actually scribe his songs for others to read and receive inspiration. And as Blake offered this poem as an introduction for his book *Songs of Innocence*, it gives insight into his artistic connection to the natural world.

> Finally, *clear* and *hear* in stanza 5 serve as both a culmination to the poem and an invitation to the rest of the book. The piper, or the poet Blake, hopes others' minds will become clear and find joy in the innocence and simplicity of childhood once they hear his songs.

There you have it. According to Julia, the rhymes Blake employs contribute to the poem's overall meaning of childhood innocence, imagination, and creativity, and the connection between nature and art. Sounds better than it "helps to make the poem flow," doesn't it?

Here are some other poems from living poets who use rhyme that will help your students practice their new 1 + 1 = 3 equation:

- "His and Hers" by Diane Gilliam Fisher
- "November 5, 1980" by Reginald Dwayne Betts
- "a remix for remembrance" by Kristiana Rae Colón
- "A Street in Lawndale" by Patricia Smith
- "Triolets in the Argolid" by Rachel Hadas
- "T.S.A." by Amit Majmudar

Narrative Poetry Using Phil Kaye Poems

This lesson comes from Oregon educator Matt Brisbin. He originally shared his lesson on narrative poetry as a post for teachlivingpoets.com.

For this lesson, as a prewriting activity, ask students to think of the first neighborhood they can remember living in. Then have them open to a fresh page in their notebooks and draw as good a map of these neighborhoods as they can in five minutes.

As they finish up their maps, ask them to place a star in all the places on their map that have stories connected to them. In mine [Matt's], you can see my friend Scott's house toward the bottom where I earned my first broken arm during a game of "ditchum" (a game that combines both hide-and-seek and tag). At the top of the page is my house, where many tree forts were built and pickup basketball games in the driveway were played. Just behind our home was a small modular house where my grandmother lived and where my sister and I would visit for an hour each night after dinner time. This neighborhood was my home for the first eight years of my life, but those eight years have so many rich stories that go with them.

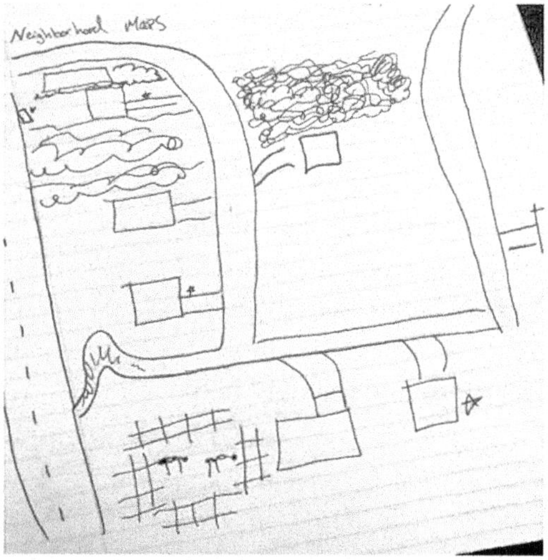

After students have starred their maps, show the video online of Phil Kaye reading his poem "Before the Internet." Give them a copy to read along with, which you can find in Kaye's book *Date and Time*.

Don't spend much time discussing the poem at this point. Instead, ask students to choose one star from their map and go around their table groups telling their stories. This is when the magic happens. Every time I've done this activity I can't help but notice the huge smiles on my students' faces as they share their childhood adventures. If you're lucky, you'll have students in the same class who grew up together and were there when these stories were happening. This is the time to just sit back and enjoy sharing the moment with your students. Try to bounce around to each of the groups and learn something about them. Share some laughs and be ready to tell them some of your own stories from your map too. When they've had enough time to share, ask students to choose one more star on the map, get up and find someone else in the room they haven't talked to yet, and share out their new stories. This is when you know you've sufficiently baited the hook.

As they finish, have students go back to Kaye's poem and read it again to themselves, thinking about how the story is told. As a class, notice and discuss devices such as narrative perspective, pacing, anaphora, tone, allusions, imagery, and specific details. And then have them write a narrative poem of their own using Kaye's as a mentor text and the tools you've just identified to tell their stories. All they have to do is choose one of the stars on their maps and go for it. Have students write for about ten to fifteen minutes, with the understanding that they'll have only a draft started at this point. Give them the chance to read out a line or two when they're done, or to finish the poem and be ready to perform a reading of it during the next class period.

This year I ended class with the follow-up poem "The Internet Speaks Back to the Author," also published in Kaye's book *Date and Time*. Ask your students what message is communicated by holding these two poems up side by side and putting them into conversation with each other. What do the poems have to say about what it means to be human and how technology affects the way we interact with one another? The way we pass the time? Ask students to think about how many stories like the first poem—and like the stars on their maps—they live in a month, and how many stories like the second poem they experience in a month. Have them consider what this tells them about their own lives and how they want it to shape the experiences they have moving forward. I don't ask students to respond but instead use the moment to emphasize the power of poetry, literature, and art in general to inform them about their own lives and the kind of people they would like to be.

Considering Diction in Poetry Using Concentric Circles with Hanif Abdurraqib's "I Tend to Think Forgiveness Looks the Way It Does in the Movies"

The idea for this lesson came from Virginia teacher Jen Flisinger. She tweeted using the #TeachLivingPoets hashtag and shared her directions with teachlivingpoets.com.

This activity works with any poem, encourages a variety of interpretations, gets students thinking analytically about specific words, and asks students to consider how overall meaning is created.

Materials needed:

- Butcher paper
- Markers

When Jen did this activity with her class, she asked her students a deceptively simple question about Hanif Abdurraqib's "I Tend to Think Forgiveness Looks the Way It Does in the Movies":

What is the most significant word?

Do the same with your students and then have them discuss in small groups what they believe to be the most important word in the poem and why. After a few minutes, once the groups seem to have settled on a word, give each group a large piece of butcher paper and some markers and show the directions in Figure 4.3 on the board.

Have students copy the three concentric circles on their butcher paper and then collaborate to fill up their circles. It's important to remind students that there are no right or wrong answers. As long as students can defend their word choice with evidence from the poem and their interpretations, it's completely acceptable if groups choose different words for their center circle.

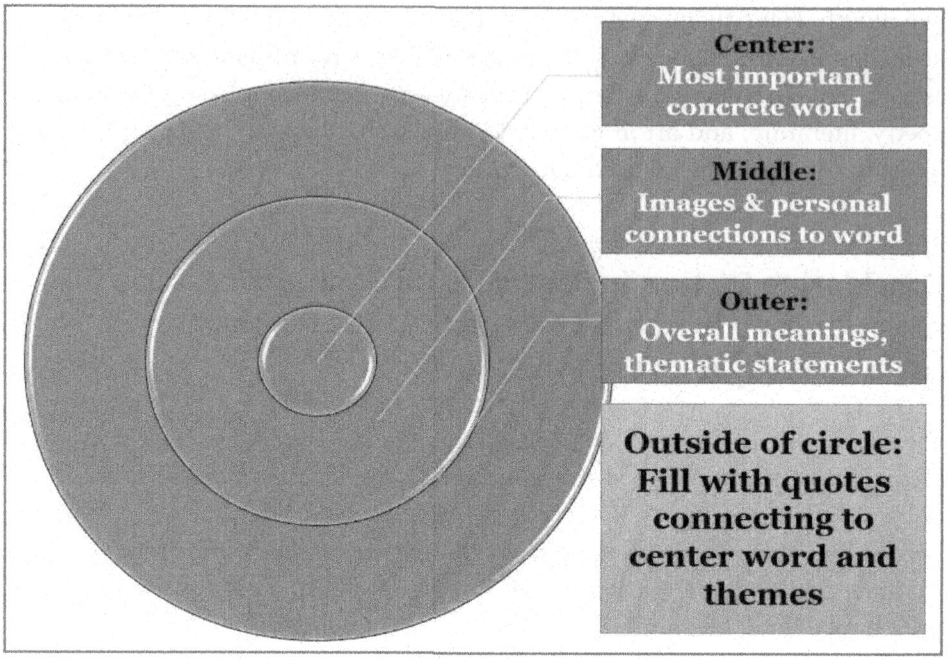

FIGURE 4.3. A Considering Diction activity.

The middle circle gets filled with images from the poem associated with the group's chosen word, as well as personal connections they have with it. The last and largest circle is filled with overall meanings (which can be written as shorter phrases) they can derive from the word and how it operates in the poem, along with a well-developed "official" thematic statement for the poem (or more, if they have time!) Last, students fill up the outside area with "sprinkle" quotes—short little phrases excerpted from the poem that connect to the rest of the ideas in the circles.

Variation: You could give all groups the same poem, or give each group different poems. If you do different poems, students could present their circles to the class or do a gallery walk afterward.

Annotating a Poem with Jimmy Santiago Baca's "I Am Offering This Poem"

This lesson was posted originally in the AP Literature and Composition Facebook group by Amber Buckley.

Materials needed:

- Jimmy Santiago Baca's poem printed out and cut into individual stanzas. I (Melissa) taped the stanzas onto index cards myself (which took forever), so to save time I suggest having students tape them.
- Large paper (large enough to include all four index cards with room to write around them)
- Tape
- Highlighters

Place the index cards in piles, along with the large paper, for students to come pick up. Index cards should not be in order. Ask for a volunteer to choose a card and read it out loud for the class. Ask for another volunteer to read a second card, any card they choose. Repeat until all four cards have been read out loud. Instruct students to place the cards in the order they believe is correct. The first one will be obvious since it includes the title of the poem. I like to start by giving them one obvious choice by including the title of the poem on the first card; it helps to boost their confidence as they begin. Once it looks like most students are finished, acknowledge that the first one was easy due to the title; then ask for someone to share what they guessed for the *last* card. Some students will notice that the final stanza is the only one that ends with a period (the rest end with a comma). Finally, ask for someone to share which card they put second and why. My classes are typically evenly split between the two options, and their reasons are varied. Once several students have shared, ask them if they would like to know the correct answer. Now that you've built up their curiosity, of course they want to know and will attentively listen as you play a video of Jimmy Santiago Baca reading the poem (easily found with a quick internet search).

Now that they know the correct order of lines, have students arrange their cards appropriately in the middle of their larger sheet of paper and tape down *one side only* of each index card.

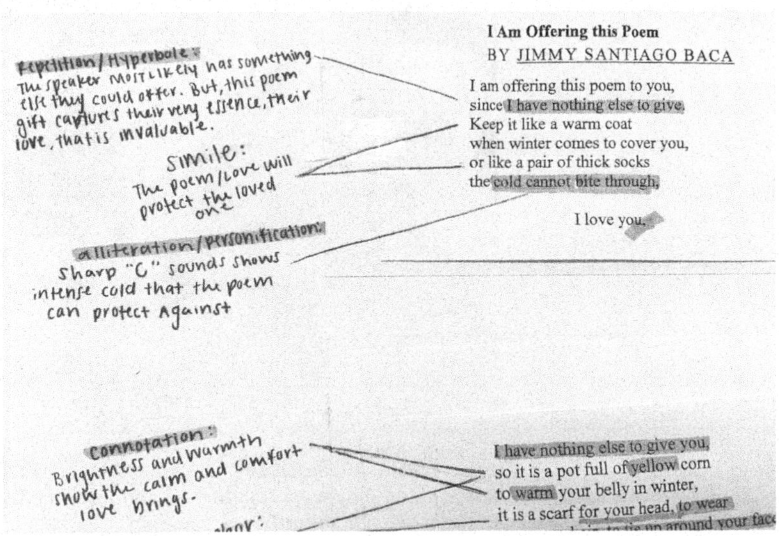

Directions

1. Try to put the poem in order. I will reveal the correct order in a few minutes.
2. Tape or staple your note cards to a larger sheet of paper on one side only (so I can still read the back of your cards).
3. On the back of each note card, paraphrase each stanza and write how the stanza conveys meaning.
4. In the right margin of the larger paper, explain how each stanza relates to the stanza before it (except the first one), and why the poet chose to separate each stanza with "I love you."
5. In the left margin, identify literary devices and explain their effect.

Allow students to work in pairs to discuss thoughts, but each student makes their own annotations around the poem. As students get to work, walk around and ask each group, "Who do you think the audience of the poem is? Who is the 'you'?" Some common answers may be a child, a loved one, or even the speaker himself.

They will be writing on the back of their cards so they need to be able to flip them over. On the back of each card, they write two things: a literal paraphrase of the stanza and their interpretation of what it means. What's Baca *really* saying? What's his message to his audience of "you"? Then, in the right-side margin of the larger paper, have students write their explanations for the order of the stanzas. How does each stanza relate to the one that comes before it? Why does Baca separate each stanza with "I love you"? Finally, in the left-side margin of the larger paper, students identify literary techniques and explain how they are working in the poem. For example, my student Nicole notices the alliteration on the letter C in the first stanza, emphasizing the sharp, biting cold. Nicole also explains the effect of asyndeton in the second stanza: "The continuous listing of uses for love reminds the audience of its importance and never-ending presence. The love will always be there to comfort and compliment the loved one."

Rayyan and Ajay work together to annotate the sequencing of stanzas in the right-side margin.

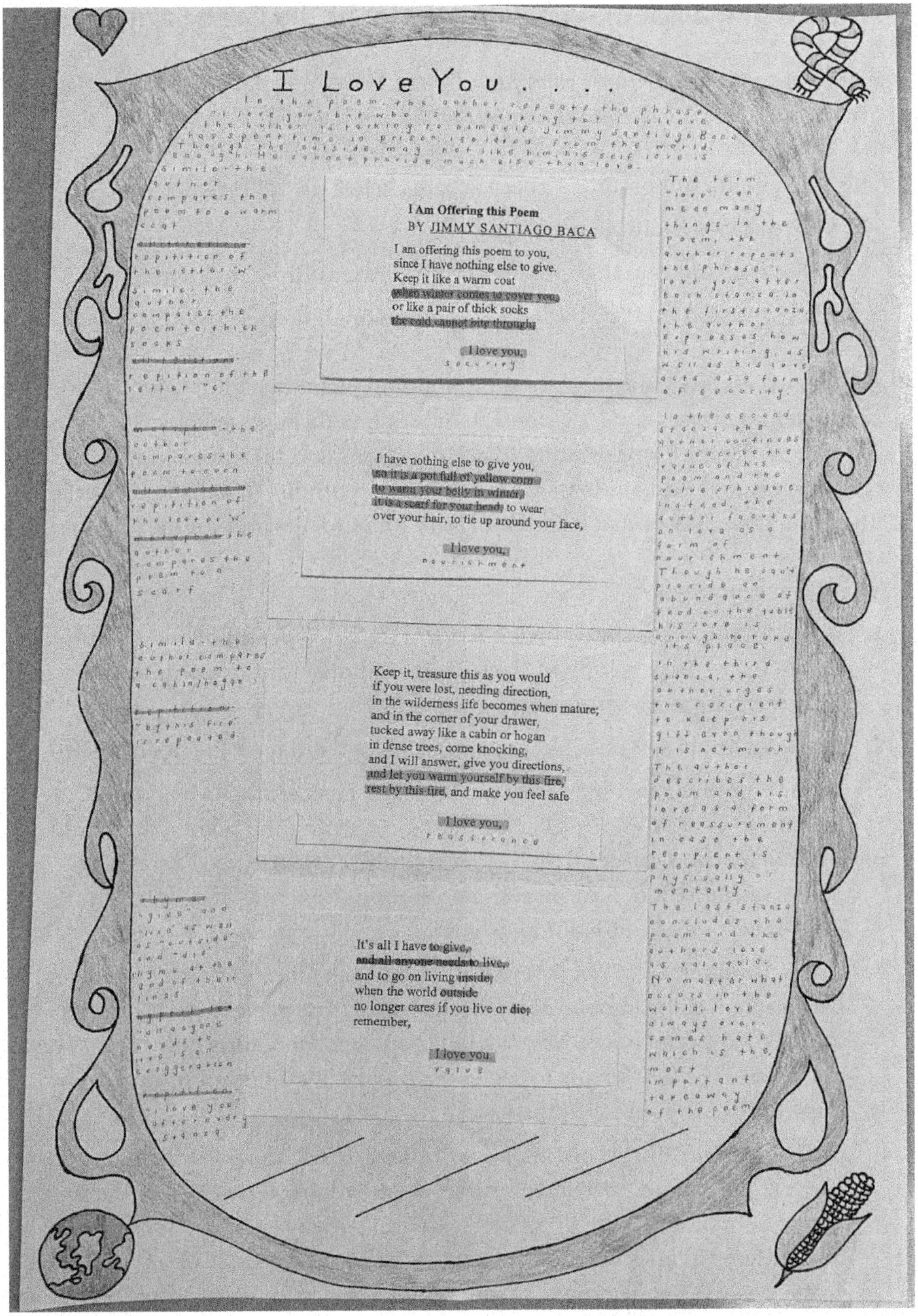

Jordyn's interpretation of the poem is that the speaker is addressing himself, reminding himself to see his worth and love himself, so she chooses an image of a mirror to frame her work.

Annotating a Poem with "Hulk Smash!" by Greg Santos

This strategy for annotating comes from Donna Vorreyer, a middle school teacher and living poet, who has published three poetry collections.

This strategy for annotating a poem accomplishes the following:

- Encourages multiple readings
- Shows changes in thought that occur with multiple readings
- Focuses students on discussion and personal interpretation

At its simplest level, the three-color annotation technique allows for a student's personal first impressions, a second chance to talk through the poem with someone else, and a third opportunity to ask questions and take notes during whole-class discussion. Can students do these things without three colors? Certainly. But using them has been a useful tool both for students and for me [Donna].

The Basic Process

1. **Read Aloud.** When introducing a poem, I always read it aloud to students before I give them a copy of the text. This allows for the poem to enter into their thinking without it seeming like a task.
2. **Read Again!** I then pass out copies of the text and read the poem again.
3. **Color Number One:** *My First Best Thinking.* I ask students to annotate or take notes using their first best thinking regarding the poem. This could include marking places they like, even if they aren't sure why; noting places of confusion; writing comments about how they feel or anything they notice and don't want to forget.
4. **Color Number Two:** *Two Brains Are Better Than One.* Students then take their second color in hand for a discussion with a partner. Each partner shares their initial notes, helps with confusions, and adds new ideas. This makes it easy for students to see that a second reading can produce new ideas and clarify initial confusions.
5. **Color Number Three:** *Instruction and Group Thoughts.* Once students have had a chance to do a second reading, we move to whole-class discussion, where I annotate on the document camera. I always start by asking what the students like—since this is a third reading, I often end up marking the entire poem! Then we move to any remaining confusions; simple ones, like unfamiliar vocabulary, we address first, and any larger issues regarding meaning I reopen to the whole class. I often ask leading questions at this

point, especially if I'm trying to use the poem as a model of certain literary elements.

When we're finished, students have a record of their thinking. The colors make it clear how their thinking has progressed through multiple readings. The colors show me how willing or able students were to comprehend the poem's content alone before discussion and instruction. As the year progresses, the three steps can become more specific: different colors could be used for finding specific literary devices, commenting on form, etc. Each student's notes are as unique as the students themselves. They are a record of their thought processes and provide excellent deep reading practice. The three-color annotation technique is easily adaptable to all levels and can be used with any poem.

"If They Come for Us" by Fatimah Asghar

Many of my students are tactile learners and digital natives, so I often incorporate some hands-on learning along with the use of technology. First, I print off the poem for students so they can each have their own copy to write notes on. We go straight to listening to Asghar read the poem from a video easily found with a quick internet search. As they listen for the first time, they simply follow along, getting a feel for the poem. The second time around, they underline key phrases and lines that stand out to them as important. They don't need to explain *why* yet, just acknowledge that the language *feels* important to them and to the poem as a whole.

Students then turn to the person next to them for a comparison of the underlined lines. Do they have any of the same ones? If so, why do they both feel those lines are important? If not, which lines does the other person find key and why? Floating around the room, I find discussions to be rich and full of analysis, and students don't even realize they are actually interpreting a poem. Some students look up unfamiliar words; others don't. Some are more interested in a particular metaphor or image. Volunteers then share their thoughts out loud for the whole class.

Next, I post these questions on the board for further discussion and exploration of the poem:

1. Who are your people? If you walked into a room full of strangers, what type of people would you naturally gravitate toward? Who do you feel most comfortable around? Who do you feel protective of?

2. How does Asghar's use of imagery and metaphor contribute to the experience of the poem?
3. How does the use of punctuation and line breaks add meaning to the poem?
4. This is the final poem in Asghar's collection steeped in the India-Pakistan Partition. Research what this is and consider how this poem relates.

Students in Melissa's eleventh-grade English class work together to create their sculptures representing "If They Come for Us."

Whenever I bring the Play-Doh box out, students—yes, even seniors—get really excited. Students pair up and use Play-Doh to create sculptures representing their interpretations of the poem. I have only one rule: they can't make literal stick-figure people. My goal with the sculptures is for them to think more symbolically and to allow for diversity in their interpretations.

Once their masterpieces are complete, students use Flipgrid to record their explanations of how their artwork represents the poem. They are required to quote phrases or lines (textual evidence support) in their reasoning. The free version of Flipgrid limits students to ninety-second videos, so explanations have to be concise and relevant. As the last step, students watch one (or more) of their peers' Flipgrid videos and leave a comment about their interpretation. A potential step further could be to end on a written analysis of the poem, whether it be a well-written paragraph or a full essay.

Olivia and Sarah's holding hands sculpture illustrates the idea of unity and togetherness in Asghar's poem.

Mash-up Poem Using Kyle Dargan's "Call and Response"

This lesson is inspired by the Young Chicago Authors blog for National Poetry Month Writing Prompt 11/30 written by José Olivarez on youngchicagoauthors.com ("Remix").

American poet Robert Frost once said, "No surprise for the writer, no surprise for the reader."

In my experience, however, students struggle to produce the same element of surprise and irony in their writing that we find in the poems of the published poets we read in class. This activity uses a Kyle Dargan mash-up poem, which comprises two or more separate texts, as inspiration for students to practice creating and achieve new and surprising moments in their own writing.

Call and Response

Our Father who art in heaven,
there's broken glass everywhere.
Thy hallowed staircase pissed on
by those who care not
for thy kingdom, thy name.
Come—thy will be the smell.
Thy will be the noise
on Earth. In heaven, no
money moves. Give us
this day our rats in the front room,
our roaches in the back,
and forgive the junkie
in the alley, his baseball bat.
But trespass in this place
we try to get away from. Repossess
those who have trespassed against us.
Lead us, but do not push—
we're so close to the edge of temptation.
Deliver us from our lost
Heads—this evil trying us.
For thine kingdom is like a jungle.
Sometimes, it makes us wonder
how your power keeps.
We go under. Glory
forever?—a ha-ha ha ha.
Amen.

As a prereading activity, students can freewrite or discuss a song that they believe holds an important meaning. They should identify the meaning, whether it's personal or not, and why they believe it's important.

Next, have students draw a vertical line down the middle of a piece of paper, creating two columns. In the left column, students make a list of:

- Songs you love and consider your own personal anthem
- Random songs you know by heart
- Favorite nursery rhyme or holiday songs

In the right column, students make a list of:

- Historic texts you would recognize if quoted or that we hold in common as a country
- Texts you have memorized (prayers, anthems, pledges)

Play the video online of Dargan reading his poem as students follow along on a printed copy. I always watch it twice, once to get the gist and the second time for a closer look. I tell students that Dargan's poem is a mash-up of the Lord's Prayer and Grandmaster Flash & The Furious Five's lyrics to their song "The Message." Provide students with printed or online copies of both of these original texts. On their copies of the poem, with two different colors of highlighter, students should highlight which parts of the poem come from which original text. Students will quickly realize that Dargan mashes up both original texts in almost all of his lines. Only a couple of lines come from solely one original text.

After highlighting, students can discuss or write responses to these questions):*

1. What lines stand out to you and why?
2. How does Dargan's juxtaposition of the prayer and the rap—his call and response—impact the meaning of the poem?
3. Which imagery resonates the most with you and why?
4. What is "found poetry" and how is this poem an example of it?
5. How does Dargan's poem create new meaning? Why do you think he chose these two texts to combine? What effect does it have?

---

*Credit to Illinois teacher Kristin Runyon for questions 1–4.

The final step is for students to write their own mash-up poems. They should choose one item from each of the columns they filled out earlier. After searching for the lyrics or texts online, have them craft a draft of a poem that incorporates both texts in each line. I share Dargan's explanation of his process in writing "Call and Response," which he provided in a tweet in a #TeachLivingPoets chat.

> Once I sensed/realized there was an accord, I just moved back and forth between them as the association allowed. The Lord's Prayer is fairly short, and most people only know the first verse of "The Message," so that actually helped focus the process.

After playing around with lines and drafting for maximum surprise, students type up a final draft, highlighting each of the original texts in different colors.

One of my students, Katie Bergmann, challenged herself by mixing together three separate texts: "I Dreamed a Dream" by Claude-Michel Schönberg from *Les Misérables* (underlined), the poem on the Statue of Liberty: "The New Colossus" by Emma Lazarus (italicized), and the Pledge of Allegiance (bolded).

I Dreamed the American Dream

I dreamed a dream in times gone by
To the flag of the United States of America
That **liberty and justice** would never *refuse*
And **one nation under God** would be forgiving

Then I was young and filled with wonder
And he *tossed the huddled masses to the* tigers
He slept the summer by *a lamp*
But they were gone when autumn came
And I pledge to God at night
With his **justice** as strong as thunder
That he tear *the wretched refuse* apart.
But my hope was used and wasted.

And I still dream he'll come to me
That we will *lift* **the flag** together
For the teeming shore is turned to shame
And I'm *yearning to breathe free.*

I had a dream **America** would be
So different from this hell I'm living
But the **Republic** cannot be
Indivisible with liberty and justice for all.

Students can close by reading their poems out loud or conducting a gallery walk. As a follow-up reflection, I ask the class what surprises they encountered in the process of writing their poems. Are there any lines or phrases they are particularly proud of? How did the original texts work together to create new meaning in your poem?

Exploring "Abandoned Farmhouse" by Ted Kooser

This lesson is shared by Ann Cox, an ELA teacher in Illinois with more than twenty years of ELA teaching experience. It was originally posted on teachlivingpoets.com.

"Abandoned Farmhouse" works well in a middle school or high school classroom for a couple of reasons:

1. It dispels two myths that my [Ann's] students often believe—that poetry is difficult to understand and that poetry must rhyme.
2. It is deceptively simple. Students find the poem easy to comprehend, but as they discuss the piece in more detail, they discover elements such as personification, figurative language, diction, and repetition.

I like to begin this lesson by projecting the photo of a sparse farmhouse bedroom. Ask students to examine the objects in the room and then make inferences about what type of person resides here. Give students a minute or two to write and then open up a brief discussion about who might sleep in a room like this. Encourage students to point out details from the photo that help support their inferences.

Once we've discussed the photograph, students are ready to examine the poem. We listen twice to a recording available online of Kooser reading the poem—the first time just to appreciate the poem, the second time to examine the poem more closely. I give students a copy of the poem and ask them to mark particular words, phrases, or lines that catch their attention. You might also want to pose a more specific question, such as "What do we learn about the people who lived here?," and encourage students to mark those details in the poem.

You might also consider asking the following questions:

- Who is the speaker in this poem?
- What do we learn about the former inhabitants of this house?

- Why did the people abandon this farmhouse?
- While this poem doesn't rhyme, it does use other poetic devices. Which ones did you notice? What effect do they have on the poem? (Depending on the level of your students, you may have to be more specific in your questioning. Ask them to find examples of repetition or figurative language, for example.)

To dig deeper into "Abandoned Farmhouse," ask students to do the following on their copy of the poem:

- Circle diction that indicates the tone.
- Select one word to describe the tone and write the word in large letters at the top or the bottom of the page. (Depending on your students' familiarity with tone, you might want to provide a list of tone words.)
- Draw a picture that illustrates the tone word you selected.

There are several extensions to this lesson that I have found to be successful:

- Use this poem as an introduction to a unit on Steinbeck's *Of Mice and Men*. Speculating on why the people abandoned their farm can lead into a lesson on the factors that caused the rise of migrant workers in California.
- Pair the poem with John Mellencamp's song "Rain on the Scarecrow." Have students compare each writer's use of imagery and diction to create different tones. You could even have students do some research on the US farming crisis in the 1980s to deepen their understanding of the song.
- Encourage students to write a poem about their own bedroom, the objects someone might find there, and what those items "say" about you. The slam poet Taylor Mali has a great ready-made handout you can use for free online. This activity might be a good alternative or extension to the "Where I'm From" poems that have become popular in many classrooms.
- This poem naturally lends itself to wondering about the former inhabitants of the house. Invite students to create the dialogue between the husband and wife that led to their departure. This would also be a great way to review how to correctly punctuate dialogue.

- Invite students to wonder what happened after the family abandoned the farmhouse. They could write a story or narrative poem that answers "Where are they now?"
- Ask students to consider how objects can tell a person's story. You could apply this idea to a character in literature (What would the character have in their backpack/car/nightstand?) or even to a short story that students might be working on for a creative writing unit.

Conclusion

The poems included in this chapter may or may not be good matches for the needs of your students. As a teacher, you know your students' backgrounds, personalities, learning styles, and interests, all of which are important factors when identifying poems to welcome into your classroom space. I try to find poems that are relevant to my students but that will also stretch them in some way. Some poems offer teachable moments about common moves in poetry; some teach us something new about the world. Whatever poem you choose, choose it first because you like it, then because you think your students might like it, and then give it a test run using one of the activities in this chapter. If the poem flops? First, give yourself credit for trying; then reflect, ask students for feedback on why they didn't like it, and adjust your selection for the next time. If it succeeds? Well, then maybe you've started something. Maybe you've begun transforming your students' perspective of poetry, and maybe by the time they leave your classroom, they will feel inspired by and more confident in their experience with poetry.

5

Teaching Single Author Collections

Probably my (Melissa's) favorite major work to teach is a single-authored poetry collection, and I don't think it happens often enough in classrooms outside of the university. Reading individual poems separate from the context of their collections is certainly worthwhile, but students really aren't seeing the complete picture of how the poem operates within the larger scope of the book it belongs in. Poetry collections offer the same instructional methods, interactive activities, and high levels of analysis as any full-length novel; in fact, I would argue that some collections will get your students thinking even more deeply and engage them even more than an assigned class novel will. Moreover, with the trend of independent choice reading, selecting a poetry collection as a whole-class text allows teachers the flexibility and time, due to their shorter length, to balance independent reading without sacrificing the shared reading experience. This chapter offers activities that can be executed with any poetry collection, as well as two full units for teaching two individual collections: *Counting Descent* by Clint Smith and *Citizen Illegal* by José Olivarez.

Once students have worked with individual poems as described in Chapter 4, they are ready to take the next step and read a single-volume poetry collection. The teaching philosophy expressed in Chapter 4 applies to teaching collections as well; direct lecture-style instruction tends to limit students' exploration and interpretation. Instead, we learn through class discussion and group collaboration. Each night students read five poems for homework. They read the poems and annotate them for things they notice, which could entail poetic devices, thematic ideas, words that stick out to them, thoughts on structure, questions brought up by the poems, or anything they feel like making note of on the page. Having read the poems and bringing them annotated to class the next day ensures that students are prepared with some thoughts to discuss and engage with their peers. Five poems a night seems like an appropriate number—not so many that students aren't reading the poems closely and enough to keep us at a steady pace working through the book.

Teaching *Citizen Illegal* by José Olivarez

I teach *Citizen Illegal* in my eleventh-grade American Literature class in which we explore over the course of the year what it means to be American. While the list of texts I teach might vary from year to year, my titles are currently *The Great Gatsby, Their Eyes Were Watching God, The Crucible, Between the World and Me, Just Mercy, How to Love a Country* (a poetry collection by Richard Blanco), and *Citizen Illegal.* At the end of the year, for their final exam, students write about what it means to them to be American, based on their readings throughout the year and their own personal beliefs and opinions. In an end-of-year survey last year, *Citizen Illegal* came out on top as students' favorite book of the year. In her survey, student Emma Viole says:

> This book definitely belongs in the American Literature class. It discusses many of the struggles of being an immigrant or first generation American. José is not afraid to get vulnerable and show his struggle to the majority of society. His book helps to talk about many values and topics that are important, such as racism that he and his family (and many others like them) have experienced, and how the American Dream isn't all it is said to be.

And student Luke Meierer says,

> *Citizen Illegal* was my favorite read. I would definitely rate this 5 stars as I loved his work. His use of pop culture and items that relate to teens really made the poetry memorable. His poem book actually inspired me to write a chapbook of poems for my final exam, and I really enjoyed writing the poems for it as a whole. Not only did Olivarez outline political, economic, and race relation issues, but it also encourages the reader to view the world in different perspectives, as well as recognize that our differences make us unique. His writing and word choice made the book so much better than my expectations, and his down-to-earth writing style made me enjoy it even more.

Getting Students Prepared to Read

After reading Olivarez's bio as a preview into the book, we watch the video online of Olivarez reading "You Get Fat When You're in Love."

You Get Fat When You're in Love

you got a little extra love
on your ankles, love hanging
over your belt line, love makes it hard
to fit inside your pants sometimes.
love got you buying bigger sizes,
need deeper pockets for all this love.
your buttons can't hold all the love
rippling up the middle of your ribcage—
love turns those shirts into accordions.
you make music with this love,
carry yourself like a song.

when you get skinny,
everyone rushes to compliment you.
they want to know what your secret is.
tell me, they say, what's your secret?
you look great.

call it the Broke Heart Diet.
love left you.
then you left you.
now all you have
is this disappearing body.

After we watch the video twice, I ask the class, "How does this poem make you feel?" *Sad, depressed, heartbroken* are popular responses, and they are spot-on. This poem is an ideal introduction to the collection because it builds students' confidence in understanding poetry. We continue our discussion with "What in the poem makes you feel that way?," "How is the first stanza different, and how does the poem shift as it moves through stanzas?," "What ideas do we have of why the poem is structured this way?" Students are able to notice that the increased indentation of the stanzas—getting farther and farther away from the left margin—relate to the speaker's "disappearing body."

I front-load thematic ideas and motifs for students to notice while they read by providing them with a reading calendar (see Figure 5.1), a list of things to annotate, and an interactive hyperdoc (see Figure 5.2), which is accessible for free online with a quick internet search.

Citizen Illegal **Reading Calendar**

Pages 3–8	Pages 9–16	Pages 17–23	Pages 24–31	Pages 32–38
Pages 39–47	Pages 48–53	Pages 56–60	Finish book	Annotations due

THEME SEEDS	MOTIFS	ANNOTATIONS
• Identity self-discovery • Love • Masculinity and vulnerability • Family • Assimilation vs. celebrating culture • Other	• Embarrassment • Body image • Religious references • Racism • Music	For every poem: • Theme • Motif (if applicable) One poem per night: • Describe structure of poem and significance to meaning • Personal thoughts, opinions, or reactions to one of the poems

FIGURE 5.1. A typical reading calendar and guide for writing annotations for *Citizen Illegal*.

The following hyperdoc is completely interactive online—each image is a link to an article, video, or resource for students to learn more about Olivarez and his work. And there are whole sections not included here of additional resources for students to explore. The hyperdoc is a collaborative effort created by Scott Bayer and Joel Garza (cofounders of #THEBOOKCHAT), Adrian Nester, and me (Melissa), all ELA teachers, for #THEBOOKCHAT. I now use the hyperdoc in class with my students as a teaching tool. Hyperdocs are also available for Claudia Rankine's *Citizen*, Ilya Kaminsky's *Deaf Republic*, Lenelle Moïse's *Haiti Glass*, and many more fiction and nonfiction titles. All hyperdocs are easily searchable on the internet and free to download and share with your students.

The following questions were created by the individuals mentioned above; we used them for a Twitter chat, but they would work just as well in your classroom as discussion questions or writing prompts:

1. "if the boy (citizen) (illegal) grows up (illegal) and can only write (illegal) this story in English (citizen), does that make him more American (citizen) or Mexican (illegal)?" Does Olivarez ever answer this question, which ends his title poem?
2. Based on Olivarez's collection, what challenges or benefits are unique to first-generation Americans?
3. Olivarez wanted his collection to feel like a block party—a joyful community event. In what ways does this collection feel like a block party?
4. *Citizen Illegal* is explicit about nationality and ethnicity. In what ways does this collection inform or complicate your understanding of masculinity and vulnerability?

Excerpts from *Citizen Illegal* Hyperdoc (Bayer and Garza)*

Poetry Readings: Click on the image to watch José Olivarez reading his work; record your thoughts and analysis in the columns.		
"Mexican Heaven" 	First reaction:	Deeper analysis:
"You Get Fat When You're in Love" 	First reaction:	Deeper analysis:
"What's Good: Angles" 	First reaction:	Deeper analysis:
"Ode to the First White Girl I Ever Loved" 	First reaction:	Deeper analysis:

COMPARE	an "after poem" with the original
"A Preface" by Idris Goodwin 	Read "Mexican American Disambiguation" and write a response that examines the influence of Goodwin's poem on Olivarez's:

*Not all of these poems are from *Citizen Illegal.* "What's Good: Angles" is from a PBS kids' special found at https://www.pbs.org/parents/whats-good/angles, and Olivarez can be seen performing "Ode to the First White Girl I Ever Loved" here: https://www.youtube.com/watch?v=IRJAM_bTfpQ.

FIGURE 5.2. Example of a hyperdoc excerpt.

5. There's a lot of Mexican American bi-ethnic duality throughout the collection. But Heaven in Mexican? Why?
6. Olivarez's speaker says, "white folks is crazy," "white folks on TV kill people every day & they don't feel a thing," and "there are no white people in heaven." How would you respond to a student, parent, colleague, or administrator complaining about Olivarez's speaker's characterizations of white people?

The final question of the chat is addressed to teachers specifically but is worth your consideration before teaching just in case you encounter a similar situation. A parent complained about the book last year because of the line "there are no white people in heaven." She questioned my decision to teach the text and asked me what other viewpoints I teach alongside it so students could see "both sides." Part of my response to her was that year after year in high school, students are forced to read a string of canonical texts written by white authors, so this book *is* a text that shows another viewpoint. As Frank Johnson writes in his article "Reinventing the World: José Olivarez's *Citizen Illegal*," Olivarez "uses the tools of his craft to create a sanctuary for others, and to present alternative realities that might finally serve, rather than pillage from, brown and black people." Because of my experience with this parent, I now front-load "Mexican Heaven" with the online video of Olivarez reading it so that students can understand the tone of the poem *before* they read. Another useful resource for approaching this particular poem is *The Adriot Journal* article "José Olivarez: How I Wrote 'A Mexican Dreams of Heaven,'" in which Olivarez explains:

> I wanted to write about my experience as the child of immigrants. My parents' decision to migrate from Jalisco, Mexico, to Chicago, Illinois, is the most transformative event of my life. It is the rupture that made me a poet. It is the event that has shaped in numerous ways all of my relationships. So how could I write about this rupture, and how could I do it as a service to my people, and how could I do more than confirm the expectations the reader was bringing to my work?
>
> One of my answers was to write A MEXICAN DREAMS OF HEAVEN, which is a way to talk about the relationship of my family to the United States. Is the United States Heaven? Is this heaven all it's cracked up to be?
>
> I want to tell you about how I got to the statement, "there are no white people in heaven." Originally, the stanza ended after the second sentence. At that point, I thought the stanza was done. I was feeling myself. Even in heaven, white people can't help but f— up. I thought I was hilarious. Later when I came back to the poem, I realized the joke was on me. I had written a poem about Mexican

Heaven and had failed to imagine an existence without gentrification and the presence of white violence. I revised the stanza by correcting my mistake: "i'm just kidding. there are no white people in heaven."

Sometimes, white people wince when I read this poem at events. Sometimes, they cheer wildly. . . . When it came time to publish my book, I changed the title of the poem to MEXICAN HEAVEN because it's more concise. I also split the poem up throughout the book. I split it up because MEXICAN HEAVEN is my favorite poem. I wanted the reader to come back to MEXICAN HEAVEN again and again. It's the chorus of the book.

"(Citizen) (Illegal)"

The titular poem of the book offers students an opportunity to explore a poet's use of punctuation. Matt Brisbin, an educator in Oregon, provides this activity, originally written as a post on teachlivingpoets.com.

In small groups, students have ten minutes to read and analyze the poem and to prepare their own dramatic reading, performed for the class, that emphasizes their insights about the text. After each performance, students explain why they made the choices they did.

(Citizen) (Illegal)

Mexican woman (illegal) and Mexican man (illegal)
have a Mexican (illegal)-American (citizen).
is the baby more Mexican or American?
place the baby in the arms of the mother (illegal).
if the mother holds the baby (citizen)
too long, does the baby become illegal?

the baby is a boy (citizen). he goes to school (citizen).
his classmates are American (citizen). he is outcast (illegal).
his "hellos" are in the wrong language (illegal).
he takes the hyphen separating loneliness (Mexican)
from friendship (American) and jabs it at the culprit (illegal).
himself (illegal). his own traitorous tongue (illegal).
his name (illegal). his mom (illegal). his dad (illegal).

take a Mexican woman (illegal) and a Mexican man (illegal).
if they have a baby and the baby looks white enough to pass (citizen).
if the baby grows up singing Selena songs to his reflection (illegal).

if the baby hides from el cucuy and la migra (illegal).
if the baby (illegal) (citizen) grows up to speak broken Spanish (illegal)
and perfect English (citizen). If the boy's nickname is Güerito (citizen).
if the boy attends college (citizen). If the boy only dates women (illegal)
of color (illegal). if the boy (illegal)
uses phrases like "women of color" (citizen).
if the boy (illegal) (citizen) writes (illegal) poems (illegal).

if the boy (citizen) (illegal) grows up (illegal) and can only write (illegal)
this story in English (citizen), does that make him more
American (citizen) or Mexican (illegal)?

—*José Olivarez*

As Matt walks around the room, he hears students having wonderful conversations about the poem and which parts should be spotlighted during their reading. They wrestle with the parenthetical interruptions and how those should be read. As a reader, they argue, we have a choice in reading what is inside the parentheses, and they debate how not reading them would change the poem. They discuss how important all the statements outside the parentheses are to helping them understand the speaker, and how the (Citizen) and (Illegal) kept distracting them from what is most important. They talk about how these disruptions in the poem are mini-representations of what the speaker must feel while trying to better understand his identity. And finally, they question whether these interrupters are coming from outside the speaker, or if they represent the confusion happening inside the speaker's own mind. Ultimately, the way they decide to read it says a lot about how they interpret the text itself.

When it's time for each group to read, it's amazing to see how many different ways there are to interpret, and to read aloud, the same text. One group stands in a circle with their backs turned to the reader in the middle. Each time the poem comes to an "(illegal)," the group angrily turns and shouts at the speaker, but when they get to a "(citizen)," the group barely looks up and speaks in an approving tone with a slight head nod.

Another group, wanting to emphasize the internal struggle of the speaker, decides to have all the participants who read "(citizen)" stand on the right side of the reader, while those who read "(illegal)" stand to the left. As the reader makes her way through the poem, the students on the left all whisper "illegal" while shaking their heads back and forth, and the students on the right whisper "citizen" while nodding their heads up and down. They also explain that they want to highlight how society forces conformity by labeling certain characteristics such as having lighter skin, going to school, or using English as the traits of

Peyton, Chris, Freddie, and Blake swap books, read one anothers' annotations, and then discuss last night's reading.

a "citizen," whereas speaking Spanish, hiding from *el cucuy*, and singing Selena songs are all considered "illegal."

Another group reads the poem straight through but chooses to emphasize a tone shift in the last stanza to represent the self-doubt caused by the societal labels interrupting the speaker's life. And one group chooses to emphasize the silencing of conformity by literally placing the "citizen" and "illegal" labels on the speakers.

What Matt likes most about this lesson is that it requires close reading of a text, without a lot of the teacher's direction or influence. It's also a lesson that can be done with lots of different poems. It rewards students for having their own interpretations and helps to point out that meaning is created in the mind of the reader; a poem doesn't have a singular message from the writer that readers have to try to uncover.

Odes

With several odes, including "Ode to Cheese Fries," which is always a student favorite, *Citizen Illegal* provides an opportunity to pair and compare canonical poems in terms of form and subject. One option is to have students read several odes without the authors' names or dates of publication and have them guess when they were written and whether or not they would fit into *Citizen Illegal*. The older poems will build students' confidence by being obvious, but some of the other contemporary odes by other authors will open up lively discussions of whether they belong in Olivarez's book. Alongside his odes, you might include the following, which are all available online in either text or video format:

- "Ode on Solitude" by Alexander Pope
- "Ode to Gossips" by Safia Elhillo
- "Ode to My Socks" and "Ode to the Watermelon" by Pablo Neruda
- "Ode to the Beloved's Hips" by Natalie Diaz
- "Ode to the Loop-de-Loop" by Clint Smith
- "Ode to the Midwest" by Kevin Young
- "Ode to the Waitress" by Kevin Coval

Allie's poem, an ode to her aerial silk instructor, is inspired by Olivarez's "Ode to Scottie Pippen."

After their reading and discussions, students can create their own definitions for the ode as a poetic form and explore how the odes by Olivarez and the other contemporary poets are in conversation with poetic tradition. What do poets write odes about? What do you see in common between all the odes? Are there any striking differences that stand out? Finally, have your students write their own odes inspired by their findings, using their favorite ode as a mentor text.

Another Teacher's Approach

Melissa Tucker, Rock Hill, South Carolina's 2018 District Teacher of the Year, teaches Citizen Illegal *at Rock Hill High School. Her approach to teaching the collection was originally shared on teachlivingpoets.com.*

Melissa Tucker's class meets every other day on eighty-five-minute block schedules, so the bulk of students' reading and annotating is done outside of class. To begin the unit, the students read and discuss Concepción de León's 2018 *New York Times* interview of José Olivarez, Jose Antonio Vargas, and Julissa Arce regarding their experiences as children of undocumented parents. After reading the *Times* interview, Melissa explains how to use two-column or LEFT/RIGHT annotations, in which everything that is *RIGHT there* on the page (e.g., unknown words, poetic devices, stated claims, etc.) is identified, and everything that is *LEFT over* (e.g., implied meaning, effects of devices, themes, etc.) is analyzed.

Next, Melissa T.'s class performs a read-aloud conga line of the first poem, "(Citizen)(Illegal)." Each person reads one sentence of the poem. She encourages students to adapt or revise their reading as they realize the different nuances in tone or when they notice a deeper meaning. They read the poem several times, including reading it without the words and phrases in parentheses. Pauses between the readings allow students time to reflect and annotate.

Students then read eight to ten poems before each class, using the LEFT/RIGHT annotations. Once they've read through Part III, students are assigned different elements to focus their annotations on, such as structure, shifts, syntax, enjambments, etc. In the past, Melissa T. noticed that students tended to identify only surface-level items; as a result, their inferences were more summary than analysis. Asking them to view the poems from different angles facilitated deeper understanding of how Olivarez develops meaning.

Because her focus for this unit is on identity, Melissa T.'s journal prompts mirror some of the universal experiences of the speaker in the collection:

- What are the advantages and disadvantages of having someone else define your identity?
- What is your most favorite gift, and what does it reveal about you?
- How and why do our values change over time?

In addition to reading and studying *Citizen Illegal*, students read Zora Neale Hurston's (1928) essay "How It Feels to Be Colored Me" and Lucille Clifton's (1993) poem "won't you celebrate with me." Hurston's unapologetic narration of race and identity supports the transition that Olivarez's speaker experiences throughout the collection. And Melissa T. knows from reading interviews that Olivarez is particularly inspired by Clifton, so she asks students to trace how he nods toward Clifton's themes and style in his own collection. Students then use these texts and *Citizen Illegal* to create questions as they prepare for a video chat with the poet.

As expected, students were super excited to participate in the video chat. The highlight for Melissa T. came when one of her shyest students asked Olivarez a question about Olivarez's use of Hispanic terms in *Citizen Illegal*. Although similar questions had been asked or discussed in class prior to and during the video chat, her question was unique. Olivarez paused and replied that hers was a really great question; he hadn't even noticed his use of these terms. He then said he'd have to reread the collection to figure that out. The student had noticed something the poet hadn't about his own collection.

After the video chat, Melissa T. had students complete a reflection in which she asked them questions about how reading an entire collection versus individual poems changed their understanding of poetry. Many students noted that this was the first time they had read an entire collection; they enjoyed the way the collection afforded them the opportunity to gain a bigger picture or story of the speaker. Olivarez's collection helped them reflect thoughtfully on their perceptions and experiences, and they all were grateful to speak with the poet. For more on how to have a successful video chat with a poet in your classroom, refer to the next chapter, "Poets in the Classroom."

Teaching *Counting Descent* by Clint Smith

Most teachers I (Melissa Smith) know who teach *Counting Descent* watch Clint Smith's TED Talk "The Danger of Silence" as an introduction to the poet and his work. As a former high school English teacher in Prince George's County, Maryland, Smith had four principles posted in his classroom that he encouraged his students to follow. These four principles now hang in the front of my classroom, guiding me and my students:

> Read critically.
>
> Write consciously.
>
> Speak clearly.
>
> Tell your truth.

Just as with *Citizen Illegal,* I provide students with a reading calendar to follow and a list of themes and motifs to guide their annotations (Figure 5.3). It helps students who may be new to reading a full collection to have a sense of direction and a goal for what they should be looking for when they read. I try not to overwhelm them with these lists, however, because I also want them to enjoy the experience of reading the poems. I have found five pages to be a nice number—enough that they will be able to find something to annotate in each poem, but not too many that they can't keep track of them all and feel overwhelmed or frustrated.

Counting Descent **Reading Calendar**

Pages 9–16	Pages 17–23	Pages 24–30	Pages 30–37	Pages 38–44
Pages 45–50	Pages 51–56	Pages 57–63	Finish book	Annotations due

THEME SEEDS	MOTIFS	ANNOTATIONS
• Innocence of childhood • Importance of family and ancestry • Racism and discrimination • Coming of age and acceptance of truth • Masculinity and vulnerability	• Water, bodies of water, swimming • The Black body • Basketball • Prison • Sky, flying	For every poem: • Theme • Motif (if applicable) One poem per night: • Describe structure of poem & significance to meaning • Personal thoughts, opinions, or reactions to one of the poems

FIGURE 5.3. A reading calendar and guide for annotations for *Counting Descent.*

The guiding questions for #THEBOOKCHAT Twitter chat hosted by Scott Bayer and Joel Garza on *Counting Descent* are also questions you could use in your classroom as discussion questions or writing prompts (see Figure 5.4):

1. Which poem in *Counting Descent* did you connect with most and why?
2. To what extent does Smith depict contemporary African American lives? Why is it important for everyone to read about these experiences?
3. What makes "Counting Descent" (pages 21–22) the ideal title poem for the collection?
4. What do you make of Smith's teachings to "the black boy" (from the ocean, cicada, fire hydrant, window, or cathedral)? Why have inanimate objects as the speaker of the poems? Who is the intended audience of these poems?
5. Beyond the "black boy" poems, how else does Smith unify *Counting Descent* as a collection? Feel free to discuss voice, form, theme, motif, language, purpose, or anything else you find significant.

Excerpts from *Counting Descent* Hyperdoc (Bayer and Garza)

Poetry Readings: Click on the image to watch Clint Smith reading his work; record your thoughts and analysis in the columns.		
"what the cicada said to the black boy" 	First reaction:	Deeper analysis:
"Counting Descent" 	First reaction:	Deeper analysis:
"When They Tell You the Brontosaurus Never Existed" 	First reaction:	Deeper analysis:

FIGURE 5.4. Excerpt of a hyperdoc for studying *Counting Descent*.

6. "There Is a Lake Here" is written after Jamaal May's poem "There Are Birds Here." What inspirations from May does Smith incorporate into his poem? How does he make it his own?
7. What makes "There Is a Lake Here" the ideal resolution to this collection?

Just as with the *Citizen Illegal* hyperdoc, this is only a small portion of the overall interactive document available for free online.

Introducing the Collection with Analogies

This introduction idea is inspired by Adrian Nester, who teaches in Virginia, and written by Susan Barber, who teaches in Georgia, originally posted on aplithelp.com.

One way to introduce a poetry collection is by having students watch a clip showcasing a designer's final collection from the Bravo channel's *Project Runway*. I [Adrian] then ask my go-to question: what do you notice? Without any prepping, students discuss how the first couple of outfits are very edgy, to get the attention of the judges, and then the outfits become more accessible for everyday wear. Students also notice how colors fit together even though everything isn't "matchy-matchy," with patterns appearing in different styles, the designer carefully choosing the order they appear in on the runway. Next, I pull up the *Thriller* album and ask students to comment on the track listing. We explore the rationale behind the progression of songs in terms of lyrics, music style, and song length; students also discuss how the songs tie together and are unified even though they all have a slightly different message. My students are then primed for thinking about a collection of poems and have some context for how these poems can fit together yet still be different, and how they are ordered in a specific way rather placed randomly. We read the first poem of *Counting Descent*, "Something You Should Know," aloud, and then students spend a few minutes thinking about it before we discuss not only the poem itself but also reasons why Smith chose it to open the book.

As the first poem in the collection, "Something You Should Know" serves as an introduction to the speaker and his sense of vulnerability.

Something You Should Know

is that as a kid, I once worked at a pet store.
I cleaned the cages
of small animals like turtles, hamsters,
rabbits, and hermit crabs.

I watched the hermit crab continue
to grow, molt, shed its skin and scurry across
the bottom of the aquarium to find a new shell.
Which left me afraid for the small creature,
to run around all exposed that way, to have
to live its entire life requiring something else
to feel safe. Perhaps that is when I became afraid
of needing anything beyond myself. Perhaps
that is why, even now, I can want so desperately
to show you all of my skin, but am more afraid
of meeting you, exposed, in open water.

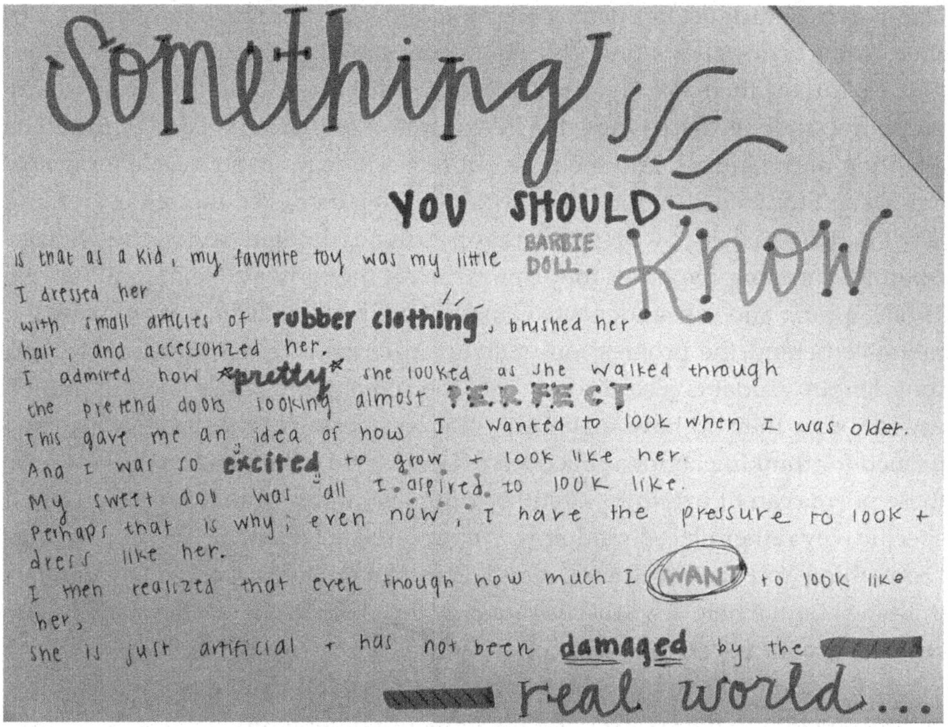

Something YOU SHOULD Know
is that as a kid, my favorite toy was my little BARBIE DOLL.
I dressed her
with small articles of **rubber clothing**, brushed her
hair, and accessorized her.
I admired how *pretty* she looked as she walked through
the pretend doors looking almost PERFECT
This gave me an idea of how I wanted to look when I was older.
And I was so **excited** to grow + look like her.
My sweet doll was all I aspired to look like.
Perhaps that is why, even now, I have the pressure to look +
dress like her.
I then realized that even though how much I WANT to look like
her,
she is just artificial + has not been **damaged** by the
real world...

Kailee's poem (above) explores the stereotypical image of female beauty, comparing herself to her dolls as a child. Her poem shifts toward the end, as Smith's does, to reveal the speaker's vulnerability. Her conclusion is a realization that many young people could relate to, a coming-of-age lesson on the reality of the human experience.

I teach *Counting Descent* early in the school year, so "Something You Should Know" provides the perfect mentor text for students to introduce themselves to me in a creative and personal way. The directions are fairly straightforward:

> Write your own version of "Something You Should Know," keeping the same title. Pretend that it's the opening poem to your collection. What would you want readers to know about you?

I love the products my students create with this assignment. I encourage them to make it "artsy," but that's not a requirement.

Something You Should Know

I'm always optimistic, or at least I think I am.
Life's thrown me curveballs
But I don't like to say that I've had the worst of it
Everyone asks how I can be so brave
What makes you get out and work
You're a miracle, we've been inspired by you
I hear it so often it's what I repeat to everyone
But I wish I could take it all back
I want to be me, the one I was before
The one that rarely got sympathy
The one that gets up because he knows he has to
Not because he's brave
I get up because I want to forget
I get up because I want to be normal
I get up because I have a life I want to live
Life throws everyone curveballs, I'm still trying to
figure out why mine had to be this.

On the surface, Brady's poem (above) sounds like any normal teenager's experience, but it takes on new meaning when you learn he was diagnosed with a malignant brain tumor the size of a lemon a year before he wrote it. Normally a reserved, quiet student in class, Brady used this assignment to share his feelings about his diagnosis.

Finally, Ethan's poem illustrates the struggle of navigating high school and becoming a young adult. Every day feels like a mountain, and every day is a new battle.

"There Is a Lake Here"

Susan Barber and Adrian Nester's ideas helped to create this lesson for the final poem in the collection.

Before reading the poem, students freewrite about a specific place they love, somewhere that gives them a sense of belonging, and describe its key features. They share with someone next to them and then move into a discussion of their school community as a place, or the town/city they live in. They divide a sheet of paper in half, one column for common misconceptions made about the place by outsiders, and the other for the TRUTH, which, as a person who belongs to the place, they know. This puts them in the right frame of mind for being introduced to Smith's "There Is a Lake Here."

I am a believer in the necessity of reading a poem out loud. A student volunteer reads it slowly while the rest of the class follows along. A second volunteer reads it again, and students underline words or phrases that stand out to them during this second time through. Students then think-pair-share about what they notice in the poem. For younger students, a simple fill-in-the-blank model might help them to organize their thoughts: *The word(s) _____ stood out to me because _____, and it makes me think/notice/feel _____.* With a poem that uses such strong imagery, students could also make drawings around their poem of images that stand out to them.

Hurricane Katrina hit New Orleans in 2005, when most of our students were too young to remember the devastation it caused. You may want to give your students some contextual information about Katrina to help them understand why Smith includes some of the misconceptions he does in the poem. If your school encourages reading nonfiction, this would be a perfect opportunity to tie in an article on Katrina or on New Orleans.

Right underneath the title of "There Is a Lake Here," Smith includes "after Jamaal May." Knowing why this is included gives important insight into Smith's poem. After you read May's poem "There Are Birds Here" (you can find it online), you should be able to see the connections and understand the inclusion of "after Jamaal May." Students read May's poem and identify the ways Smith uses May's poem as inspiration and a model. Chicago-based poet H. Melt also has a poem in their chapbook *On My Way to Liberation* modeled after May's poem. Melt's poem is titled "There Are Trans People Here."

Other poem pairing options for "There Is a Lake Here" are Nikky Finney's "Left" and Patricia Smith's "Siblings," which are also about Hurricane Katrina.

Clint Smith himself wrote more poems about Katrina, which were published after *Counting Descent* came out: "After the Storm They Attempted to Identify the Bodies" published by *The Rupture*, and "August, 2005," published as the final poem in *The New York Times Magazine 1619 Project*. Most of these poems are available online in either print or video format. As an extension activity, students can discuss how each of the poems handles the topic of Katrina and how meaning is enforced in each of the poems.

Assessment Ideas

In her post for teachlivingpoets.com titled "Teaching a Poetry Collection with Clint Smith's *Counting Descent*," educator Adrian Nester offers a summative assessment based on the concepts of constructing solid paragraphs. Her paragraph format follows the acronym PEE. Making a **P**oint (claim), providing **E**vidence (short integrated quotes), and **E**xplanation (insight) are the building blocks of each question.

> Directions: You will construct a paragraph using the PEE (point, evidence, explanation) paragraph format for each of the following literary devices: tone, imagery, poetic syntax, and word choice. You must choose four different poems (one per device) and integrate quotes from the poems as evidence. The final **E** of explanation will be where you emphasize the SO WHAT? How does that literary device contribute to the meaning of the poem? Maybe even to meaning of the collection as a whole?
>
> Paragraph 1: Tone
> Paragraph 2: Imagery
> Paragraph 3: Syntax
> Paragraph 4: Diction
>
> Last, choose one of the following:
>
> - Draft your own version of "There Is a Lake Here" or "There Are Birds Here" about a place where you have lived.
> - Briefly discuss the following: How does the title and/or poem order of this collection create an overall theme in *Counting Descent*? What is that theme? Use specific poems as evidence.

Additional Writing Prompts, Assignments, and Discussion Questions

The following questions are from Texas teacher Tolly Salz, written for the Dallas-Fort Worth Interscholastic Colloquium at The Episcopal School of Dallas (along with Colloquium team members and educators Joel Garza, Jared Colley, Gary Nied, and Jennifer Boulanger).

1. Clint Smith's written works are textured, layered, and rich with meaning. So, too, is his spoken word poetry. Watch several videos of Clint Smith performing his poems (using the hyperdoc). As you think about writing and expressing something deeply meaningful to you and your experiences/thoughts/beliefs, consider crafting a performance poem that utilizes cadence and rhythm, plays on words and words from play, and sound and silence in a deliberate art form. Submit a written copy of your poem as well as a video clip of your performance.
2. Select one of Smith's poems and create your own original short film that utilizes your narration of the poem combined with a visual complement to the piece. Your original creation should be no longer than four minutes.
3. Explore Smith's craft as a poet. In doing so, consider how he honors traditional poetic conventions as well as how he modernizes them; how he reveals the power of language and utilizes juxtaposition and imagery to convey purpose and theme.
4. Study these additional Clint Smith poems not in *Counting Descent*: "Your National Anthem," "FaceTime," "Why we shouldn't forget that US presidents owned slaves." Then, explore how these poems, stylistically and thematically, connect to this collection.
5. Consider pairing one of Smith's poems from the collection with the poem of another poet, canonical or contemporary. The following list of poems is merely a suggestion of where to begin, though you should feel free to select your own poem for the purpose of meaningful comparison with analysis and evaluation: "A Small Needful Fact" by Ross Gay; "Riddle" or "The Tradition" by Jericho Brown; "Let America Be America Again" and "Theme for English B" by Langston Hughes.
6. Craft a "golden shovel" poem for Smith's "Canon" (44). Consider the structure of the poem you will create. How might you utilize this new

poetic form to craft your own "argument" of sorts? (For more on the golden shovel form, see "Breaking Down Line Breaks" in Chapter 4.)

7. Reading and listening to Clint Smith's words about James Baldwin and his "A Talk to Teachers," consider how Clint Smith explores racial identity, particularly as it pertains to youth—students—in his collection *Counting Descent*. Based upon your exploration and evaluation, what should "critically responsive" education look like, and what must teachers and students do to create such?

8. In an interview for LitHub.com by Peter Mishler titled "Clint Smith on Protest, Art, and Protest-Art," Smith opined: "Art, I think, is inherently a protest of some sort. The role of the writer is to operate in the space of the imaginative, and thus it demands a rejection of the world as it is and movement toward what it might otherwise be." What is the "protest" inherent in this collection—and for what possible world do Smith's poems advocate? Drawing upon specific poems, explore how Smith uses his writing as truth-telling and/or truth-seeking; consider bringing in additional, related research to support your inquiry and evaluation.

9. In his TED Talk entitled "The Danger of Silence," Smith calls for students and teachers to speak their truth. Using his talk as inspiration, craft your own oration not to "[tell] people the things they [want] to hear," but "instead . . . the things they [need] to." Imagining that there is "a microphone tucked under [your] tongue, a stage on the underside of [your] inhibition," cease your silence as you deliver, poetically and deliberately, your own truth. Submit a written script for approval and be prepared to perform your TED Talk for the class.

10. Compare/contrast Clint Smith's exploration and depiction of identity in *Counting Descent* to the treatment of identity in another work of literature that you've read recently, whether novel, short story, or poem.

11. Peruse—and then read closely—the following collections: the *New York Times Magazine 1619 Project* or Bryan Stevenson's website for the Equal Justice Initiative. Selecting one for further inquiry, evaluate the texts, resources, and ethos of the collection as a whole. Then, connect some aspect of this collection to that of Clint Smith's. What do you notice? Of what do you despair? How does this resource, in conversation with Clint Smith's, contribute to your understanding of systemic racism and injustice?

Additional Engaging Activities for Teaching Poetry Collections

Poem Posters

This activity is ideal for implementing early on in your work with the collection, as well as in the middle. I print out five poems students have already read and tape each one (separately) onto the middle of five larger poster boards. I create five groups of students, one for each poem. Each group has a different color marker, so I know which group is responsible for which writing on the poster. The groups each start with one of the five poems, read it out loud, and then write their answer to question number 1 (see the list below) in the blank space of the poster board. After about eight to ten minutes, they switch to the next poem, read it out loud, and answer question number 2. Again they spend about ten minutes, then rotate again until all five poems and questions have been covered. The final task for each group is to return to their first, original poem poster, read everything the other groups have written, and discuss everything together. Do they agree with the other groups' notes? Do they have anything to add? Students can discuss the poem further in conversation, or they can reflect on the poem one last time in writing.

5 Questions

1. What is the poem about? Define unknown words.
2. Consider form—is it in couplets, tercets, prose, other? How is the form appropriate to the meaning?
3. Unique, interesting, or surprising images—what do they convey to you?
4. Line structure—end-stopped vs. enjambed lines, caesura. Is there any interesting use of punctuation or text manipulation (e.g., italics, white space).
5. What else do you notice? Figurative language, wordplay, title significance, point of view, shifts, sound devices (alliteration, consonance, assonance, sibilance), other?

I have fifty-minute class periods, so by the time students settle, get directions, form into groups, and rotate through the five poems, it has taken almost two full class periods to finish the poems.

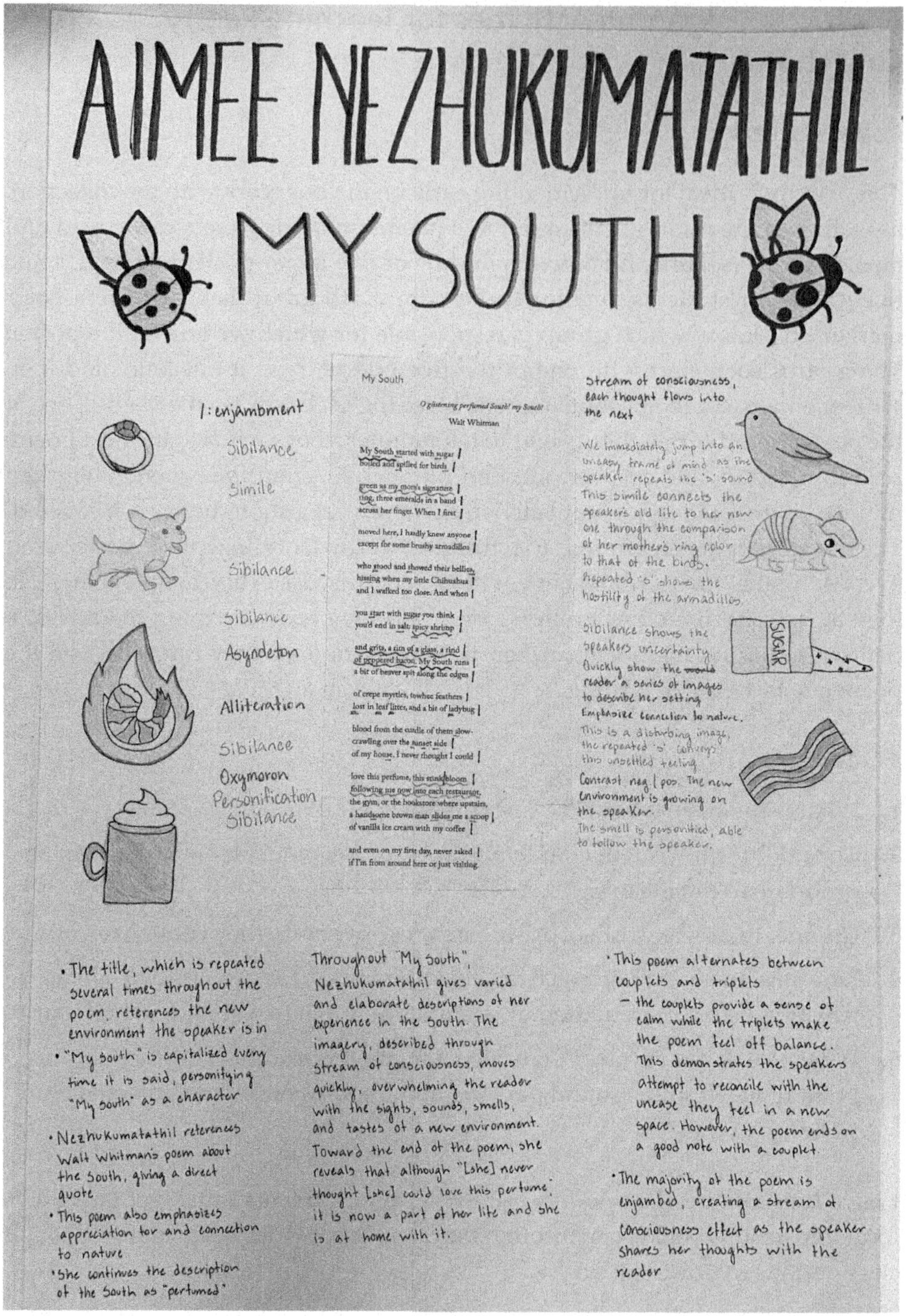
AIMEE NEZHUKUMATATHIL
MY SOUTH
/: enjambment
Sibilance
Simile
Sibilance
Sibilance
Asyndeton
Alliteration
Sibilance
Oxymoron
Personification
Sibilance
My South
O glistening perfumed South! my South!
Walt Whitman
My South started with sugar /
boiled and spilled for birds /
green as my mom's signature /
ring, three emeralds in a band /
across her finger. When I first /
moved here, I hardly knew anyone /
except for some brushy armadillos /
who stood and showed their bellies,
hissing when my little Chihuahua /
and I walked too close. And when /
you start with sugar you think /
you'd end in salt: spicy shrimp /
and grits, a rim of a glass, a rind /
of peppered bacon. My South runs /
a bit of beaver spit along the edges /
of crepe myrtles, towhee feathers /
lost in leaf litter, and a bit of ladybug /
blood from the cuddle of them slow-
crawling over the sunset side /
of my house. I never thought I could /
love this perfume, this stink/bloom /
following me now into each restaurant,
the gym, or the bookstore where upstairs,
a handsome brown man slides me a scoop /
of vanilla ice cream with my coffee /
and even on my first day, never asked /
if I'm from around here or just visiting.
stream of consciousness, each thought flows into the next
We immediately jump into an uneasy frame of mind as the speaker repeats the 's' sound
This simile connects the speaker's old life to her new one through the comparison of her mother's ring color to that of the birds.
Repeated 's' shows the hostility of the armadillos
Sibilance shows the speakers uncertainty
Quickly show the ~~world~~ reader a series of images to describe her setting
Emphasize connection to nature.
This is a disturbing image, the repeated 's' conveys this unsettled feeling
Contrast neg / pos. The new environment is growing on the speaker.
The smell is personified, able to follow the speaker.
SUGAR
• The title, which is repeated several times throughout the poem, references the new environment the speaker is in
• "My South" is capitalized every time it is said, personifying "My South" as a character
• Nezhukumatathil references Walt Whitman's poem about the South, giving a direct quote
• This poem also emphasizes appreciation for and connection to nature
• She continues the description of the South as "perfumed"
Throughout "My South", Nezhukumatathil gives varied and elaborate descriptions of her experience in the South. The imagery, described through stream of consciousness, moves quickly, overwhelming the reader with the sights, sounds, smells, and tastes of a new environment. Toward the end of the poem, she reveals that although "[she] never thought [she] could love this perfume", it is now a part of her life and she is at home with it.
• This poem alternates between couplets and triplets
– the couplets provide a sense of calm while the triplets make the poem feel off balance. This demonstrates the speakers attempt to reconcile with the unease they feel in a new space. However, the poem ends on a good note with a couplet.
• The majority of the poem is enjambed, creating a stream of consciousness effect as the speaker shares her thoughts with the reader

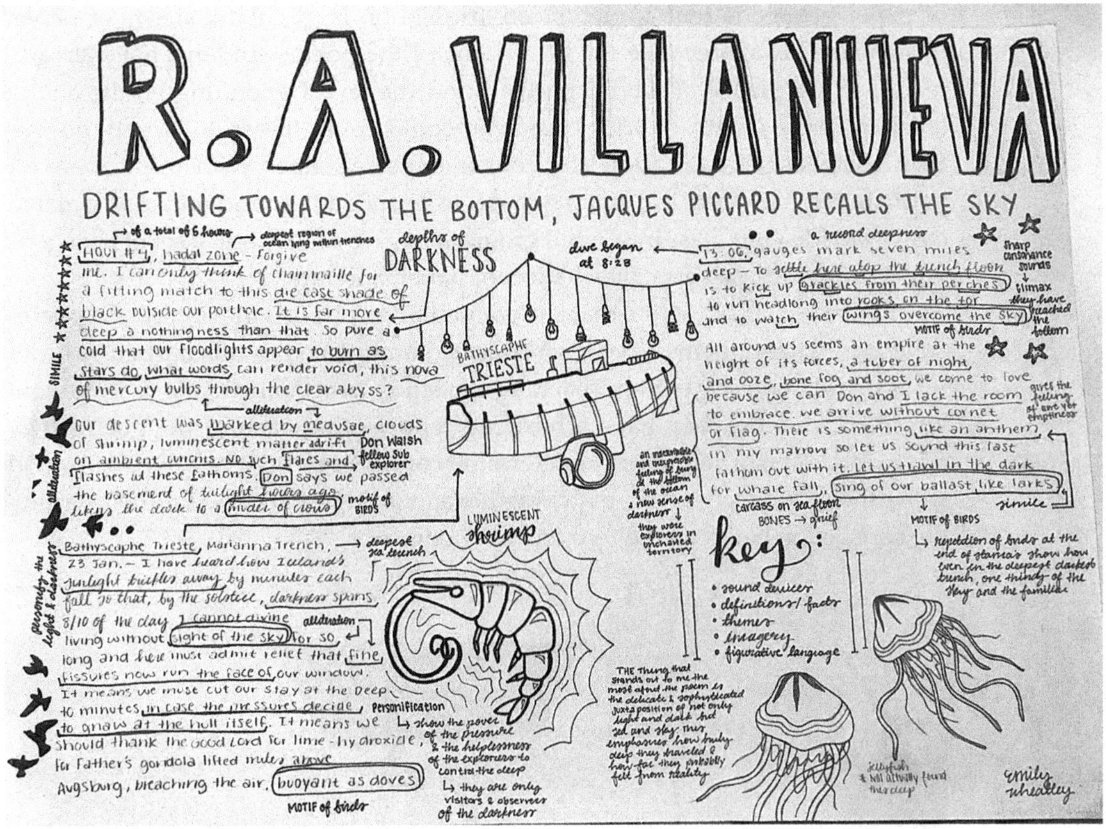

Variation: I do the same poster board setup with the five different poems in the collection, make five student groups again (different people this time in the groups), but instead of rotating poems for each question, the groups all stay with the same poem for the entire time, meaning that they answer all five questions for the same poem. I offer an extra credit point for the best poster, which helps motivate students to write quality annotations.

Hexagon Maps

The idea for Hexagon Maps comes from Tia Miller, an English teacher in southern West Virginia. She is currently working on a PhD from Marshall University and was kind enough to share this activity as a post for teachlivingpoets.com.

Teachers often know where they want to start and end when teaching a full collection, but the middle can sometimes be challenging to navigate. Hexagon Maps work perfectly in the middle of a poetry collection. To begin, create a series of paper hexagons that students can arrange on large, blank sheets of paper. Inside each hexagon, write the title of one of the poems students have already read, leaving plenty of white space around the text. Depending on the ability level and time length of your class, you could cover fifteen to twenty poems. Five hexagons per page allows for convenient-size shapes, with ample room for your students to write but small enough to be moved around and manipulated easily. Divide your class into small groups and give each group a set of hexagons with poem titles, scissors, blank sheet of paper, and tape.

In her post, Tia explains that she wanted to emphasize the nature of a poetry collection. These poems have been collected and placed in this particular order for a reason; one way of approaching the study of a collection is to figure out why. Tell students they have a hexagon representing each of the poems they have read so far. Their job is to determine connections between the poems and show those connections by matching hexagons edge to edge and then writing the connection between the two touching edges.

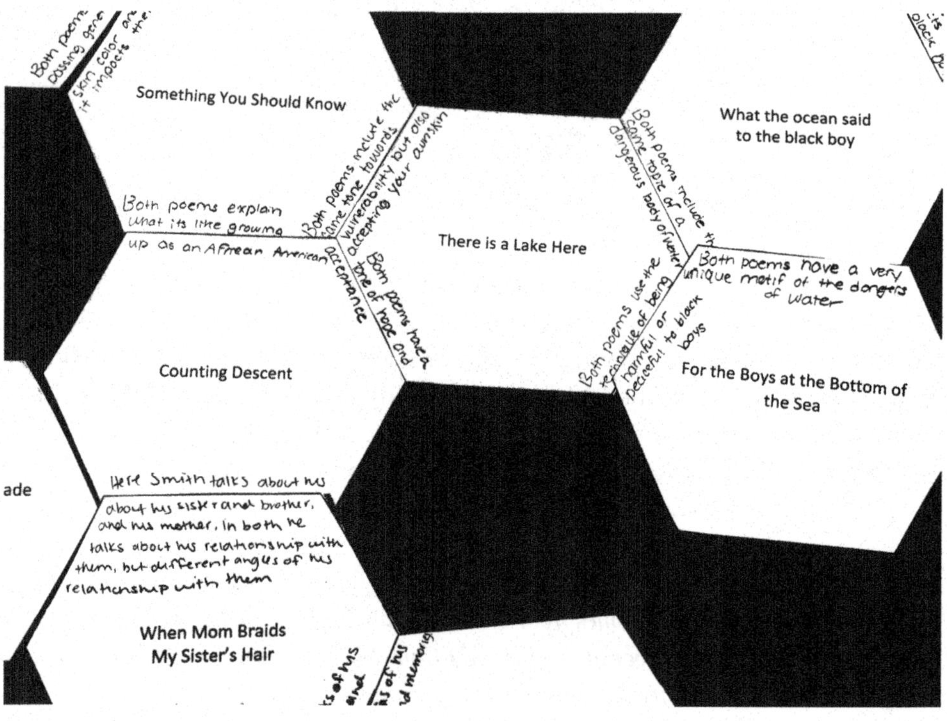

Encourage students to think outside the box; push them to consider connections between the poems beyond subject matter. Do they notice similarities in structure, use of image and details, point of view, etc.? They are essentially making a map of connections between poems. If they put two edges together, a connection must be found between those poems. If they feel that more than two poems connect in some way, corners could also be used, but in the end, if two "poems" are touching, there has to be an established connection between them.

(from left to right) Chiagozie, Aaliyah, Tre', and Jordyn explore how individual poems connect in Clint Smith's Counting Descent.

What excites me most about this activity is that no two final maps are the same. Every group finds different ways of connecting and making sense out of the poems. Once students tape all the hexagons together, they can be displayed in your classroom.

Madison, Matt, and Mehar work with the rest of their group to explore connections between individual poems in Citizen Illegal *by José Olivarez.*

Once groups are finished, they can share out, perhaps focusing on the two most insightful connections each group made. Assigning a written reflection following the activity allows students to demonstrate their learning. They can explain new connections they noticed, start to formulate thematic ideas, and incorporate textual evidence from the poems to support their insights.

Envelope Game

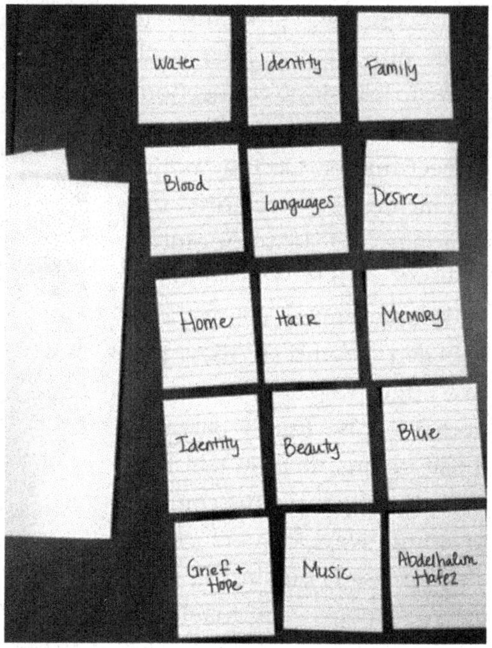

The envelope game was born when I was teaching Safia Elhillo's *The January Children*, but it can be adapted for any text. This activity works best toward the end of a collection. To prepare for the envelope game, you will need a list of about fifteen theme seeds, symbols, motifs, and images important to the collection. You can provide the list yourself or let your students collaborate to compile their own list.

For *The January Children*, our list started with these themes and motifs we had been exploring through annotations while reading:

THEMES	MOTIFS
Grief and hope	Blood
Language	Blue
Identity and place	Music
Gender issues	Brother
Memory and imagination	Relationship with mother and grandmother
	Hair
	Water

Kailee pulls out her group's items to explore how they work together to create meaning in Safia Elhillo's The January Children.

Once you have your list set, you will need however many envelopes as groups you want to have (I had five envelopes for five groups). You will also need cut up index cards or pieces of paper, each with one of the items from the list written on it.

Place three cards in each envelope. Each card has written on it a theme, motif, symbol, or image important to the book. Mix up the cards to make them random and hand an envelope to each small group. The instructions are simple: Draw connections between the three items in your envelope and describe how they work together throughout the collection to tell a story. Discuss and write a group explanation using support from the text. I keep this activity pretty basic, but I can also image variations using Venn diagrams, sketch notes, or Flipgrid instead of writing. Walking around the room, I found that students' discussions were insightful, engaging, and analytical. Again, this activity could be done with *any* collection—or any text, for that matter—with any mix of items for the envelopes.

Theme Debate

This is one of my favorite activities, and it really gets students motivated through competitive spirit. Ideally, this activity would be best at the end of the collection, probably on the day students return from reading the last five poems for homework. I use extra credit to the winning group as encouragement, along with bragging rights for crushing their opponents. While working throughout the collection, you will need to create a list of theme seeds to explore. We were fortunate to be able to ask R. A. Villanueva via Twitter direct messaging which themes he believes to be integral to navigating his book *Reliquaria*. Villanueva provided us with five theme seeds: memory, masculinity, joy and grief, faith, and family. You will need as many theme seeds as the number of groups you would like to have for your debate. We were given five themes, so we formed five groups, with each group assigned a different theme. Students had an entire class period to go through the collection to find textual evidence that would allow them to argue that their theme was *the most important theme* to the book. Students gathered ideas, collected quotes, and prepared a list of reasons to use the next day in our debate.

We started the next day off with opening arguments. Each group had one minute to present a brief introduction to their assigned theme. After all groups had shared, each group then had three minutes to argue in Round 1. They could all take turns talking in the group, or one person could talk for three minutes straight—the choice was up to them. After each group presented their Round 1 argument, I had the rest of the groups take a one-minute break to jot down notes for crafting a formal rebuttal. After Round 1, it was time to start the

Students hunt for textual evidence to support their theme for the class debate.

rebuttals. Each group had two minutes to address the other groups and negate the Round 1 arguments. After all groups had a chance to rebut, I, as the official judge, ruled out two of the five groups with the weakest arguments. These two groups now became my co-judges to decide the overall debate winner. The remaining three groups had two minutes each in Round 2, after which we ruled out another group. The last two groups presented their closing arguments.

After the closing arguments, the groups no longer in the running helped me choose the winner. It was a lot of fun; the students really got into the competition, and everyone was engaged the entire time. In total, from gathering textual evidence to picking a winner, the activity took us three fifty-minute class periods to complete.

Extension: Students could follow up the debate with a written argument for the importance of their theme. They've already done all the research, evidence gathering, and considering potential counterarguments, so they are well-equipped to transform their claim into writing.

Threading Poems

This activity works best toward the end of a collection or once students have completely finished reading all the poems. The idea came to me when I was trying to think of a way for my students to display their understanding of how a collection's themes are threaded throughout, from first poem to last. The word *thread* got me thinking. What if students actually *use* thread to represent thematic cohesion between poems, along with other patterns they notice? To set up the activity, you will need poster boards for each group you want to have (the thickness of poster board works better than butcher paper to hold the materials placed on it). Choose five poems from the collection that you feel best represent the book as a whole. Print out and tape the five poems onto each poster board, four in each corner and one in the middle. Cut lengths of brightly colored yarn to represent the connections. I chose to have one color represent themes, a different color to represent motifs, another for literary techniques, and a fourth for

Kailee and Hope consider each poem's annotations and how they can relate ideas in multiple poems.

other connections students can find. You might also assign a color for structural connections, images and symbols, or whatever you want your students to explore.

The first day of class is spent annotating the five poems in their small groups; the yarn doesn't come out until the next day. Groups work together to make notes and illustrations of what they notice around each of the five poems. Because students have read most or all of the collection at this point and have engaged in class discussions prior to this activity, I don't give them any specific criteria for their annotations. At this point in their exploration of the book, they feel confident in identifying themes and other literary elements since they've been practicing doing so all along.

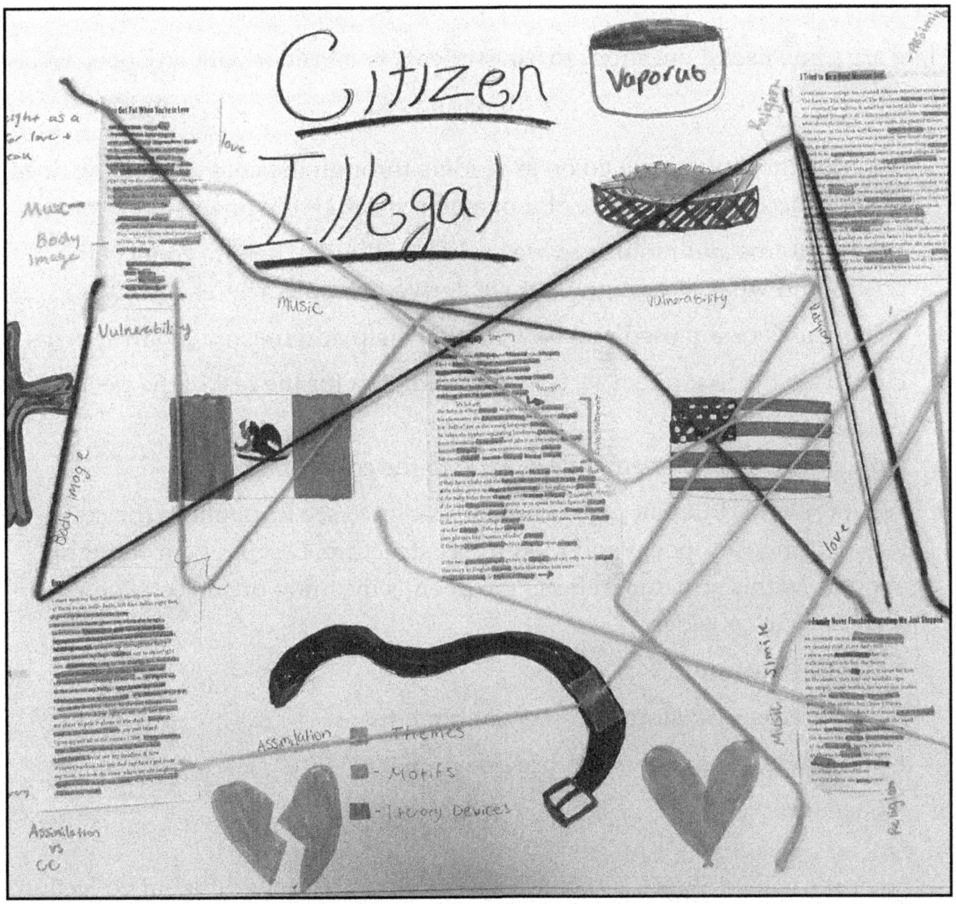

A finished product of poem threading using five poems from José Olivarez's Citizen Illegal. *Threading poems could work as a culminating activity for any poetry collection or group of poems you read in class.*

On day two, pass out colorful yarn, tape, and scissors and instruct students to show the connections between the poems using the yarn. A single piece of thread might connect only two of the poems, or it might weave through four of them, perhaps even all five. If the thread stops at one of the poems with a piece of tape, then that poem includes whatever that piece of thread represents. Students create a key on their poster to show what each color of yarn signifies. To assess the posters, I give a completion or participation grade and offer a little extra credit for the poster that I deem is the best portrayal of the collection as a whole. The extra credit carrot gets students motivated and encouraged to make the best poster.

Guiding Questions for Reading Any Collection

Here are some useful questions to ask students to consider with any poetry collection:

1. Describe the journey we go on as readers through the collection. How does the poet accomplish a sense of movement through the poems?
2. What patterns and motifs can we see? How do they help to connect the poems and what meaning(s) can we derive from them?
3. What allusions are used and how do they help add meaning to the poems?
4. How does the first poem serve as a foundation for the rest of the poems in the collection?
5. How does the final poem give closure to the collection?
6. What types of different poetic structures do we see throughout the collection? Choose a poem and identify its structure. Discuss your thoughts about how this structure reflects the poem's meaning or subject. Poetic structures to consider:
   - Stanza structure
   - Line breaks: end-stopped vs. enjambment
   - Form (ode, elegy, sonnet, prose poem, free verse, etc.)
   - Caesura

Whether it's *Citizen Illegal, Counting Descent,* or an entirely different collection, we encourage you to try teaching a full collection, as we have found them to be equally successful as traditional texts in getting students to examine language, to think critically, and to feel a relevant urgency and personal connection. Whether you read the collection as a whole-class text or in small-group literature circles, with the engaging hands-on activities described in this chapter, your students will build confidence in reading poetry. Finally, writing their own poems using mentor texts empowers students to share their own voices and grow as writers.

6

Poets in the Classroom

When I (Melissa) started to teach living poets with purpose in my classroom, I asked myself, "What would be the best-case scenario? How can I make this the most enjoyable and educational for my students?" I quickly came to the conclusion that students would learn best from the poets themselves. When I teach poetry, I'm really just a middlewoman, a transference role between the poet and the student. To me, the best scenario involved the students learning directly from the source, the professional—the poet. Students benefit from being able to ask poets questions and have conversations with them about what they write and why they write it. Having a poet in your classroom in person allows students to realize that poets are regular people just like them. And by being able to interact with them, hear their stories, and learn about their processes, students start to realize that they can write poems too. This chapter discusses some of the ways a poet visit could look, ranging from virtual visits to in-person classroom visits, along with poet-led professional development sessions for teachers.

Virtual Visits

Being able to have a face-to-face conversation with a poet allows for a new level of student engagement. Skype, Google Hangouts, and Zoom are free and easy ways to invite a poet into your classroom. To have the most successful conversation, have your students read several poems (if not an entire collection) by the poet, learn about the poet's biography, have lots of discussions in class, come up with quality questions ahead of time, and, finally, do a practice run with someone else (it can even be a student in your class on their phone) to work out any technical difficulties. Video chats are effective and successful because they don't involve the time and expense incurred with a face-to-face visit, yet students can experience what the face-to-face visit affords: a sense of the poet's voice and personality and how their poems are embodiments of those qualities. It's fairly

Melissa's AP Literature class Skyped with Clint Smith after reading his collection Counting Descent *for summer reading. Read more about teaching* Counting Descent *in Chapter 5. (Photo by Jamie Lord.)*

straightforward to get a poet to agree to a virtual visit—all you have to do is ask. Let them know which poems your students have read, some things students appreciate about their work, some questions or issues students are curious about, and some dates and times as options for a video call.

Skyping: A Teacher and a Poet Share Their Story

Kelly Herrera, a teacher in California, had her students read poet Nicole Tong's book How to Prove a Theory. *Kelly and Nicole originally posted their story on teachlivingpoets.com.*

Kelly Herrera teaches English at Buena High School in Ventura, California, and has been an English instructor for twenty years. (Kelly also shares how teaching living poets has impacted her classroom in our concluding chapter.) Nicole Tong is a poet who received her MFA from George Mason University. She is a recipient of the President's Sabbatical Award from Northern Virginia Community College, where she is a professor of English. Washington Writers' Publishing House announced Nicole Tong's debut collection *How to Prove a Theory* as the 2017 Jean Feldman Poetry Prize Winner.

Kelly's Story

When I first learned about #TeachLivingPoets, I wanted to immerse myself and my classroom in poetry. Through a grant from the Ventura Education Partnership, we purchased poetry collections from many of the authors featured on teachlivingpoets.com. I also wanted to provide a video conferencing experience with a living poet for my students, but I wasn't sure how to make it happen. I had many questions and apprehensions. First, how would I set it up? I had never contacted an author before. I wondered about scheduling, and what would the poet think about the idea of working with a group of high school students. I kept thinking about all the *what ifs*. Finally, would my students be ready? How would the poet react to their observations?

I ripped off the Band-Aid and took a deep breath as I read through Nicole Tong's website. On her contact page, I read, "Notes are Nice," so I sent one explaining what I hoped to set up for my class. I heard back from her later that day, and over the course of a few emails, we set up a video conference for the following week.

As for technology, I asked Melissa Smith what she does, and I contacted my teacher librarian Joel Levin, who is our go-to tech person on campus. My school had little experience with videoconferencing, and Joel was more familiar with FaceTime, so we chose to use that medium versus Skype. We connected a MacBook to my projector with speakers and a USB microphone, and Nicole offered to do a test run the day before.

I quickly learned that my apprehensions about videoconferencing and contacting an author were unnecessary. Nicole was accommodating and gracious, and as I hung up from the test run, I was geeking out!

The students and I worked through *How to Prove a Theory* in sections. Students read and annotated on their own, and we discussed in small groups. My AP Literature students might have been hesitant to work on more academics right after the AP exam, but as they got into Nicole's words, the stress of the exam melted away. They wrote questions, they expressed emotion, they identified with what they read. We talked about lines that stood out:

> "To save anything you must risk its loss."
>
> "Even emptiness yearns for something."

"Suppose happiness waits like finish lines."

"Grief is a color you can't see through."

As we moved onto themes that we saw emerging in the work, we started to wonder and to formulate questions:

- Are all of the Hypothesis poems connected? Same for theory poems? How are they connected?
- In "Marathon," what's the purpose of structure? Is it meant to be a concrete poem?
- Who is Anna, and what is her significance?

Our brainstorming covered the whiteboards with insights that showed growth and confidence. We were ready for our call with Nicole.

The day of our videoconference, Nicole captivated my students. She started the call by sharing her biography and how she got into writing, and then transitioned into her process with publishing *How to Prove a Theory*. She delighted us by reading some of her work, and afterward shared the inspiration for some of her poems. Learning about Nicole's inspiration provided an intimate insight that answered many of the questions my class had pondered.

I fought back tears as I listened, and students felt the emotional impact as well. The last part of our call was a Q&A, and students had the opportunity to approach the microphone and talk to Nicole directly. Before we hung up, we crowded around the screen to take a group photo with our new friend.

As we prepare to close out the school year, one of the assignments my seniors are working on is an inspiration poem that takes one of the poems we've studied during the year and uses it as a mentor text for their own. After our day with Nicole, I have a feeling I'll be reading about some "theories" with a personal connection.

Nicole's story

I was so happy to hear from Kelly a short time before I met her class virtually; her request proves how the #TeachlivingPoets virtual library does the great work of expanding the reach of living poets and the "breathing" elements of the genre—the live reading, in particular. Before I met her class, Kelly provided about two pages of typed notes the students had generated a class ahead of our meeting about the poems in *How to Prove a Theory*. From those notes, I suggested an agenda for our time together that included my background, writing habits and practices, the evolution of the book, a reading of five poems (I selected the most discussed in their notes), and live questions from students present. During our time together, I shared a few "book secrets," including a former title of the collection (and my impetus for changing it), as well as some biographical context for a few of the elegies in the collection—"Grief Theory" and "How to Prove a Theory," specifically. Because high school students move from class to class on a strict schedule, it is important to know how much time you'll have together and to propose or request some points of focus to make the most of the visit.

While I have read to high school audiences before, it was striking to me how many students had questions or comments about "Grief Theory," which is a poem about my dear friend dying unexpectedly. I wanted to address students' comments and questions while also reassuring them that the manner in which my friend died was rare. Whether or not students have experienced a profound loss at their age, many of Kelly's students could empathize with the situation of the speaker, who begins, "Grief wakes me, insists I play your voicemails / in the bathroom in the middle of the night." The pattern of their questions and their gratitude make me want to write more poems to and for younger readers. Generally, the visit reminds me that students are ideal readers because of the ways in which they see patterns, uncover themes, ask questions, and empathize.

Specifically, since the reading, I've given myself the assignment to write a sonnet or an ode to a living friend because, while elegy is important, it is equally important to let those who mean a great deal to us know that while they are still

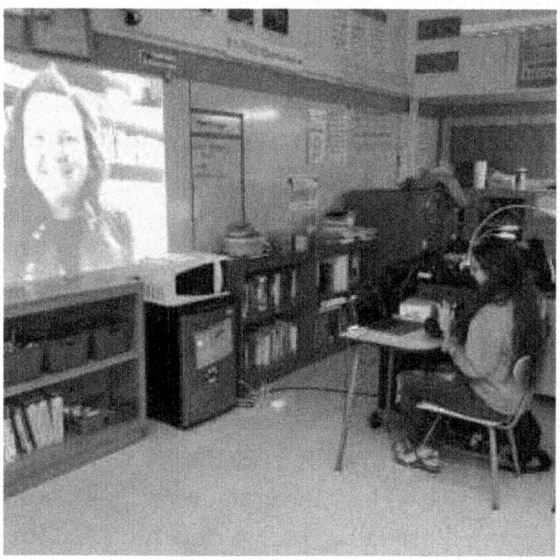

Photos by Kelly Herrera

here. I am still hashing out the ode, but if it makes it into my second collection, I'll have this class to thank—as will a new set of readers, perhaps.

• • • • •

Providing your students with an opportunity to talk to a poet is one of the most rewarding and inspiring classroom experiences. Not only do students get their questions answered and learn new insights about the poems they've been reading, but they also get to see that the author is a living, breathing person, not just an abstraction of a name on a book spine. After Skyping with poet Victoria Chang, author of numerous books of poetry, including *Barbie Chang*, which my class had read, my student Olivia commented that it was eye-opening to see that Chang was just a "normal person" like her. And if Chang is a normal person and can write poetry, maybe Olivia as a normal person can write poetry too. Hearing Olivia's comment affirmed my reasons for teaching living poets and inspires me to continue connecting my students with poets, and to share our experiences for other teachers to do the same.

How to Plan a Successful Virtual Visit

1. Read work by the poet, preferably an entire collection.
2. Contact the poet (email is probably the preferred tool of communication for most poets) to ask if they are willing to videoconference with your class. Once the poet agrees, discuss dates and times for the virtual visit.
3. Prepare specific questions ahead of time and have them available during the conversation for reference. Go over with students what makes a good question, and identify any potential questions to maybe avoid, such as those that verge on too personal or invasive.
4. Get help if you need it. I have a phenomenal technology facilitator who is willing to be there at the start of every Skype just in case there's a technical glitch (which there usually is). They can help to set up an account and decide which platform will be best to use (Zoom, Skype, Google Hangouts, etc.).
5. Arrange a location. I have a classroom camera mounted in the front of my room, but if you don't, you need to go to a room in your building that does. Or you will need to set up a computer with a camera at the front of your group to get as many students in the frame as possible.
6. Test the sound and video quality beforehand. Sound quality is tricky. It never seems to be loud enough for the poets when I Skype because the microphone is also on that camera mounted in the front of the room, so it

picks up all ambient noise from the entire room (the AC unit, shuffling papers, creaking chairs, whispering, etc.). So audio is usually my biggest challenge—getting kids to be quiet when they aren't speaking and projecting (basically, yelling to the camera) when they are. I always do a test-run with someone else beforehand to iron out kinks and adjust things as necessary before the real deal. This also helps the kids get used to talking to the screen. And even then, you never know what might happen on the poet's end with their technology. I've had experiences when there was no video and we were just listening to a voice in the sky, as well as times when the feedback was horrible—and many times when it worked perfectly. You just never know! I always ask our tech person to be in the room when we start to help with settings and tech issues if they arise.

Melissa's eleventh-grade American Literature class Skyped with José Olivarez after reading his collection Citizen Illegal. *Read more about teaching* Citizen Illegal *in Chapter 5. (Photo by Jamie Lord.)*

7. Predetermine which students will ask the first few questions, and in what order, to keep the conversation flowing.
8. Be flexible! Have someone on hand to help you with tech.

Don't forget to take pictures to share with social media and tag #TeachLivingPoets.

9. Finally, send a thank-you note to the poet signed by all your students and, if you are able to, a small gift card to compensate them for their time.

School Visits

Local Poet-Teachers Lead Professional Development

One of the best resources for teaching poetry is probably a lot closer to you than you think. Professors who teach in the English department, especially creative writing classes, at the higher ed institution near you may be willing to come to your school and provide a professional development session for you and your colleagues. If your school will allow you to arrange a content-specific professional development session, this is a highly effective option for gathering new teaching methods and materials from educators who live and breathe (and often write) poetry. Search your nearby colleges' English department pages to see who teaches courses focusing on poetry. Are any of the syllabi online? Have they published any poetry or instructional resources themselves? My school was fortunate to bring in Alan Michael Parker for a half-day PD event highlighting strategies for teaching the reading (and understanding of) poetry. Parker is an essayist, poet, novelist, and teacher of creative writing at Davidson College. He has taught some of my all-time favorite poets, including Clint Smith and Rebecca Hazelton.

In his half-day session, Parker shared activities for reading and understanding poems, as well as for creating engaging writing prompts we could immediately take back to our classrooms. He first directed us in compiling a list of words or phrases that completed the sentence "*A poem is* ____," and led us in a discussion of what makes a poem a poem. Initially, some of us had more rigid views of what is considered poetry, and he encouraged us to think outside of typical forms we are used to seeing in textbooks and old anthologies. Parker went around the room and asked us random questions with simple answers, such as "What did you do last night?," "What is the first thing you did when you woke up this morning?," and "When was the last time you were alone?" He wrote our responses on the board in a list-like format and then asked the group, "Is this a poem?" Some of us said *yes* and some said *no*, and a discussion ensued as to why or why not. I admit, I was one of the people who said *no* at first, but after thinking it through and listening to my colleagues, I changed my mind. By the end of the discussion, our definitions of poetry were broadened, and we were ready to start digging into some poems. Parker's opening activity can be used at any grade level as an introduction to poetry. I used it on the first day of my Creative Writing class to set the tone for the year of an inclusive and open view of poetry.

Local Poet Class Visits

Jay Ward started our workshop with a performance of his poem "Posthumous," modeling his tips for giving a successful slam performance.

Living near a large city like Charlotte, North Carolina, means I have a wealth of poets at my fingertips. Think of the biggest city near you and do a little digging to see if there is a poetry scene and how you can get connected. It just so happens that Charlotte is home to one of the best poetry slam teams in the world. Slam team member and poet Jay Ward is a performer, teaching artist, and author of *Sing Me a Lesser Wound.* He represented Charlotte at the Individual World Poetry Slam three consecutive years and at the National Poetry Slam for two consecutive years. Jay was Charlotte's 2016 Poet of the Year and the 2018 Charlotte Grand Slam Champion. The Slam Charlotte team went on to win the 2018 National Championship and the 2019 Individual World Poetry Slam. Jay was kind enough to visit my Creative Writing class during our slam poetry unit. Who better to guide students than a slam world champion?

For slam performances, Ward's tips are:

- **Slow down.** Give the words the weight they deserve.
- **Square up.** When standing in front of a crowd, you need to find your base. Set your feet hip-width apart, stand up straight, don't sway. Pretend there is a frame around your face (he referred to it as a "box") and that any movements outside of this frame, such as fidgeting, hand gestures, or rocking, are distracting. Build any movements in where they make sense with the poem and then return to your base.
- **Let the words dictate the performance.** The words tell you what you need for the performance. Any movements should be purposeful and meaningful, in sync with the language of the poem.

- **Stick the landing.** Don't trail off at the end. The emotion and volume of the last words should match the rest of the poem. End it with the same intensity you began with.

And, of course, a slam poet needs to *write* a poem before they can step on the stage to slam. For writing poetry, Ward's advice to young writers is:

- Don't edit as you write. Everything exists in a first draft. Don't stifle creativity as you go. Don't be afraid of being too cheesy. Let it all into your draft.
- Find yourself in the work. Ask yourself why you are writing this poem. Avoid generalities and get as specific to your experience as you can. The more specific you are, the more inviting you will be to your audience.
- Consider why it's important to you. Tell a story. What is the poem really about to you on a personal level? Poetry can often help us heal, as well as provide a source of healing for others.

After his reading and sharing his tips, Ward joined the class as an audience member for student group slams. He listened to their poems and offered his professional feedback on their strengths and what they could work on to improve.

Creative Writing students Sophia, Bryce, and Pearce listen to Jay Ward's feedback after performing their group slam poem. Sitting in the back of the class, Ward participates as an audience member and then provides groups with his feedback and insights.

Poets in Town for Other Events or Readings

One Class Period Visit: Kate Partridge and L. A. Johnson

Following the annual Association of Writers & Writing Programs conference, poets L. A. (Liz) Johnson and Kate Partridge visited my Creative Writing class on their way up the east coast for readings and book tour events. Johnson was touring for her new book, *Little Climates*, and Partridge for *Ends of the Earth*. My class had read some of their poems earlier in the week, so each poet started off with a mini-reading. Partridge began by reading "Say When" and "I Like the Muscles on That One," which we had previously spent some time discussing in class and that students had some questions about. Students were especially curious about the fly in the bottom of the vase in "Say When," first published in *RHINO*.

Say When

I learned a recitation
from one woman, and have

taught it to no one.

Something peaceful in that—
enough of the rolling

forward. Enough
of rivers. Enough

sea. Whatever lingers is
not sorrow. The fly remains

at the bottom
of the rose vase.

After hearing students' interpretations, Partridge shared her thought process behind crafting the poem. She was exploring what happens when someone tells a story but then no one repeats it—how it just ends or stops. And how that then connected in her mind to thoughts about death and mortality. She explained that her short line length mirrors what she was thinking about as she wrote it.

She said there was actually a fly at the bottom of a vase sitting on her writing desk, and she thought the image fit with the poem. She wanted a poem as tight and restricted as a flower vase, hence the poem has a skinny column-like structure. Her enjambment shows breaks between a thing *being* and *NOT being*—the life of a story in existence versus stopped. She followed her explanation with a reading of "I Like the Muscles on That One" and shared her inspiration for writing it, which was taking online personality quizzes.

Before Liz Johnson read, she spoke about poetic structure, specifically in regard to couplets and tercets, and why a poet would choose to write using either. She explained that, to her, couplets create a sense of unity in a poem; because they are in neat pairs, they allow for a balance and an opportunity to play between them. Tercets, on the other hand, create a lack of unity and an off-balance, odd feeling. Johnson mentioned that she lives out west, so she often uses California and seasonal imagery, along with dream-like states. She read several poems that my students had read in class, one of which was inspired by a missing person story she saw in her local newspaper. My students were inspired by both Partridge's and Johnson's poems, which taught students that they can write a poem about anything—like taking online quizzes or a news story.

We transitioned into a mini-lesson on the poetic line by reading "Party Ship" by Kay Ryan, which Partridge and Johnson had rewritten in paragraph form. In small groups, we tried to figure out where Ryan put her line breaks. This activity was challenging because the poem has several rhyming words, but it also has punctuation that doesn't always come after the rhyming words, so the line breaks could occur after either of the rhyming words. Or both. Or neither. This poem certainly offered an interesting discussion on structure, and we were all dying to see the actual poem, which the poets then revealed.

The last part of class was spent on a prompt to write a six-line poem in either couplets or tercets using (but not limited to) words from a provided word bank written on the board. Some of the words included were *green, hand, music, skin, sing, sleep, bridge, stars, face, wave, darkness.*

We had just enough time at the end of class for students to volunteer to share their poems out loud. I was proud of my students, who are mostly ninth and tenth graders, and how invested they were in everything Partridge and Johnson had to say. They began to understand that stanza structure and line breaks are purposeful decisions that poets make, and how these poetic elements can affect a reading of a poem. Even long after this visit, my students would refer back to what they had learned about couplets versus tercets and apply that knowledge in their own poems.

Half Day Visit: José Olivarez

Before José Olivarez's visit, we read "Ode to Cheese Fries" and "(Citizen)(Illegal)" as a whole class, showcasing small-group performances of poems of choice from *Home Court*, coauthored with poet Ben Alfaro. With poems about father-son relationships, basketball, crushes, feeling alienated, and love, their poems span the range of my students' interests, and students found the poems easy to relate to and accessible. This visit happened before Olivarez's collection *Citizen Illegal* was out, which we discuss in detail in Chapter 4.

Olivarez began the workshop with a freewrite he called "I don't believe you." We started writing about the events of our day, beginning with getting up in the morning, not paying attention to grammar or mechanics—just keeping the pencil moving. The twist came when every few minutes Olivarez announced, "I don't believe you," as a signal for us to shift our story 180 degrees into something different. He suggested the option of starting the next sentence with "Actually, I . . ." to help us avoid writer's block when we needed to veer our story. One second you might be walking to the bus stop in the early morning fog, and the next moment you've decided to hitch a ride with a friend who drives by your block. Some stories ended up sounding pretty wacky, and students laughed over what they had written. Besides warming up our creative writing juices, one of the goals of this activity, I suspect, was to recognize and practice shifts in writing and to be inspired to include surprising turns in the poems we were to write later.

This dynamic writing activity was followed by a longer, uninterrupted prewrite describing a place that is special to us, which got us geared up for reading "Space Is the Place" from Adrian Matejka's *Map to the Stars*, about the two neighborhoods the speaker grew up in as a child. The poem begins:

> I would rather be back in Carriage House
> stashing away stale bread
>
> than in this abundance of landscaped dirt
> where the neighbors' dog-walk
>
> greetings are twice as loud
> as their arguments.

From just the first six lines, students ascertained that the speaker prefers his old home in Carriage House to the artificiality of his new neighborhood. Olivarez led the class in a discussion of what we learn about the speaker and his relationships to each place mentioned in the poem. After discussing the poem and

sharing our place prewrites, we all wrote poems about a place, Olivarez's final prompt for us.

As we ate lunch following the workshop, Olivarez and I asked students to write on the board favorite lines from the poems they had just written, creating a community of writers and an artifact for the day. The second half of the visit included a reading and Q&A—Olivarez read poems we had read in class as well as new poems, several of which are now in *Citizen Illegal*.

Full Day Visit: Ron Villanueva and Kaveh Akbar

Before this event, my students had just finished reading *Reliquaria* by R. A. Villanueva and *Portrait of the Alcoholic* by Kaveh Akbar. When choosing titles, I had a clear mission—to get these poets to come to my classroom and talk with my students. We had Skyped the year before with Villanueva, and I had had some interaction with Akbar on Twitter, but I thought my mission was a little insane, and probably impossible. Good thing I like a challenge.

We started the day with breakfast as a large group. With about sixty students, we had to split into halves for the morning workshops. Half started off with one poet, and then we switched after a short break. To open each workshop, a student who had worked closely with each respective poet's work (as their poem for their Poetry Project, described in Chapter 8) read an introduction about the poet.

Workshop 1: R. A. Villanueva

To get our minds engaged and ready for the day, Villanueva started off his ninety-minute workshop with a collection of fourteen "catalysts"—little bits of texts and quotations by living writers about writing. As we read them out loud, he encouraged us to underline or circle words and phrases that stood out to us,

or to write notes in the margins. Afterward, as a collective, we discussed the catalysts to investigate the conversation they were having with one another and the threads running through them, referring back to them for specific textual evidence.

Next, we each divided a blank sheet of paper into four boxes. We filled in one box at a time with as many words as possible in a two-minute time allotment for each of the following categories:

1. parts of the body that give you pain (doesn't necessarily have to be physical)
2. bodies of water you have a relationship with and/or memories of
3. nouns that are also verbs (e.g., *eye, box, gaze, bridge*)
4. (split in half) 1st: beautiful, joyful, wondrous things, people, or phenomena; 2nd: monstrous, terrifying, unsettling things, people, or phenomena

We then flipped our papers over and drew a self-portrait. Next, we made a list of things we saw in our illustrations—what did we include? Then we wrote a second list of things we'd left out. We then watched a YouTube video of a rehearsal excerpt from *Untitled America* featuring choreography by Kyle Abraham. With plenty of inspiration, language, images, and ideas at the ready, it was time to start writing a poem. Our constraints were as follows: the title must be "Self-Portrait as _____" or "Self-Portrait with _____," using words from all four lists. After we had written for a while and wrapped up our poems, Villanueva informed us that this wasn't the end of our poems, but instead a shift. Our next line had to signal the shift using a transitional word, and he provided a list of potential words on the board. In this last section of the poem, he wanted us to consider the relationship between our self-portraits and the video we had watched, including performance, dance, and music.

To end the workshop, we went around the room and shared something out loud about our experience, whether it was our thoughts about the process of writing, pieces of our poems, or something we had learned in our time together.

For me personally, the ninety minutes flew by. Villanueva kept us at a swift pace, moving seamlessly from one activity to the next, but I never felt rushed. His energy was incredible; he kept us engaged the entire time, and we all walked out of his workshop with a draft of a poem we felt proud of. In talking with my students afterward, I found that they were surprised at how easy it was to write a poem in such a short amount of time, and how inspired and creative they felt heading into our next session.

Workshop 2: Kaveh Akbar

After a short break, we headed into Akbar's session and started off with introductions, which included our name, preferred pronouns, and something that fills us with wonder. This was a brilliant way to start off the workshop; not only did I learn new things about my students and their interests, but also we quickly created a community of inspired thinkers. Akbar responded to each student's individual sense of wonder and followed up with a question or a comment, building bridges between himself and the students, as well as among the group, by weaving our wonders together. By the time we got to the last person, Akbar had spun a spider web of magic and awe.

He explained how the best poems orbit around a sense of amazement or marvel, and how "language orbits the nucleus of wonder." Poets use specific objects and images, a "cloud of particulars," to orbit the center of the poem, and it is "through these that we can shape or ascertain the nucleus." In other words, we don't just say "I am so sad my dog died" in a poem, but we use concrete images to shape a sadness.

To collect our own arsenal of images, we passed around books by living poets from my classroom library. Students took a random book, opened to a random page, and wrote down the first word they saw. We spent a good amount of time with a book before we traded books with someone next to us; we traded three times. At first, it was a flurry of page turning and writing spurts, but as time went on, the page turning slowed down, and we started reading more, spending more time on each page with each poem. It felt like a very organic process.

Once we had filled our papers with words and phrases, connecting words that seemed to work together, it was time to draft a poem. We could add words as we felt necessary, and compared to Villanueva's workshop approach, there weren't really any constraints at all. In talking to students afterward, I found that some preferred the more open nature of crafting a poem using Akbar's method, while others preferred Villanueva's more structured method.

After we spent some time writing, our next activity had us in groups of three. We listened to an audio of poets Joshua Beckman and Matthew Rohrer creating an improvisational poem, one word at a time and taking turns, titled "Laundromat of the Cosmos." As we listened, Akbar transcribed the poem (now our mentor text) on the board, modeling the role of the third person in the group. In groups of three, two of us took turns playing the poets while the third assigned the topic for the poem and transcribed.

When crafting the poem, the two poets had to make choices on the spot:

1. Say a single word.
2. Add on a suffix to the previous word.
3. Say, "end of sentence."
4. Say, "end of title" or "end of poem."

What was great about these poems, which I found to be very challenging to write but also had us laughing, was the surprising twists they would take mid-line. There was time for some volunteers to share at the end of the workshop, and the span of topics and tones was immense.

Anyone can write. About anything.

Afternoon Schedule: Reading, Q&A, Book Signing

After lunch, we headed back as one big group for a reading. Each poet read for about twenty minutes, and then we moved right into the Q&A. We got through several questions, but I'm pretty sure everyone wished we'd had more time because it was a special opportunity to be able to ask them our questions in such an intimate setting, and after we had shared the day together. I say *share* because that's how it felt—Villanueva and Akbar are so down-to-earth, humble, and kind. They worked *with* us, shared the space of poetry, and treated us as equals. We had moments of vulnerability, experimentation, wonder, laughter, and friendship.

The following year, after such a successful event with Villanueva and Akbar, I expanded the workshop even more and was able to bring in a third poet, Safia Elhillo, author of *The January Children*.

Student responses to the poets' visit underscore how significant this experience was for them:

Student Testimonials

For me, this workshop was very emotional for a reason I am not sure. The poem I wrote was the most genuine thing that I think I have ever put on a page, and I am thankful for RA for providing us with time, as well as inspiration to be able to create. Being able to acknowledge my emotions truthfully was something that I never really do. The space that RA created stirred something inside of me and allowed me to open up, something that I am very grateful for and that I hope to continue in my own writing. —Lauren G.

I felt so intellectually nourished, and for two hours, I felt like a poet. When I went home that day, I actually kept working on the poem I wrote during his class because I couldn't leave it alone; I wanted to write more, and it's been a long time since I felt inclined to write by my own accord. —Evelyn G.

RA's workshop enabled us to write more and active poetry by kind of guiding us through it. It was as if he was teaching us how to swim, and rather than just pushing us in the pool, he walked down the steps and got in with us. His lesson on the catalyst and how everyone could be a poet or writer gave me insight on how poetry could impact and be a part of everyone's lives regardless of profession. —Joe F.

It allowed me to write about an event that I had struggled to put into words for a while. This was also the first real attempt I took in writing a legitimate poem. Therefore, this workshop will always hold a special place within me. —Joshua P.

I learned more about myself as I wrote my poem. It was the first time in a long time that I have enjoyed writing. —Julia W.

They forced me to think more introspectively and face insecurities. The insecurity that I ended up writing about is one that I often try to ignore, but writing about it was unbelievably healing for me. They made me want to find the time [to write] because I felt like the emotional effect it had on me was valuable. —Johannah P.

I remember R.A discussing how he created the Wryneck poetry form to express an unresolved fear or emotion that is inescapable in the end. After he said this, I couldn't help but think about my own experiences, my own fears about life about myself or my family and I realized that the poets of today aren't writing about themselves in particular, but rather the human experience and all the emotions that are associated with it. —Jelani S.

I honestly think I will remember this experience for a long time to come. It's one thing to read poetry on your own or for class, but it's another thing to actually meet real, live poets in person and to interact with them. I think this visit truly opened up my eyes to the world of poetry. I feel all English students should get this experience to find out how relatable and down-to-Earth these poets are, and how accessible poetry truly is to anyone. —Tyler K.

Before the workshop, the poets went around my classroom and examined the work students had done with their poems. This moment is ingrained in my memory as one of my favorites of the day. They were so quiet, so attentive, and took pictures of my students' work to post to social media. They slowly made their way around the room and spent time with each poster and each piece of work. I can't imagine a more authentic audience for my students than the poets themselves. Now I tell my classes, "Don't do it for me. Don't do it for a grade. Do it for the poet!"

How to Plan a Poet Visit

So how do you make poet visits happen in your class? First of all, you need to do a little research. Check out local literary events and university websites. Look up your favorite poets' reading tour schedules on their professional webpages for any coming to a location near you. Try participating in Poetry Out Loud or a slam poetry competition. Share your love for a poem or poet on social media. Reach out to a poet for a potential class visit.

I'm no booking agent, but I have individually planned poet visits to my school, so maybe telling you about my process will help you to give it a whirl as well. And I sincerely hope you do because it is a remarkably inspiring experience your students will remember for a long time.

1. *Check with admin.*
I'm more of an *ask for forgiveness, not for permission* kind of person, but some things are too big a deal to go that route. I am fortunate to have extremely supportive administrators who see the value in students learning from professionals, but I understand this might not be the case in all schools. So you might need to have your justification prepared for convincing your principal that an event like this is worth it—both educationally and financially. Be prepared to answer the following questions:
    - How will the visit impact students' learning?
    - How is it aligned with the curriculum?
    - What is the cost, and what ideas do you have for where this money will come from? For example, are you asking for money from the school or relying on fundraisers?
    - How many students will be impacted?
    - What are the benefits of having a real-world context, and why is it more beneficial than a virtual visit (via Skype, Google Hangouts, etc.)?

2. *Contact the poet well in advance to secure a date.*
Poets are busy professionals; many have full-time jobs and spend much of the year traveling for readings, workshops, and literary events. I suggest looking at potential dates during the previous spring for the following school year you wish them to visit. Getting your school on the poet's official calendar early will help to secure your ideal date. The more popular the poet, the earlier you should ask. Check out *who* you should be asking, as well, which you can usually find on their website. Does the poet maintain their own schedule, or do they have a manager you should be working through instead?

3. *Read works by the poet.*
Spend quality time with the poet's work in class. Read their entire collection if you can. You want your students to be well versed (pun intended) in the poet's work so they can have the most meaningful and engaging experience possible. In my opinion, reading just a couple of poems doesn't cut it. I put both Villanueva's and Akbar's books on my syllabus as required reading for the class. We spent more than a week on each book, holding class discussions, annotating, writing reflections, debating themes and symbols, analyzing structure, making posters, shooting videos—we got dirty with the poems.

4. *Budget carefully.*
Poet visits are typically not free, so you may need to get creative to make this happen. If a poet is in town, you could get lucky with a volunteer visit. If not, you will most likely need to pay an honorarium and cover any travel and hotel expenses. **The experience your students will have will be well worth the cost.** The honoraria I have paid range anywhere from $150 to $1,500. For Akbar and Villanueva's visit, the grand total came to just over $4,000 to cover everything, including honoraria, flights, hotel, catered lunch, poets' dinner, welcome bag of goodies for the hotel, and Uber/Lyft rides.

5. *Raise money.*
Some schools have instructional budget allotments, booster clubs, and/or PTOs you could ask for funding. You could set up a Go Fund Me or DonorsChoose. You could do your own fundraisers, such as bake sales, T-shirts, restaurant nights, etc. We held several fundraisers, including restaurant nights and Matchmaker surveys. In addition, each of my students paid a small fee to attend the whole-day event—kind of like a field trip, except we didn't technically go anywhere. We also invited guests from a nearby school and charged them a fee too. A chunk was donated by local businesses and family members as a tax write-off. Finally, a portion was paid for through my school's instructional budget. Parents also helped immensely by donating items for breakfast and lunch treats.

6. *Book hotel and flights—three months ahead of time.*
Ask the poet the best way to go about this. Usually, the poet or the poet's manager will research flights and send you a request for you to book for them. Or they might book it themselves and you then reimburse them. For the hotel, send them a couple of nearby options to choose from, and once they choose, book it for them. You should also ask them about payment—do they need to be paid prior to the event, or is sending a check afterward okay? I've had to do both, so knowing this ahead of time may save your event if they need payment before the visit. Also, check with your school's financial business office regarding what you will need from the poet to pay them, such as a W-9 form or an invoice.

7. *Make a schedule for the day of the visit.*
To make your event run as smoothly as possible, you need to map out a schedule. Workshops typically run between one to two hours, readings twenty minutes, and Q&A about thirty minutes. If you have a half-day workshop, it could look like:

11:30–12:45 Workshop

12:45–1:30 Lunch

1:30–1:50 Reading

1:50–2:20 Q&A

2:20–2:45 Book signing

For a full-day workshop, I made the following schedule. I had a large group of sixty students and two poets, so we split in half for the morning workshops.

7:45–8:15 Breakfast (donated by parents)

8:20–10:00 Workshop with Poet 1

10:00–10:20 Break

10:20–12:00 Workshop with Poet 2

12:00–1:00 Lunch (catered by local pizza/pasta place, with desserts donated by parents)

1:00–1:20 Poet 1 reading

1:20–1:40 Poet 2 reading

1:40–2:20 Q&A with both poets

2:20–3:00 Book signing

8. *Two weeks before the event:*
   - **Confirm** everything (Hotel, lunch, staff affected by event)!
   - Ask about any poet dietary restrictions or allergies, as well as what **equipment** they will need. Villanueva needed video capabilities, and Akbar needed a supply of poetry books to pass around. Ask the poet what they will need to have a successful workshop so you can prepare ahead of time. Also, in this email you should include the information your school may need in order to pay them. I needed a completed **W-9 form**.
   - Now would be a good time to create **SignUpGenius** for any donated items or volunteer help needed. I made easy-to-accomplish slots (e.g., bring in a dozen donuts, cream cheese, a dozen cookies for lunch, a box of utensils) and put in the descriptions of where and when the items should be dropped off. I also needed a couple of parent volunteers to set up the breakfast while I was out picking up the poets,

as well as to set up lunch while we were in the workshops. I am so grateful to the parents who helped out, and I think they were happy to support their senior student in one of the last school activities they were ever going to have!

- Prepare **introductions**. Poets deserve a good introduction, and intros are so much more meaningful when they come from students who love the poet's work. In each of the workshops, we started with a student introduction for the poet, written by the students themselves. Introductions included awards, publications, and what the poet's works meant to the student personally.
- Get a **substitute** to cover any of your classes that are not participating in the event. You can't be in two places at once!
- Find places to **displace your other classes** not attending the event. They will have a sub, so that makes it easier; you won't need to ask any colleagues to cover. I begged some of my colleague friends to borrow their classrooms during their planning period so that the sub and my students could relocate there. I made sure to give my students plenty of meaningful work, both to keep them busy and to ensure that the sub wouldn't need to use the classroom computer (except perhaps for attendance), which meant that my colleague could still work in the room while my class was in there.
- **Notify other teachers** as needed to give them a heads-up that they might have a lot of "absent" students. As an AP teacher, I felt a sense of duty to email the other AP teachers, as we share a lot of the same students; they might not want to schedule a big assessment or super important activity for that day, especially if it's close to AP exam time.
- **Secure a large space or more chairs** (and someone to help set them up) for any large-group events. I had to bring thirty additional chairs into my room for the whole-group afternoon events: the readings and the Q&A. The chairs were generously placed in my room by one of our custodians while we were in the cafeteria at lunch.

9. *Two days before the event:*

- Email the poet to see if they have any handouts that need to be copied. Double check on the equipment needed and send the poet the schedule for the day.

- Have your students prepare questions for the Q&A. You certainly want to avoid a crickets-in-the-room situation. You could even identify a brave student ahead of time to ask the first question to get things started.
- Check and practice the introductions your students have written.
- Also send the finalized schedule to administration, and anyone else involved, especially the secretary—secretaries are the glue that holds a school together, right? Touch base again with any custodians you may need help from.
- Email a list of the students attending the event to the necessary people so that they are not marked absent. Inform students that they are responsible for any work they miss in their other classes.
- Email SignUpGenius parent volunteers a friendly reminder—and a thank-you for their contribution.

10. *The day before the event:*

- Drop off a welcome bag (labeled with the name) for the poet so they will receive it when they check into the hotel. I got a mix of sweets and healthy snacks. After a long day of travel, some dark chocolate and dried mangos sounds really good. I also included a more personal thank-you gift, a specially made coffee mug with the #TeachLivingPoets hashtag on it, because that's my favorite little gift to give to people who love and respect poetry.
- Stick to your schedule so things don't get chaotic. And it's okay to feel nervous. I was a hot mess the entire week leading up to the event; I felt anxiety and stress like I haven't felt in a long time. It was the biggest school-related event I had ever planned, and I wanted so badly for it to go well. I was nervous about meeting the poets in person, and I didn't want to let my students, my school, and especially the poets down. My fear of things somehow not going smoothly was fierce.

11. *Enjoy yourself!*
Now, in hindsight, I realize I should have taken some deep breaths and reminded myself that I had double-triple checked with *everyone* about *everything*. I managed to get it together the morning of the visit so that I could enjoy the day with my students and the poets. Because I had planned everything so meticulously, I was able to appreciate and delight in playing student and participate as an equal with them in the workshops.

7

Writing Poems from Prompts

In the introduction, we briefly mentioned the findings of Dan Melzer's research on writing assignments across the curriculum in higher education, but the findings bear repeating here: only 3 percent of the more than 2,000 writing assignments collected in the study could be characterized as expressive in nature. Though the argument can be made that giving students the opportunity to write poems develops linguistic and rhetorical dexterity (it does), Melzer's findings show that students are probably not getting the chance to express themselves in writing as much as they need to in order to make writing meaningful to them.

This chapter presents prompts for writing different kinds of poems. Each prompt begins with a brief description of the kind of poem students will be writing, including examples poems, followed by the prompt. Since the example poems act as primers for the prompt and give students ideas for their own poems, share at least two with your class to provide enough time for reading, discussing, and pointing out craft elements that students can emulate in their own poems. One way Melissa has supported students' reading of the example poems is featured on the #TeachLivingPoets website in a post where she describes printing the example poems on poster boards, along with the poet's picture and biographical information. In small groups, students read the poem, share their impressions of the poem, annotate it with definitions of unfamiliar words, and paraphrase the poem. Student groups were also asked to identify

the main shift in the poem (sometimes called a turn or volta) and to identify figurative language, literary devices, or other moves they recognize.

Given the description and example poems as their guides, some students will feel confident enough to write their own poems without the prompts. Others will want more explicit, step-by-step instructions, and for those students the prompts will support their writing efforts. Some students have even asked to "go off prompt" and write an entirely different kind of poem than the one described in the prompt, to which I (Lindsay) always answer, "Absolutely." The aim isn't to have students write an ode or an abecedarian; the goal is to use language in a way that's meaningful to them. This is their chance to sit in the driver's seat, to become a poet.

Color Poems

Color words appear often in contemporary poems because they enhance the vividness of a poem's imagery. Some poems focus on a single color, like Brenda Shaughnessy's "Why Is the Color of Snow?" and Melissa Range's "Shell White," while some writers populate their poems with splashes of different colors, like Ross Gay's red-headed vulture and purple okra in "Sorrow Is Not My Name" or Ada Limón's fuschia and green in "Instructions on Not Giving Up." Other poems repeat the color word, the repetition like the ringing of a bell, as in Li-Young Lee's "Spoken For" and Simone Muench's "The OED Defines Red-Hot." Lindsay's poem "Cobalt" was written from a similar prompt:

Cobalt

my name when I was a jazz musician
cobalt—
    a better daughter than blue
because the word
    comes close to metal—
    its consonants and long o
    fall out of the mouth like a ball
the color cobalt
    is the color cold and wet
    electric fish
the color cobalt
    repeats in circles around
    the hard purple center of a bruise

she is the color of the ink
    of words ricocheting off my guitar
cobalt
    the clash feud rocket boat—
    the velvet hat I throw offstage
    at the end of the show
cobalt's the color of the neon letters
    above the bar, and so it
    can be the color of light through glass
but really
just another name for blue

Other color poems your students might enjoy include the following:

"application for the position of abdelhalim hafez's girl" by Safia Elhillo

"Blue" by Carl Phillips

"Instructions on Not Giving Up" by Ada Limón

"The OED Defines Red-Hot" by Simone Muench

Section 12 of "Dear P." by Victoria Chang

"Shell White" by Melissa Range

"Sorrow Is Not My Name" by Ross Gay

"Spoken For" by Li-Young Lee

"Synesthesia" by Mahtem Shiferraw

"Why Is the Color of Snow?" by Brenda Shaughnessy

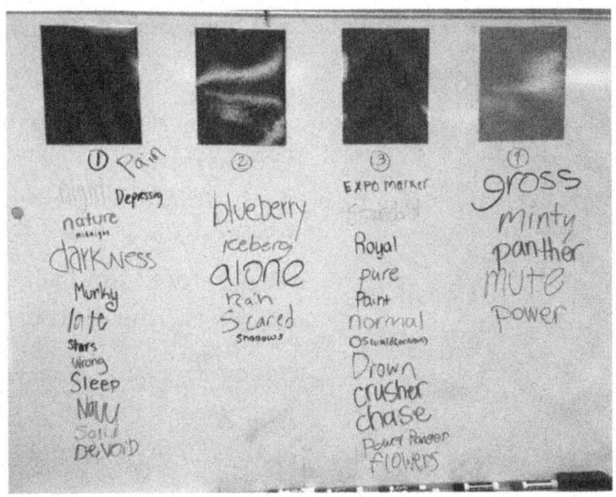

Color Poem Prompt: Write a poem inspired by a color. Include multiple references to the color in your poem. As a prewriting activity, display different hues of the same color and ask students to describe each hue with at least three words they associate with objects of that color or actions related to the color. Then ask students to pair the words they used for the different hues in surprising or unexpected ways (for blues, my students came up with "shy blueberry" and "electric sleep"). Instruct students to use at least two of the unexpected pairs they wrote in the final version of the poem.

Odes

The ode traces its historical roots back to the Olympics in Ancient Greece. They were written to celebrate the winners of the games. The form survives because of its connection to one of the most basic reasons poets write poems—to praise, to lift up, to call attention to a person, thing, or idea. These poems are about cultivating joy, a practice of gratitude.

Because Pablo Neruda's "Ode to My Socks" is often included in children's poetry anthologies, students may appreciate starting with it because they remember being introduced to it in elementary school. "Ode to My Socks" is also connected with other contemporary iterations of the ode because it simultaneously celebrates the mundane and the unexpected, calling our attention to the obvious and ordinary wonderful things in life, as does Olivarez's "Ode to Cheese Fries," which begins "golden goo of artificial delicious." In another Neruda poem, "Ode to the Lemon," the halved lemon is compared to a cathedral with "acid stained glass," a "cool architecture."

Ode to Cheese Fries

golden goo of artificial delicious
what probably lines
my stomach with sunlike grease for weeks after
eating the yellow
so yellow it could only be manufactured so what
if it's fake

as much cheese content as Apple Jolly Ranchers
i come from
a city of foreclosure empty lot city
where we got
dollar store brand action figures so what
my Wolverine didn't

have retractable claws or the right uniform
so my joy
at Pano's my favorite fried everything spot

the cashier's voice
a box of Newports filtered through throat
i didn't know

i would miss this home where the patties
come from freezers
and maybe not ever from cows or even animals
i live in
a city that brags about its organic fair trade
quinoa fed beef

of course i miss the 90's pop playing the restaurant
the Backstreet Boys
live in Cal City where the band never breaks up
the song plays
on repeat as the cashier takes my order say it with me
cheese fries please

give me everything artificial including cardboard fries
the bread fresh
out of some Walmart cloning experiment throw in
a cold pop
i want a joy so fake it stains my insides and
never fades away

Odes you might have students read include the following:

"Ode to Kool-Aid" by Marcus Jackson

"Ode to the Hotel Near the Children's Hospital" by Kevin Young

"Ode to the Lemon" by Pablo Neruda

"Ode to the Letter B" by Aracelis Girmay

"Ode to the Tampon" by Sharon Olds

Ode Prompt: Choose an ordinary thing that's important to you, something that deserves celebration or praise. Then make a list of similes and metaphors with the object of your ode as the vehicle. For example, "A lemon is like a _______" or "A lemon is a _______." Generate at least ten similes and metaphors. Next, play around with stringing these similes and metaphors together, omitting the name of the object you're writing about. Sometimes a pattern emerges, an organizational structure that allows grouping sets of similes or metaphors into stanzas. Return to the example poems for ideas to conclude the poem. Consider closing your ode with a poetic apostrophe.

The List Poem

In the title of Chen Chen's book, *When I Grow Up I Want to Be a List of Further Possibilities,* we find named one of the most generative kinds of poems—the list poem. You can see an example of this in several of his poems, including "For I Will Do/Undo What Was Done/Undone to Me," in which he begins by listing things he will pledge allegiance to, as a springboard to the rest of the poem, which praises mutability, partiality, and the paradoxical. Similarly, Ilya Kaminsky's poem "A Toast" is a list of things he's toasting: "to pine, redwood, sworn-fern, peppermint, / to hyacinth and bluebell lily, / to the train conductor's donkey on a rope, / to smells of lemons, a boy pissing splendidly against the trees."

When I Grow Up I Want to Be a List of Further Possibilities

To be a good
ex/current friend for R. To be one last

inspired way to get back at R. To be relationship
advice for L. To be advice

for my mother. To be a more comfortable
hospital bed for my mother. To be

no more hospital beds. To be, in my spare time,
America for my uncle, who wants to be China

for me. To be a country of trafficless roads
& a sports car for my aunt, who likes to go

fast. To be a cyclone
of laughter when my parents say

their new coworker is like that, they can tell
because he wears pink socks, see, you don't, so you can't,

can't be one of them. To be the one
my parents raised me to be—

a season from the planet
of planet-sized storms.

To be a backpack of PB&J & every
thing I know, for my brothers, who are becoming

their own storms. To be, for me, nobody,
homebody, body in bed watching TV. To go 2D

& be a painting, an amateur's hilltop & stars,
simple decoration for the new apartment

with you. To be close, J.,
to everything that is close to you—

blue blanket, red cup, green shoes
with pink laces.

To be the blue & the red.
The green, the hot pink.

List poems your students might enjoy include the following:

"Algebra is ____________. (fill in the blank)" by Daye Phillippo

"Bronzed" by Dean Young

"A Field of Onions: Brown Study" by Vanessa Angélica Villarreal

"For I Will Do/Undo What Was Done/Undone to Me" by Chen Chen

"Siblings" by Patricia Smith

"60 Songs about Quilting" by Sammie Bordeaux-Seeger

"Through" by Sam Pittman

"A Toast" by Ilya Kaminsky

List Poem Prompt: Write a poem that is a list. If it's helpful, use Chen Chen's opening "I pledge allegiance to . . ." and then list all the things you would pledge allegiance to, which will lead to some conclusion that can be drawn from the list generated. Another approach is to write a sentence like the one in Daye Phillippo's title and then fill in the blank multiple times to create the lines of the poem.

Abecedarian Poems

Abecedarians are acrostic poems made up of the letters of the alphabet. Each letter is the first letter of the line, starting with *A* and ending with *Z*. The best abecedarians are the ones that aren't obvious when you start reading the poem—and then you notice the letters. The most difficult lines of the abecedarian are the closing lines, the *x*, *y*, and *z* lines. Perhaps it's the expectation of those verbal gymnastics in the closing lines that makes abecedarians so appealing for poets. It's the challenge.

In Natalie Diaz's "Abecedarian Requiring Further Examination of Anglikan Seraphym Subjugation of a Wild Indian Rezervation," the speaker warns that if you see an angel on the rez, it's probably going to march you to "Zion or Oklahoma, or some other hell they've mapped out for us." Ashley M. Jones finds "Zion" a compelling occasion for the *Z* in her poem, "Avian Abecedarian," about the life of Harriet Tubman; it ends: "You there, Master—now you see her, now you don't. / Zion call her beyond the snub of your colonizing thumb." In Jessica Greenbaum's "A Poem for S.," the speaker writes to a fellow lover of words, someone known to read the dictionary, to whom the poet relates a story that imagines the alphabet as a kind of prayer, ending with the hope that the addressee's wife's "X-rays return with good news, may we raise our / Zarfs to both your names in the Great Book of Life." A zarf is a goblet.

Abecedarian Requiring Further Examination of Anglikan Seraphym Subjugation of a Wild Indian Rezervation

Angels don't come to the reservation.
Bats, maybe, or owls, boxy mottled things.
Coyotes, too. They all mean the same thing—
death. And death
eats angels, I guess, because I haven't seen an angel
fly through this valley ever.
Gabriel? Never heard of him. Know a guy named Gabe though—
he came through here one powwow and stayed, typical
Indian. Sure he had wings,
jailbird that he was. He flies around in stolen cars. Wherever he stops,
kids grow like gourds from women's bellies.
Like I said, no Indian I've ever heard of has ever been or seen an angel.
Maybe in a Christmas pageant or something—
Nazarene church holds one every December,
organized by Pastor John's wife. It's no wonder

Pastor John's son is the angel—everyone knows angels are white.
Quit bothering with angels, I say. They're no good for Indians.
Remember what happened last time
some white god came floating across the ocean?
Truth is, there may be angels, but if there are angels
up there, living on clouds or sitting on thrones across the sea wearing
velvet robes and golden rings, drinking whiskey from silver cups,
we're better off if they stay rich and fat and ugly and
'xactly where they are—in their own distant heavens.
You better hope you never see angels on the rez. If you do, they'll be
marching you off to
Zion or Oklahoma, or some other hell they've mapped out for us.

Abecedarian poems your students might enjoy include the following:

"Avian Abecedarian" by Ashley M. Jones

"Elementary" by Savon Bartley

"A Poem for S." by Jessica Greenbaum

"Siblings" by Patricia Smith

"Twenty-Six Imaginary T-shirts" by Terrance Hayes

Abecedarian Poem Prompt: Several approaches to writing abcedarians can yield good results. The first approach is to start the first line of the poem with a word that begins with *A*, continuing with the line until a word starting with *B* is written, and so on. In this approach, the on-deck letter becomes an invention device, with the writer creating ways to get to the next letter word. Another approach is to treat the abecedarian like a list poem, with the title functioning as the category or question that the poem's content answers.

Reverse Poems

Reverse poems express a common human desire: to turn back time, to go back to a time before something has happened. In reverse poems, we get to undo some undesired event, or we get to see the unfolding of something we want to relive or understand. These time travel poems show us in reverse a montage of images. If you're looking for a correlative example in another medium, watch the music video for Coldplay's "The Scientist." What makes reverse poems accessible for students is their apparent simplicity, describing the actions of a story in reverse, ending with an image from the beginning, which resolves the tension of the poem.

The final image of Matt Rasmussen's "Reverse Suicide," the speaker and his brother scattering fallen leaves from garbage bags, takes the speaker back to a time before his brother died by suicide. In Nate Marshall's "palindrome," the act of scrolling down through social media creates the effect of going back in time, "unmeeting" his first love, a slow fall into sweetness, and the speaker realizing her name was a palindrome. Writing a poem that brings her father back, Warsan Shire imagines "teeth sinking into gums," becoming an infant again, in "Backwards." In Yanyi's "Dream Diary," the poem ends with ghosts becoming alive (or, if not alive, glowing).

Reverse poems your students might enjoy include the following:

"Backwards" by Warsan Shire

"Dream Diary" by Yanyi

"palindrome" by Nate Marshall

"Reverse Suicide" by Matt Rasmussen

Reverse Poem Prompt: Reverse poems rely on capturing the action of a series of scenes and describing the action as if we were watching the scenes on rewind. To write one, start the poem with the "the end" scene, with each subsequent line going to a previous scene. Another approach is to write a list of five scenes in story order and use the outline you've created to draft the poem, moving from the last scene to the first. Using photographs or thumbnail scene sketches can also aid in the composition of reverse poems. Finally, reverse poems can be created from stories that are already written (either by the student or something the student has read) in an ekphrastic mode.

If you think your students need additional support writing this kind of poem, you might want to create a prompt that asks students to write directions to complete a task, such as making a peanut butter and jelly sandwich. Once students write the step-by-step set of instructions, they can use the steps as the basis for the reverse poem. For example, "spread the peanut butter with a knife on one slice of the bread" might become "with the knife, carefully scrape off the peanut butter from the bread and put it back in the jar."

Bestiary Poems

Bestiaries are a literary genre, a collection of stories or poems about or from the point of view of different animals. Donika Kelly's collection *Bestiary* is an example of this literary form. Bestiary poems perform the opposite of personification: the person becomes animal.

Love Poem: Centaur

Nothing approaches a field like me. Hard
gallop, hard chest—hooves and mane and flicking
tail. My love: I apprehend each flower,
each winged body, saturated in a light
that burnishes. I would make a burnishing
of you, by which I mean a field in flower,
by which i mean, a breaching—my hands
making an arrow of themselves, rooting
the loosened dirt. I would make for you
the barest of sounds, wing against wing,
there, at the point of articulation. Love,
I pound the earth for you. I pound the earth.

Other bestiary poems your students might enjoy include the following:

"The Elephant" by Dan Chiasson

"Golden Retrievals" by Mark Doty

"Siren Song" by Margaret Atwood

Bestiary Poem Prompt: Write a poem from the point of view of an animal—real or mythical—who is contemplating the characteristics that make them unique, connecting these characteristics with the emotional. Think of the animal as a totem or emblematic of your unique qualities, or you can randomly choose an animal, and some of the same emotional aspects of yourself will be present. Any animal you choose will allow you to explore aspects of yourself that aren't immediately evident if you were to describe yourself directly.

The Self-Portrait Poem

In *Calling a Wolf a Wolf,* Akbar's poems tell a story about his recovery from alcoholism. Some of the poems, like my favorite, "Portrait of the Alcoholic Floating in Space with Severed Umbilicus," use the self-portrait, or selfie mode, to paint us a picture of the poet. In this poem, the poet is an astronaut running out of air (that's the "severed umbilicus") and using his last bit of air to recount some moments in his life. Then, at the end, in a strange reversal of logic that sometimes happens in someone's last moments (or so we imagine), space itself becomes small—a cave—and the stars, diamonds. Akbar isn't the first poet to write a poem that is the textual version of the painter's self-portrait. In the United States, one of our most famous poems, Whitman's "Song of Myself," is in effect a self-portrait poem.

Other self-portrait poems your students might enjoy include the following:

"application for the position of abdelhalim hafez's girl" by Safia Elhillo

"Autumnal Self-Portrait" by Dean Rader

"Phosphorescence" Cynthia Cruz

"Self-Portrait as C-Section Scar" by Aimee Nezhukumatathil

"Self-Portrait as Daedalus, Writing the First Draft of His Autobiography" by torrin a. greathouse

"Self-Portrait with Reader" by Dean Rader

Self-Portrait Poem Prompt: Imagine you are painting a self-portrait. What is the setting of the portrait and what are you doing? Wearing? What expression is on your face? What are you thinking? It may be helpful to do an online search for famous self-portraits for inspiration. It also might be helpful to sketch your self-portrait. After this prewriting work, write a self-portrait poem from the point of view of a viewer of the self-portrait, starting with what the viewer notices first.

Cliché Poems

In cliché poems, poets breathe new life into overused words or phrases, imagining new contexts, new meanings, or doubling down on the cliché's logic with surprising outcomes. Take Leila Chatti's "The Rules," a poem composed of poetic clichés that manages to confirm the reason that stars are clichés in poems: they are wonders to behold, the poet admitting at the end, "I nearly wept on the sidewalk at the sight of them all."

The Rules

There will be no stars—the poem has had enough of them. I think we can agree
we no longer believe there is anyone in any poem who is just now realizing

they are dead, so let's stop talking about it. The skies of this poem
are teeming with winged things, and not a single innominate bird.

You're welcome. Here, no monarchs, no moths, no cicadas doing whatever
they do in the trees. If this poem is in summer, punctuating the blue—forgive me,

I forgot, there is no blue in this poem—you'll find the occasional
pelecinid wasp, proposals vaporized and exorbitant, angels looking

as they should. If winter, unsentimental sleet. This poem does not take place
at dawn or dusk or noon or the witching hour or the crescendoing moment

of our own remarkable birth, it is 2:53 in this poem, a Tuesday, and everyone in it is still
at work. This poem has no children; it is trying

to be taken seriously. This poem has no shards, no kittens, no myths or fairy tales,
no pomegranates or rainbows, no ex-boyfriends or manifest lovers, no mothers —God,

no mothers—no God, about which the poem must admit
it's relieved, there is no heart in this poem, no bodily secretions, no body

referred to as *the body*, no one
dies or is dead in this poem, everyone in this poem is alive and pretty

okay with it. This poem will not use the word *beautiful* for it resists
calling a thing what it is. So what

if I'd like to tell you how I walked last night, glad, truly glad, for the first time
in a year, to be breathing, in the cold dark, to see them. The stars, I mean. Oh hell, before

something stops me—I nearly wept on the sidewalk at the sight of them all.

Other cliché poems your students might enjoy include the following:

"Downhearted" by Ada Limón

"Famous" by Naomi Shihab Nye

"I'M GOING TO BE LATE" by Paige Lewis

"In Defense of 'Moist'" by Hanif Willis-Abdurraqib

Cliché Poem Prompt: Pick a cliché or overused word. Make a list of all the different ways people use the phrase or word, including situations. Next to each example you listed, come up with a new word or phrase that conveys the meaning using active verbs and concrete nouns. From this set of new ways of thinking about your phrase or word, group them or string them together. At the end of your poem, think about closing with an affirmation of the phrase or word (as in Chatti's poem) or with a rejection of the word. As an alternative prompt, write a poem defending a cliché or overused word in the style of Hanif Abdurraqib's "In Defense of 'Moist.'"

America Poems

When we reflect on our complicated history in the United States with regard to oppression and freedom, it probably comes as no surprise that poets write poems addressed to America. America poems reflect that complication: they celebrate and interrogate, criticize and elegize, offer hope and blame. As Ada Limón's poem below states, "the truth is, every song of this country / has an unsung third stanza, something brutal / snaking underneath us." These poems find their origins in the American poetic tradition, exemplified by Whitman's "America." We even have a recording of Whitman's voice reciting the poem (which Levi's used for an interesting commercial that you can find on YouTube).

A New National Anthem

The truth is, I've never cared for the National
Anthem. If you think about it, it's not a good
song. Too high for most of us with "the rockets
red glare" and then there are the bombs.
(Always, always, there is war and bombs.)
Once, I sang it at homecoming and threw
even the tenacious high school band off key.

But the song didn't mean anything, just a call
to the field, something to get through before
the pummeling of youth. And what of the stanzas
we never sing, the third that mentions "no refuge
could save the hireling and the slave"? Perhaps,
the truth is, every song of this country
has an unsung third stanza, something brutal
snaking underneath us as we blindly sing
the high notes with a beer sloshing in the stands
hoping our team wins. Don't get me wrong, I do
like the flag, how it undulates in the wind
like water, elemental, and best when it's humbled,
brought to its knees, clung to by someone who
has lost everything, when it's not a weapon,
when it flickers, when it folds up so perfectly
you can keep it until it's needed, until you can
love it again, until the song in your mouth feels
like sustenance, a song where the notes are sung
by even the ageless woods, the short-grass plains,
the Red River Gorge, the fistful of land left
unpoisoned, that song that's our birthright,
that's sung in silence when it's too hard to go on,
that sounds like someone's rough fingers weaving
into another's, that sounds like a match being lit
in an endless cave, the song that says my bones
are your bones, and your bones are my bones,
and isn't that enough?

Other America poems your students might enjoy include the following:

"America, I Do Not Call Your Name without Hope" by Dean Rader

"An American Sunrise" by Joy Harjo

"Dear White America" by Danez Smith

"Exile and Lightning" by Robert Pinsky

"One Today" by Richard Blanco

America Poem Prompt: Freewrite some lines, a paragraph, or a journal entry in which you talk about common (positive or negative) qualities, ideas, experiences, or institutions that are thought to be "American." Using the ideas, words, phrases, and lines generated by your freewriting, write a poem addressed to America. End the poem like Ada Limón's, with a question.

Body Poems

The human body is a site for politics: who gets to be beautiful, what we get to talk about with others, the way our bodies move in the world (and are moved). For that reason, poets take up issues of the body often in contemporary poetry. Early poems like Lucille Clifton's "homage to my hips" show up in the work of poets whose bodies are in conflict in some way with the world, becoming what poet Emilia Phillips has called a "poetics of body positivity":

> It is a movement of poetry that celebrates the body, doesn't shy away from the body's full experience; it expands the scope of poetry's engagement of the body and privileges the diverse lived experiences of people with bodies, all types of bodies. It rejects the appropriation of others' bodily experiences. It is imperfect, and it sometimes recognizes that one's own bodily acceptance is a process, a struggle. ("Poetics of Body Positivity")

Other body poems your students might enjoy include the following:

"Cardiology" by Rafael Campo

"Hair" by Elizabeth Acevedo

"Mad about Cows" by Jacob Saenz

"There Are Lungs" by Victoria Chang

"why you cannot touch my hair" by Eve L. Ewing

Body Poem Prompt: Write a poem celebrating some part of your body. Describe the way it looks and feels. Identify experiences that you associate with this part of the body. What secrets does it have? What do you wish about the body part? What would it say if it could talk?

Name Poems

Like faces and bodies, our names are part of our identities, powerful sites of self-fashioning. For poets, writing about their names gives them an opportunity to own and shape something that was given to them. In the example texts for this prompt, poets grapple with the experience of having a name that isn't part of the dominant culture, claiming for their names power in the face of forces meant to disempower.

Name poems your students might enjoy include the following:

"Alternate Names for Black Boys" by Danez Smith

"Choi Jeong Min" by Franny Choi

"etymology" by Airea D. Matthews

"first name cassandra, middle name remembrance" by Cassandra Anouthay

"Her Name Was Name" by Matt Hart

"How I Got That Name" by Marilyn Chin

"My Mother's Name Lucha" by Juan Felipe Herrera

"On Listening to Your Teacher Take Attendance" by Aimee Nezhukumatathil

"Say My Name" by Idris Goodwin

Name Poem Prompt: In the middle of a sheet of paper, write your name in large block letters. Around your name, draw lines like rays coming from a cartoon sun. Make the lines extend to the edge of the page. On each ray, write a memory associated with your name or details about the meaning or history of your name (lots of online sources are available to help with this part). In a prompt for the *Young Chicago Authors* blog, José Olivarez suggests listing nicknames you've been given, nicknames you've given yourself, mispronunciations of your name (if that applies), family names that are important to you, people you were named after, pet names you've been given, pet names you've given others, what you call your close friends, any groups/frats/sororities you've been a part of. Using the lines you composed for each ray, write a poem about what your name means to you or that in some way reclaims the power of your name.

Writing Good Prompts

Other kinds of poems that lend themselves to poetry prompts are contronym poems (with a word or words that mean opposites), haibuns, villanelles, ekphrastic poems (poems about works of art), and even love poems. This chapter could go on forever toward a horizon that will always be out there because as long as people are living, they will be writing new poems, and those poems will present new opportunities for writing prompts.

Writing prompts for poetry exercises begins with noticing similar ways of treating a subject or similar themes in poems. This depends, of course, on first cataloging and curating poems, as discussed in Chapter 1. Once you identify a pattern or theme and collect enough example poems (aim for at least three), dramatize the origin of the story, like a superhero's origin myth. In other words, try to imagine the context in which the poet got the idea for the poem or how they might have written it. At this step in the process of writing prompts, it's helpful to remember William Carlos Williams's adage about a poem being a machine made out of words: how do the example machine poems work? What's under the hood of those poems that might be instructive for students who will be composing similar poems? Finally, imagine active-learning approaches to generating the steps for creating such a poem. Melissa's #TeachLivingPoets website has some great examples of doing this (especially, in Lindsay's opinion, for the color poem), which can serve as mentor texts for lessons and prompts that you will develop for your class, your curriculum, and your teaching style.

8

Writing Projects for Contemporary Poetry

In "Slay the Monster! Replacing Form-First Pedagogy with Effective Writing Instruction," Kathleen Dudden Rowlands highlights the paradox of the persistence of the five-paragraph essay:

> Teaching the five-paragraph essay is a deeply entrenched instructional habit, repeated unquestioningly across the nation. Ironically, few teachers notice that the five-paragraph form they require from students has no connection to the rich variety of forms found in their pleasure reading. (53)

When thinking about the development of the assignments offered in this chapter, we tried to keep in mind the kinds of content we like to consume: podcasts, dynamic presentations, content shared on blogs (like TeachLivingPoets.com!). The assignments reflect Kathleen Blake Yancey's call to develop new approaches to writing in the twenty-first century, writing that engages with technology and also writing that is participatory and public, writing that comes as close as possible to Deborah Brandt's concept of self-sponsored writing.

Of course, assignments are by definition excluded from self-sponsored writing, but certain aspects of self-sponsored writing are sustained in some of these assignments. First, students retain ownership of their writing labor because of the public nature of the assignments (blogs, podcasts, etc.), an important but often overlooked aspect of student writing. When students are asked to write on demand for assignments without real audiences, the value of the writing is reduced to the grade. Once a grade is given, the artifact itself becomes disposable in the eyes of students. This view of their own writing as devalued was one of the findings of the Stanford Study of Writing (ssw.stanford.edu). Another way these assignments are similar to self-sponsored writing is that they ask students to write in genres that exist beyond the classroom, or *wild genres*, a term researcher Mary Soliday coined for genres that people use in their everyday lives. We share these assignments because we've found them to both enhance students' understandings of poetry and help them grow as writers.

Poetry Blogs

When creating their blogs, students choose designs, themes, colors, fonts, titles—all of the building blocks that go into making a webpage. Their blogs truly are a reflection of their personalities and offer them an opportunity to design a space to publish and share their writing. They can add pictures, links, other media; there are so many options.

Importantly, blogging provides students a rare opportunity to write for an authentic audience, a whole world of people beyond their teacher, what Dan Melzer in *Assignments across the Curriculum* refers to as the "Teacher-as-Examiner" audience. Partly because students understand public audiences better than they do the more abstract "Teacher-as-Examiner," the quality of student writing in a blog is often better than the quality of their assigned essays. They report feeling more comfortable and relaxed when writing blog posts compared to writing essays. Their blogs require the same analytical writing found in analytical essays, but the posts are often of higher quality, more fluid and expressive than more formulaic essays. Students enjoy the blogging experience so much that it was one of the major focuses in a student-led professional development session for teachers at Melissa's school, where students taught the teachers what works best for them: how they learn best, what engages them, and so forth.

In my (Melissa's) AP Literature class, as the focus for their monthly poetry blog students choose any living contemporary poet who has published at least one collection with a university or other respected press. I supply them with a long list of options and point them toward the #TeachLivingPoets Virtual Library (created by me and Scott Bayer); we also use Split This Rock's online poetry database, "The Quarry: A Social Justice Poetry Database," to select a perfect poet for each student. We spend a whole day in class researching different poets (thus exposing students indirectly to a diverse group of quality poets) because students will be spending an entire year focusing on one particular poet's work. Some students choose based on identifying with a poet's ethnicity, geographical region, or religion; some choose based on similar beliefs such as feminism or environmental advocacy; and others just like the poet's name or their author headshot online. Regardless of the reason, the choice is completely theirs. Finding a poet who speaks to them personally increases their enjoyment of studying poetry and deepens their engagement with the assignment, an outcome that results from empowering student choice in independent reading, widely discussed by literacy specialists such as Penny Kittle (*Book Love*), Donalyn Miller (*The Book Whisperer*), and Jennifer Serravallo (*Independent Reading Assessment: Fiction*).

Blogs are a fantastic and easy way to connect your students with poets who are active on social media. When students create their class blogs, I let them know that they will be public and shared with a wider audience. One of my favorite things to do is send the student blog link via a tweet, tagging the poet they are writing about. Sometimes poets are generous and respond with a comment, which pleases students. And sometimes poets go so far as to gloss poems with additional links or information about their work. For example, poet Kyle Dargan commented with some explanation about why he wrote a particular poem, as well as adding a link to a motion poem that offered more insight into the poem originally mentioned.

Poetry Blog Directions

Poets are alive and poetry is thriving! Let's take a closer look at some poets of literary merit who are currently writing. Please pick a living poet as the focus for your blog, and try to stick with this poet through the entire year. Your poetry blog should convince me that you have read and thought carefully about your poet and their poems. To a limited extent, it is true that a poem means what the reader thinks it means; you must, however, be able to explain your interpretation by specific references to the poem. Your grade is based on what you have to say and how well you say it—your personal reaction to the poem and your explanation of the logic that led to your interpretation. [Some of these requirements are taken from Ms. Effie's Literary Response Journal directions at http://mseffie.com/assignments/poetry/poetrylrj.html (Effinger)]

You MUST include the following in every poetry blog:

- The poem's title in quotation marks and the author's name
- A link to the poem, a picture of it from a book, or the poem typed out and cited on your blog page
- Quotations from the poem integrated with your own sentence, properly punctuated, and commented upon as necessary to show why you cited that particular line

After you've included the five MUSTs above, choose at least three of these MAYBEs to guide your response:

- A general statement of the poem's content
- An analysis of the speaker/persona
- A discussion of the title's significance
- A detailed response to a specific line or lines
- An examination of poetic techniques used, such as rhythm, simile, metaphor, personification, allusion, etc.

- A close analysis of the poet's diction, perhaps noting specific word choices or connotation and denotation
- An explanation of where the poem's shift (or shifts) occurs
- A discussion of the writer's life and its relevance to the poem
- A statement relating the poem to your experience or ideas
- An explanation of problems you had in understanding the poem
- An analysis of the structure of the poem
- Your opinion/personal reaction to the poem, good or bad, supported by specific references from the poem

Thank you to Sarah Soper, English teacher extraordinaire at Northwest High School in Jackson, Michigan, for making a poetry blogs rubric, shared in Figure 8.1.

Since students are blogging every month, here are some variations, created by Virginia teacher Adrian Nester, to offer more choice and variety:

1. Connect your poem to a visual text or piece of art (include the visual in the blog post) and discuss how these two works complement or relate to each other.
2. Connect your living poet's poem to a poem written by a nonliving poet. Include a link to this poem as well; include the author's name and the year the poem was written or published. Explain how the two poems are in conversation with each other.
3. Write your own mentor text poem inspired by a work from your poet. Include in the title "After ______" or "On Reading ______." Discuss how the poet's work influenced your own, and by doing so analyze the original work.
4. Answer the question: What is enduring about your poet's work? Support your claim with examples from at least three of their poems.
5. Connect your poet's poem to social commentary and societal happenings referenced in the poem. Be sure to hyperlink to respectable news sources and possibly to social media to show reactions. Bring it all back to the analysis of the poem.
6. Find two poems by the same poet that are contrasts in some form (e.g., tone, form, style, etc.) and discuss the choices and their effect.
7. Connect one of your poet's poems to a song by a current musical artist.
8. Create a vlog to post to your blog site. This must be a well-edited full analysis of the poem.

Successful 30/30	These are well-written blogs that respond fully to the poem and cover all the required elements. The best responses show a full understanding of the poem and support their points with appropriate textual evidence and examples. Writers of these responses demonstrate stylistic maturity by an effective command of sentence structure, diction, and organization. The writing need not be completely without flaws, but it should reveal the writer's ability to choose from and control a wide range of elements of effective writing.
Satisfactory 26/30	These blogs also respond to the poem well and cover all required elements, but their responses may be a bit less thorough or less specific than the essays in the top range. These essays are well written in an appropriate style but reveal less maturity than the top blogs. They do make use of textual evidence to support their points. Some lapses in diction or syntax may appear, but the writing demonstrates sufficient control over the elements of composition to present the writer's ideas clearly.
Adequate 23/30	These blogs respond to the poem, but the analysis may be simplistic or imprecise; they may be overly generalized, vague, or inadequately supported. These responses refer to textual evidence, but they are less specific. These blogs are adequately written but may demonstrate inconsistent control over the elements of composition. Organization is attempted, but it may not be fully realized or particularly effective.
Developing 21/30	These blog responses attempt to deal with the poem but do so either inaccurately or without support or specific evidence. They may show some misunderstanding or omit pertinent analysis. The writing can convey the writer's ideas, but it reveals weak control over diction, syntax, and/or organization. These responses may contain excessive and distracting spelling and grammatical errors. Statements are seldom supported with specific or persuasive evidence, or inappropriately lengthy quotations may replace discussion and analysis.
Unsuccessful 19/30	These blogs fail to respond adequately to the poem. They may reveal misunderstanding or may distort the interpretation of the poem. They compound the problems of the developing papers. Generally, these responses are unacceptably brief or poorly written. Although some attempts to answer the question may be indicated, the writer's view has little clarity and only slight, if any, evidence in its support.

FIGURE 8.1. Sarah Soper's poetry blogs rubric.

Multimodal Project

One of the primary assignments I give students all year is a multimodal project I call the Poetry Project. Students work on it over the course of a month. This is a good project for those times during the year when in-class time is being spent on other projects. For example, I assign the Poetry Project during a month when my class is reading and acting out a Shakespeare play. The Poetry Project has two main components: a digital presentation and an essay.

Digital Presentation

Using PowerPoint, Google Slides, Prezi, or Canvas, each student presents to the class their findings on and interpretations of a randomly assigned poem. In a class of twenty-five to thirty students, it takes a good bit of time to get through all the presentations. Some teachers might not feel comfortable devoting that much class time to student presentations, but I continue to do it year after year because I find the activity valuable. Students are not only practicing their public speaking skills, but they also become masters of their poem. Knowing the poem inside and out, having wrestled with it for a month, gives them a sense of ownership and confidence in understanding the poem that no other assignment I've given does. The poem becomes forever a part of them, and many who come back to visit years later say they still have parts of their poems memorized.

I also find the presentations to be extremely beneficial for the audience as they listen to their classmates. The students take notes on each presentation, writing directly on the poems I print off in a packet for the class. By the end of all the presentations, every student has a mini-anthology of annotated poems. Because I make sure to include a wide variety of poems from all time periods and types of writers, students are exposed to deep analysis of a broad spectrum of poetry in a quick time span, and the active learning component of the assignment means that students are engaging more deeply with the information than they would if I were relying on lecture-based lessons. Sure, I can teach them the definition of *anaphora* and show them examples, but when they see the same techniques again and again in their peers' presentations, the repetition seals the definition in their minds. And, perhaps more important, they get to see all the different ways poetic techniques, like anaphora, can affect a poem's meaning. And maybe, just maybe, one of those ways will help them in future poetry analysis when a technique is operating in a similar way in a brand-new poem they've never seen before, or even help them to understand prose texts that employ anaphora with similar effects. Many of my students say they feel like they didn't really "get poetry" until after completing, presenting, and listening to others present their Poetry Projects, which is why, even though it requires a time commitment, I continue to assign the project.

I provide students with a handout that outlines the information they should cover in their presentation:

- Author
  - Brief biography (accent on brief)
  - Anything in personal life that relates to the poem specifically?
- Historical context of poem
  - Date of publication and a couple of major events of that time period
  - Was anything going on that is important to know when reading this poem?

- Genre, type/form
  - Characteristics of genre/type
  - How does the genre/type lend itself to the poem's overall effect and/or meaning?
- Themes and how they are created (which can be discussed throughout presentation)
- Tone—connotations of certain words
- Ideational dimension—*What is the poem about?*
  - What is the main topic of the poem?
  - Are there any main characters in the poem? If so, who are they? What are their relationships to each other?
  - What happens in the poem on a literal level?
  - What is the setting in time and in place?
- Interpersonal dimension—*What does the poem do?*
  - What is the point of view of the poem? How does it help to create meaning in the poem?
  - Who is the speaker?
  - Does the poem include allusions? If so, what is the effect of those allusions?
  - What is the poem's chief impact on the reader? Does it want the reader to know something, do something, and/or feel something?
- Textual dimension—*How does the poem work?*
  - Scansion—meter, rhyme
  - Is there a shift in the poem? Where? Why? How does it operate?
  - End-stopped vs. enjambed lines—discuss the linear construction of the poem
  - Sound devices
  - Figurative language
  - Syntactic structure
  - What accounts for the overall structure of the poem? Does it raise (and answer) a question, tell a story, make a request, evoke a feeling or mood, describe a scene, celebrate an event or person, criticize an event or person, or something else?

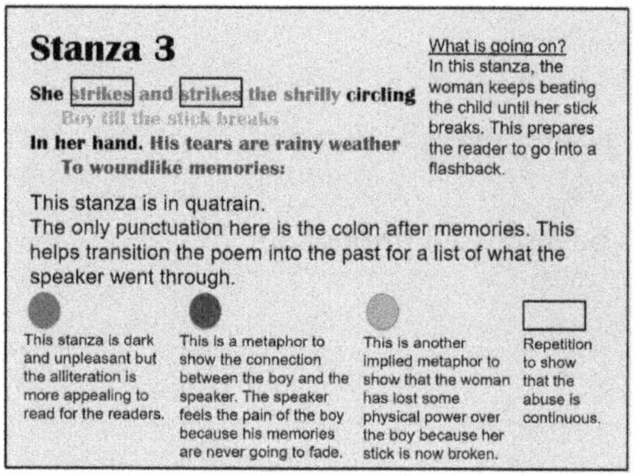

A slide from Mackenzie's presentation on Robert Hayden's "The Whipping," in which she identifies and discusses the effects of metaphor, repetition, punctuation, and alliteration. For her comparison poem, Mackenzie chose "Boy & the Belt" by José Olivarez.

Most students organize their presentations so that they first give information about the author and historical context, genre and type, move on to an overview of tone and themes, major characters and speaker, and then start a walk-through of their poem. Depending on how long their poem is, the walk-through might be line by line or stanza by stanza or somewhere in between. It is in their walk-through that they identify and discuss the effects of the different literary devices and how they work in the poem to create meaning.

On presentation days, to determine who will present, I draw student names randomly. This way, everyone needs to be ready on the first day. We begin by finding the poem in our packets and either listening to an audio of the poet reading the poem, if available or listening to the student reading the poem aloud. Then the student starts their presentation as the rest of the class takes notes on the poem in their packet. After the student is finished, the class can ask the presenter questions. We typically get through two or three presentations per fifty-minute class period. I collect the packets after all presentations are completed for a small grade and return them to students to keep as a poetry resource.

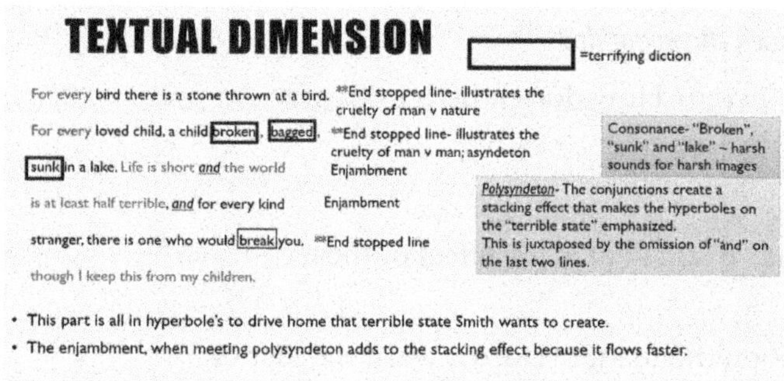

Nolan chose "Buen Esqueleto" by Natalie Scenters-Zapico as his comparison poem for his project on Maggie Smith's "Good Bones." Scenters-Zapico's poem is written as an after poem for "Good Bones." This is one of Nolan's slides analyzing Smith's poem.

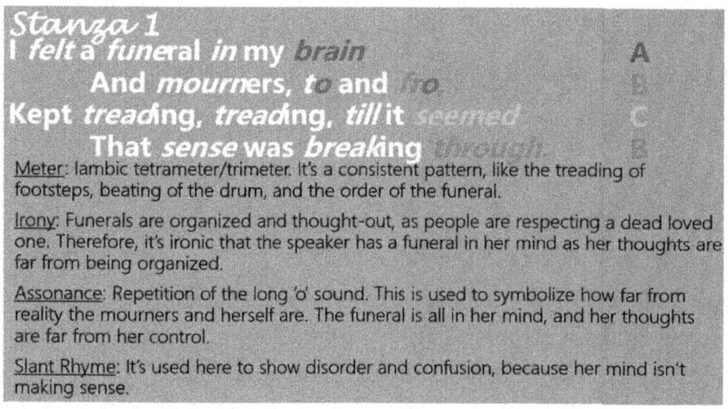

This slide from LingLing's presentation on Emily Dickinson's "I felt a Funeral, in my Brain" discusses how poetic devices like meter and rhyme operate in the poem. She chose Neil Hilborn's "OCD" for her comparison poem.

Essay

For the essay portion of the project, students write a compare-and-contrast essay on their assigned presentation poem and a contemporary poem of their choice. If their assigned poem is a contemporary poem, they must choose a different author. The poem they choose ideally should be similar in subject, form, or theme. Most students choose a poem on the same subject and explore each poet's treatment of that subject. I encourage students to choose carefully, to find a poem they feel confident they understand. The essays discuss how meaning is created through literary devices, form, and structure.

Essays that score high will:

- Demonstrate that significant attention has been paid to the poems as a whole, rather than a section
- Trace the poets' use of elements of craft throughout the poems, citing specific lines
- Give specific and detailed explanation of how the craft element is employed and what effect that has on the poems
- Focus on *how* the poets achieve certain effects rather than explicating the topic and meaning of the poems
- Be clear and well written, with sophisticated diction and varied syntax
- Be the student's original work; any research and/or critical work about the poem being discussed is cited using MLA format
- Show a clear and sophisticated understanding of the meaning and craft of *both* poems
- Balance insights and analysis between the two poems equally
- Maintain an organized structure that effectively elucidates the students' interpretations and analysis of both poems in a comparative manner

The biggest challenge for students is being as thorough in their discussion of their chosen poem as they are with their assigned poem. They know their assigned poem so well by the time they write their papers, and most likely have *a lot* to say about it (enough to fill a twenty-minute presentation), that their chosen poem tends to get overshadowed. I encourage students to find a balance between the two, but their biggest hurdle continues to be a lack of equilibrium in discussion and analysis.

Here are some of the poems I assign, which students choose randomly from a bag. I like to make a big deal out of the moment and tell them that "you don't choose the poem; the poem chooses *you.*" And for some students, I truly believe that, as when Janais serendipitously pulled Kaveh Akbar's poem. The list includes a mixture of canonical poems and newly published poems, so students experience a wide variety across the poetic spectrum.

- "Dulce et Decorum est" by Wilfred Owen
- "The Whipping" by Robert Hayden
- "The World Is Too Much with Us" by William Wordsworth
- "O Captain! My Captain!" by Walt Whitman
- "I felt a Funeral in my Brain" by Emily Dickinson
- "Harlem" by Langston Hughes
- "To His Coy Mistress" by Andrew Marvell
- "Because I could not stop for Death" by Emily Dickinson
- "Ozymandias" by Percy Bysshe Shelley
- "Out, Out—" by Robert Frost
- "Siren Song" by Margaret Atwood
- "The Tiger" by William Blake
- "Introduction to *Songs of Innocence*" by William Blake
- "Instructions on Not Giving Up" by Ada Limón
- "The Flea" by John Donne
- "We Real Cool" by Gwendolyn Brooks
- "Sound and Sense" by Alexander Pope
- "Sonnet 66" by William Shakespeare
- "The Second Coming" by William Butler Yeats
- "Music Lessons" by Mary Oliver
- "On Listening to Your Teacher Take Attendance" by Aimee Nezhukumatathil
- "An American Sunrise" by Joy Harjo
- "Mirror" by Sylvia Plath (89)
- "Woman Work" by Maya Angelou (89)
- "somewhere i have never travelled, gladly beyond" by e. e. cummings
- "Chicago" by Carl Sandburg
- "Good Bones" by Maggie Smith
- "Handsome Man" by Rebecca Hazelton
- "yasmeen" by Safia Elhillo
- "What Marked Tom?" by Tyehimba Jess
- "Mine will be a beautiful service" by R. A. Villanueva
- "Mass" by R. A. Villanueva
- "Portrait of the Alcoholic Floating in Space with Severed Umbilicus" by Kaveh Akbar
- "application for the position of abdelhalim hafez's girl" by Safia Elhillo
- "Declaration" by Tracy K. Smith
- "I Wouldn't Even Know What to Do with a Third Chance" by Kaveh Akbar
- "Duplex" by Jericho Brown
- "We Lived Happily during the War" by Ilya Kaminsky
- "Hammond B3 Organ Cistern" by Gabrielle Calvocoressi
- "In Praise of My Manicure" by Aimee Nezhukumatathil
- "To the Notebook Kid" by Eve L. Ewing

Poetry Podcasts

To introduce students to making podcasts, I use as a mentor text *The Slowdown* podcast, which is hosted by former US Poet Laureate Tracy K. Smith and guest

---

Thank you to Matt Brisbin and Jori Krulder for their contributions to making podcasts a successful endeavor in my class.

hosts such as poets Brenda Shaughnessy and Tina Chang. If you've never listened to *The Slowdown*, it's a five-minute podcast in which the host introduces a poem with an anecdote, personal story, historical or current event, or some explanation that eventually leads in to what the poem she is reading on that particular episode is about. Then she reads the poem. It's a relaxing, thought-provoking, poetic five minutes very well spent.

To start our podcasting adventure, we listen to two episodes together in class. Students take notes as they listen, not on the content or what Smith is saying, but on the *structure* of it. I ask students to notice the sections. For example, every episode opens with the same theme music, the host introduces herself, and then we get more music, an introduction story, the poem reading, and last, acknowledgments and thank-yous to close out the episode. Students think-pair-share their noticings, and we make a list together as a class on the board of the sections we notice. This list becomes my students' requirements for their own podcasts.

As I am always open and honest with my students, I disclose my novice status regarding podcasting (I'm describing my first attempt) and ask them to raise their hands if *they've* ever tried to make a podcast. Zero hands. Cool, so this will be a learning experience for all of us. I ask students to please provide me with feedback throughout the process so we can tweak things as we go, which I believe gives them a sense of authority and ownership of their own learning in our podcasting adventure.

We draft a rough outline of a schedule together. I ask students what they think they can get accomplished in class each day, and this is what we end up with:

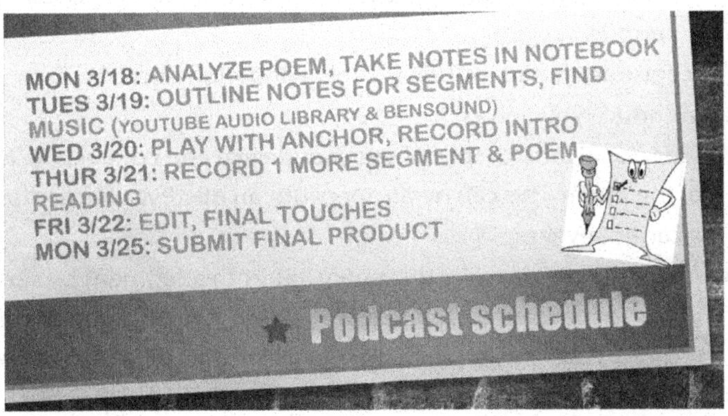

The first order of business is to find a poem. We use the #TeachLivinigPoets Virtual Library, Poets.org, and Split This Rock's "The Quarry: A Social Justice Poetry Database" to search for poems that are of personal interest to the students. They have full freedom to choose whatever poem they want, provided it is written by a living author.

We use Anchor to record our podcasts and YouTube's audio library and Bensound to find music. My students inform me that using the Anchor app rather than the website is smoother and more user-friendly. At the beginning of class each day, we touch base to see if they have accomplished their goal for the previous day.

I debate whether to hold a "listening party" in class of all the students' podcasts. Since telling a personal story as an introduction to the poem is involved, and because I cringe whenever I hear my own voice recorded and played back, I decide to spare students the embarrassment. I let them know at the beginning of the process that I will be the only one listening, although *they* have the option of sharing their podcast with anyone they wish using Anchor's shareable link feature.

Podcast Assignment Directions

Using *The Slowdown* podcast as a model, record a podcast episode that discusses a poem of your choice. Using Anchor, you will upload and edit recordings of your discussion and reading of the poem to produce a polished and professional podcast. If you choose, you may publish your finished episode.

Requirements:

- Provide a written summary for each segment. What do you plan on saying? This should *not* be a word-for-word transcription you read from but instead some organized notes to guide you.
- The episode should be between three to five minutes long.
- Your episode should have a title that relates to the poem and theme of your episode.
- Your episode should include the following segments:
  1. Introduce yourselves.
  2. A personal intro that hooks your audience and connects to the theme of the poem. This can be an anecdote, an observation, or discussion of a current event.
  3. A section of "why I like this poem." Start this segment by saying, "I like this poem because . . ." and state at least two reasons. One must be a technical reason—something the poem does structurally or with literary techniques. The second reason should be more personal, a reader-response reaction to either a specific line or image or to the poem as a whole.

4. Read the poem.

- Your episode must transition in and out of each segment smoothly.
- Include theme music in a way similar to that in *The Slowdown*—as part of your intro and in between segments.
- Although this is likely your first podcast, you need to do everything you can to make this as professional as possible. I need to see evidence of an extended effort on this project [see Figure 8.2 for the rubric assignment].

	4	3	2	1
Introduction	Catchy and clever introduction. Provides relevant information and establishes a clear purpose that engages the listener immediately.	Describes the topic and engages the listener as the introduction proceeds.	Somewhat engaging (covers a well-known topic) and provides a vague purpose.	Irrelevant or inappropriate topic that minimally engages the listener. Does not include an introduction, or the purpose is unclear.
Content: Intro segment	Creativity and original content enhance the purpose of the podcast in an innovative way. Accurate information and succinct concepts are presented. Keeps focus on topic.	Accurate information is provided succinctly. Stays on the topic.	Some information is inaccurate or long-winded. Occasionally strays from the topic.	Information is inaccurate. Does not stay on topic.
Content: Why I Like This Poem segment	Technical reason and personal reason are both clearly explained, interesting, and enhance the meaning of the poem.	Technical reason and personal reason are both explained and enhance the meaning of the poem.	One of the explanations is lacking in effectiveness, but the other is still clear and clearly grounded in the poem. Explanation may be too broad or too short.	Explanation is incomplete and/or ineffective.

FIGURE 8.2. Rubric for the poetry podcast assignment.

continued on next page

FIGURE 8.2. Continued

Delivery	Well-rehearsed, smooth delivery in a conversational style. Highly effective enunciation, expression, and rhythm keep the audience listening. Correct grammar is used throughout the podcast.	Rehearsed, smooth delivery. Enunciation, expression, pacing are effective. Correct grammar is used during the podcast.	Appears unrehearsed with uneven delivery. Enunciation, expression, rhythm are sometimes distracting. Occasionally incorrect grammar is used during the podcast.	Delivery is hesitant or choppy and sounds like the presenter is reading. Enunciation is not clearly understandable, expression and/or rhythm are distracting throughout the podcast. Poor grammar is used throughout the podcast.
Music enhancements	Music enhances the mood, quality, and understanding of the presentation.	Music provides supportive background to the podcast.	Music is of poor quality or provides somewhat distracting background to the podcast.	Music is missing or distracting to presentation.
Technical production	Podcast has minimal background noise or interruptions. Transitions are smooth, and the volume of the speaker and any other sound effects enhance the project.	Podcast has some background noise or interruptions that slightly disturb the audience. Transitions are generally smooth. The volume of the speaker and other effects is somewhat inconsistent.	Podcast has noticeable and distracting background noise or interruptions. Transitions are somewhat choppy, as is the volume of the speaker and other effects.	Podcast has very noticeable and distracting background noise or interruptions. Transitions are absent. The volume of the speaker and other effects are poorly implemented.

Reflecting on the assignment, I am so happy I decided to take a risk and try something new to me and my students. None of us knew what we were doing, but we figured it out together. I learned new things about my students through their personal stories, and I truly enjoyed listening to each one. Next year I will encourage all students to use the Anchor app, not the website. And to use a microphone of some kind to record, even if it's just the little one on an earbud cord. Student feedback was resoundingly positive and unanimous in agreeing that I should assign this activity again next year.

Poetry-Inspired Tasting Menu

This activity is inspired by a tweet by Ada Limón. The credit for this lesson goes to Lake Norman Charter colleagues Angela Massingale and Noel Poynter.

Scrolling through Twitter one night after the kids were put to bed, I came across this tweet by one of my favorite poets, Ada Limón, author of several books, including *Bright Dead Things* and *The Carrying*, which won the National Book Critics Circle Award for Poetry.

If students don't believe that tasting menus can be inspired by poetry, I present evidence exhibit A, Limón's tweet. I also show them examples online of what a restaurant tasting menu looks like to use as mentor texts.

Directions

Students will use Google Drawings to create a first page, a menu page that has the title of the menu with a brief description. Then they hyperlink each poem they've found to the Google drawing to make an online poetry menu experience.

In small groups, students create a poetry menu. To brainstorm, ask students to think of their favorite restaurants. What types of things do they have on their menus? How are the menus organized into sections? What are other identifying factors? Restaurants can also fall into categories—Italian, Indian, Mexican, steakhouse, seafood, casual or fine dining, etc.

I ask students to think of the following:

1. How can the metaphor of a menu work for a poetry menu? Your poems can have a similar theme. The name of your restaurant will highlight this theme.
2. What images will go with your menu to make it graphically pleasing and relatable?
3. The type of poem will dictate whether you think it is an appetizer or starter, an entrée, or a dessert. You will create a hyperlink to the poem.
4. What types of "food" could you bring in to represent your poem menu? You will also have an end page that describes the themes you see in your poems and how the theme relates to your restaurant name. You will also justify why you classified each poem as a starter, entrée, or dessert.

Students must include:

- A restaurant name indicative of the theme
- An aesthetically pleasing layout of the menu page with images that correlate to the theme and look like a graphic-designed menu
- Four poems under each label: Appetizer, Entrée, Dessert (twelve poems in all)
- A brief summary of each poem under the label on the main menu page
- A hyperlink for each poem and thorough annotations for each poem that discuss the use of language, structure, and style
- A hyperlink to an end page of the menu that describes the themes you see in your poems and how the theme relates to your restaurant name. You will also justify why you classified each poem as a starter, entrée, or dessert.

On the due date, students bring in five copies of their menus and poems, along with a food dish to pass (of at least five servings) that relates to their menu. In groups of five, students spend the class reading one another's poems and menus and sharing their food. It's an effective way to build community in your class and expose students to many poems in a short and highly enjoyable amount of time.

• • • • •

Early in my teaching career, I was taught that poetry analysis meant a TP-CASTT chart, in which students fill out the correct answer for the poem's title, paraphrase, connotation, attitude, shift, title (again), and theme. I used this chart for years. I also was very aware of my students' antipathy toward poetry during those years. Poetry study boiled down to trying to figure out what the teacher wanted, not engaging with the poems. Since I've ditched the charts and started really listening to what my students have to say about poems, I realize I was doing those students early in my career a disservice. The assignments provided in this chapter move beyond analysis-by-acronym and allow opportunities for your students to formulate insights organically and the freedom to use their voice.

9

Becoming Connected Educators

Every year the federal government and local school districts spend billions of dollars on professional development for teachers. As someone who is responsible for writing faculty development on my campus (Lindsay here), I confess that I struggle to make professional development meaningful and impactful. Sure, I use outcomes assessment to plan workshops and share current research, but I also remember being a new teacher in PD workshops and feeling, well—uninspired. Where I was learning the most about becoming a better teacher was through conversations with other teacher-researchers who shared my interests, in going to sessions at conferences that felt relevant to me and my students' needs, and in my own writing and research in my areas of interest. The difference between the professional development "opportunities" that were delivered to me and the ways I was learning to be a better teacher (and help others become better teachers) was a matter of *agency,* my sense of power and motivation to find the answers to questions and problems that were most important to me. When researchers interested in the effectiveness (or ineffectiveness) of professional development write about this, they call it *teacher agency.* Teacher agency is "the capacity of teachers to act purposefully and constructively to direct their professional growth and contribute to the growth of their colleagues" (Calvert 4).

I didn't know the name for what was working for me—being part of a professional learning community (PLC)—but I felt strongly that it was through the experience of giving and receiving feedback on projects and ideas, having conversations with like-minded faculty, and meeting new people who shared my interests that I was growing professionally.

(Melissa here.) There are many options for teachers to get involved in a professional learning community outside of their schools, but it does take a little time and effort. I started my personal journey on Twitter, but that doesn't mean it's the only option available. There are prominent ELA educator groups on

Facebook, writing groups at local libraries, poetry workshops at universities, slam poetry events, prominent poets and educators to follow on Instagram, to name a few. You need to find an avenue that suits you and has the ability to connect you personally with other teachers. Some specific Twitter groups I find welcoming and helpful are #NCTEvillage, #aplitchat, #THEBOOKCHAT, and #DisruptTexts. A simple Google search will show the times at which each group is actively chatting so you can join in the conversation and start forming connections.

Following poets on social media will also help to keep you knowledgeable about any upcoming events in your area, new work, and social issues they are passionate about. Sharing their posts, retweeting, and supporting them may help them feel more inclined to agree to a virtual visit with your class or to come for a school visit. Post pictures of your students reading their poems and actively engaging with their work. Become an advocate for #TeachLivingPoets by publicly sharing ideas, lessons, and the impact it has on your students. Sharing your experiences will open doors for your students and extend their learning outside of the classroom in authentic ways.

Creating Meaningful and Authentic Connections for Your Students

Connections via Twitter

Once you form some connections with other educators in other schools, you can start planning ideas together for ways to get your students engaged with one another. By maintaining communication with the #aplitchat group, which is active on both Twitter and Facebook, I (Melissa) have been able to create opportunities for my students (whether they are in AP Literature or other classes) to interact with other students in other schools. One of the first activities my students engaged in was a Twitter chat about a selected poem with other students across the nation (sometimes referred to as intra-institutional collaboration).

For students in different time zones to participate in the chat, we planned a slow Twitter chat, which means a new question is posed every hour on the hour with a searchable hashtag. With ten questions throughout the day, no matter if a student is in California or Maine, they can still see other students discussing the same questions at the same time they are. You can hold a chat with several classes, or just one other class. You can even get a chat going with another English class in your school. Do all ninth-grade teachers in your building teach

Romeo and Juliet? You could arrange a Twitter chat between your class and the other classes; they could see how their peers are experiencing the play and learn from each other.

One of the great benefits of a Twitter chat is that all students are equal active participants. As much as I encourage participation in my classroom, I find it is often the same students who raise their hands every time, and the same kids who are too shy or unmotivated to participate. A Twitter chat, which doesn't involve vocalizing ideas in front of the entire class, creates equity and allows every student's voice to be heard.

And don't be shy about using Twitter to engage with poets. In one class, students wanted to ask a poet whose work we were reading, Adrian Matejka, a question on Twitter, so we did. In minutes, Matejka was answering us directly. This won't be the experience every time you interact with writers online, but overwhelmingly we've found that writers are generous and willing to be part of our discussions of their work. Through experiences like these, I've learned that students value poetry more when our teaching methods extend beyond teacher-led instruction. From interacting on social media to workshopping with published poets in person, there is a world of educational and inspirational opportunities available to students outside the physical walls of the classroom. When teaching living poets, students are able to see that poetry is happening right now; it is relevant to them. When students engage with others outside of the classroom space, they become literary citizens, entering into a community of readers, writers, and thinkers. But their access to this space is contingent on their teacher being an active member of the literary and teaching community.

One way to engage with other like-minded educators is by participating in the monthly #TeachLivingPoets Twitter chat. We hold a conversation about a preselected poem for thirty minutes one evening each month. Engaging in the chat not only exposes you to new poets and poems but it also provides you with a wide array of perspectives and interpretations of the poem from an insightful group of educators. We usually include teaching ideas as part of the chat as well, so if you decide to bring the poem we chat about into your classroom, you'll be ready. This has happened to me more times than I can count! I'll fall in love with a poem we chat about, get some amazing ideas from teachers in the chat, and *need* to teach the poem the next day. Students can feel my excitement; they can tell I am genuinely curious to see what *they* think about the poem, and they usually have insights that were not covered in the chat. They will teach me something about the poem, which makes me giddy and makes them feel empowered. You can go to teachlivingpoets.com to see archives of previous #TeachLivingPoets chats.

Virtual Connections: Classroom to Classroom

If you can manage to arrange a time that works for both you and the person you're calling, you could also Skype or use Google Hangouts with another class about a common text. The timing of a virtual video call needs to be more precise, so it might not be as easy to plan. But if it's possible, video calls are valuable opportunities for your students to see how a different class in a different school understands the same text they are reading in your class. My (Melissa's) class in North Carolina Skyped with a class in Massachusetts about *Othello*. In preparation, the other teacher and I shared a Google Doc in which we cocreated questions for our classes to prepare to discuss for our Skype. Both of our classes benefited from hearing another group's understanding of the text and having the opportunity to discuss the play with new voices. My focus of instruction was not the same as the other teacher's, so when our students were talking, they were learning from each other and seeing the play in a whole new light.

Whether you are Twitter chatting or Skyping, I suggest giving your students the questions they will be discussing ahead of time to avoid a deer-in-the-headlights, "I don't know what to say" situation. Having some ideas ready to go, maybe some notes jotted down, will help them to feel more comfortable about jumping in and joining the conversation.

We discuss in more depth Skyping with poets in Chapter 6. Skyping with a poet is always one of the best experiences of the year. It sparks in students a realization that poets are real people and not abstractions of a name on a book. When students realize that poets are normal people, they start thinking: *She's a normal person and can write poetry; I'm a normal person, so maybe I could write poetry too.*

Connections via Slams and Poetry Competitions

If social media use is blocked in your school, or even if it's not, there are other ways to expand student learning into the literary community. You could try slam poetry. Check out Brave New Voices, a nationwide poetry organization and competition for high school students. There's also Louder Than a Bomb, which has roots in Chicago but has grown into an international competition. What's so great about these organizations is that students can see themselves in these young poets—they *are* the kids on stage and in the videos on YouTube. Poet Nate Marshall got his start as a student participant in Louder Than a Bomb, and when my students watch the *Louder Than a Bomb* documentary (which can be found on YouTube or ordered from their website, along with an entire curriculum), they can see how Marshall was once a student just like them. Marshall's

Photo by Noel Poynter.

story could very well inspire a student to say, "If he could do it, maybe I can too." They can see for themselves that poets are not only old, white, balding men wearing spectacles; poets can be kids who look and sound like them.

Just about every major city has a slam poetry scene. I encourage you to do some online research to see if the nearest major city around you has a slam team. Living in Charlotte, I am extremely lucky to have an international championship-winning adult slam team, as well as an active teenage slam team. Team slams are often looking for volunteer judges, which provides a perfect opportunity to network with other teachers and artists in your community. Also, go to an adult slam performance. Afterward, find your favorite poet, introduce yourself as an educator, tell them you enjoyed their poems, and ask them if they have a book available. That's how I met poet Jay Ward, who visited my class (see Chapter 6 for more details about Jay's visit).

Sponsored by the National Endowment for the Arts, Poetry Out Loud (POL) is also an incredible experience for teachers and students. It's a great introduction to the power of poetry, and it's a little easier on the nerves because students aren't performing their *own* written work but instead works already published by renowned authors. POL's poetry database covers works from the 1500s to present day and is filled with phenomenal poems by living poets. When participating in Poetry Out Loud, students compete with other local students in memorizing and reciting published poems. Local winners advance to districts, districts to states, and states to nationals. Being a POL school immerses students in a community of poetry that helps them realize there are other students out there who love it as well. At the competitions, contestants engage in discussions with one another about the poems they picked and uplift each other to do their best. It's a welcoming, supportive organization advocating for the arts; after the first year of participating with my class, I was hooked. All it takes to get involved is a quick email to your state's POL representative listed on their website to point you in the right direction.

Connections via Blog Sharing and Commenting

As discussed in the previous chapter, blogs give students an opportunity to write for an authentic audience. By becoming a connected educator, you can team up with other teachers for a blog share. Assigning your students to make comments and leave feedback on other students' blogs is an excellent way to expose students to more poetry and other students' analysis. Be sure to review what makes for an appropriate comment. West Virginia teacher Karla Hilliard encourages her students to introduce themselves, comment on the analysis, and extend the student's analysis with a new thought or question. If you want to keep students accountable for comments or even grade them, I recommend creating a Google Form for them to copy and paste in their comments.

Creating a blog share with other classrooms can be a way to provide an additional authentic audience as well as feedback through comments. Find other teachers in your district or on social media who would like to do this assignment. Create a calendar of due dates for both blogs and comments for the year and who will comment on whose work. Hearing from students from California, Oregon, North Carolina, West Virginia, and Georgia definitely added another element of excitement and accountability to my students' blogs.

Leaving comments on other students' blogs gets your students thinking like writers. They are not only getting exposed to a new poem, but they are also evaluating writing and providing feedback, an act that ultimately strengthens their *own* writing. Here are a couple of blog comment examples:

> Hi! My name is Ethan and I'm in Mrs. Smith's class in NC. I thought your analysis of Matthew Zapruder's poem, "I Wake Up Before the Machine," even though you mentioned that you weren't able to understand some of it, was very in depth and really insightful. I liked how you compared the literal and metaphorical meanings of the title to show the significance of the title on the poem. I do agree with you that the machine represented the routine of life. It seems like life operates like a machine or even like a factory through its repetitive nature and I think that shows in this poem. I also liked the way you explained that the connotations in the line "daylight is coming/but dreams do not go away" give way to a tone shift. Overall, I really enjoyed your analysis on Matthew Zapruder's poem.

> Hey! My name is Ryan, and I am currently a senior in Mrs. Smith's class in NC. I thoroughly enjoyed reading your poem analysis and how you explained Kemp used

Thank you to Adrian Nester, who wrote a post on blogging for teachlivingpoets.com, some of which is shared here.

> the sun to "brighten the effects of cold and winter." When I read the poem, this is something which jumped out to me as well. Moreover, I loved how you mentioned the significance of the title and how it related to the poem. Maybe, just a suggestion, you could have expanded a little more after you gave that line reference to show the pessimistic side of loneliness. I also loved how you explained you had to rephrase the first line to understand it. In fact, I had to read it a couple of times to understand it as well. I also think it acted as a double negative, when I first started reading. All in all, I enjoyed reading your poem.

Local Higher-Ed Institutions

Establishing connections with professors like Alan Michael Parker at nearby higher-ed institutions will help you feel more confident in teaching poetry and could also garner some special opportunities for your students. For example, after Parker's PD session at my school, we remained in contact, and later in the year he invited my class to a private Q&A with poet Clint Smith. My students had read Smith's book *Counting Descent* for summer reading, and they were excited to meet him in person in a more intimate setting and to get their books signed. To be invited to a smaller event like a private Q&A was a unique and memorable opportunity for my students, provided by professional connections I had formed. Local colleges and universities are great places to look for free events and readings, and some of the best professional development you could ever get.

Becoming a Literary Citizen and Engaging with the Literary Community

Local Organizations—Readings, Writing Groups, Workshops

What organizations in your area might help facilitate your growth as a writer? It's commonly said that "teachers of writing should be writers," so I encourage you to visit a writing group or literary organization outside of school. These groups will sometimes host readings and open mics, providing further opportunities for networking with authors and sharing your own writing. For example, Charlotte Lit is an organization near me that brings in writers for readings, hosts workshops, and provides writing spaces to work. Charlotte Lit hosted poet Terrance Hayes for a reading and a workshop, which I signed up for the second it opened. The Friday evening of the reading, I offered to volunteer with setup and passing out programs—to help, of course, but also to form closer connections with Charlotte Lit for the future. And because I had posted about it on social media, some of my former students still in the area came too. Before the reading began, Hayes was sitting in the first row alone. I pondered whether to introduce myself, because I didn't want to interrupt him or bother him if he was trying to prepare, but I figured if he was out there amongst the crowd and not in a room backstage, then maybe he wouldn't mind. So I sat down next to him, offered a handshake, and introduced myself. I told him that I was a teacher and that one of my students had just done their Poetry Project (discussed in Chapter 8) on one of his American sonnets. We had a brief chat about the poem and my students' insights, and I told him I was looking forward to his workshop the following morning. The next day at the workshop he recognized me and remembered our chat, and I was so happy I had introduced myself to him.

Photo by Melissa Tucker

I went to the workshop for two main reasons. First, I love Terrance Hayes's work and I wanted to bask in his brilliance. Second, I was hoping to pick up new strategies for teaching and reading poems. Hayes started off by explaining his theories on how poems *move* (technical aspects) and how poems *are moving*, followed by a discussion of two poems; then we wrote our own. My goals for attending the workshop were met beyond my expectations, along with a third "goal" I hadn't even anticipated, which was writing a draft of a poem I was proud of.

My attendance at the reading and the workshop also demonstrates a very practical way to support writers as a literary citizen—paying for their services and their words. This means subscribing to literary journals, attending ticketed events, and taking classes with them. Request books for purchase at your school and local libraries. Seek grant funds for building classroom libraries for ELA teachers in your district (the local NCTE affiliate in New England offers grant funds up to $2,000 for such projects). It's easy to dance around the obvious, but poets need money to live, and our patronage (money) enables a world in which writers can have the time and a place to write (and health insurance!).

Write about Poetry

As a member of NCTE and state affiliate, I have plenty of options for publishing writing on ELA education. NCTE has multiple journals you can submit to, including but not limited to *English Journal*, *Talking Points*, and *Voices from the Middle*. What do you do in your classroom as best practice that you could share with other teachers? You could also submit educational writing to sites such as Edutopia and Prestwick House, or to your local newspaper's Education or Arts section.

ntertainment

Arts Q&A

Class teaches poetry as an art form

Melissa Smith is a teacher at Lake Norman Charter High School and teaches AP Literature, honors English and creative writing. She uses poetry in her lessons as often as possible to both educate and inspire her students. Herald Citizen spoke with her about why poetry is such an important expressive art form.

Herald Citizen: How do you incorporate poetry into lessons?

Melissa Smith: In creative writing, we read and discuss poems written by living poets as mentor texts for writing prompts. We use poems as inspiration, pulling language from our favorite poets to spark our own ideas.

For AP Literature, a major part of the college board curriculum is the close reading and analysis of poetry. The biggest project of the year involves them mastering a poem and teaching it to the class.

AP Lit students also keep a monthly poetry blog. One of my favorite things to do is to send their blog links to the poets via Twitter and when the poets respond to my students.

We also work with Poetry Out Loud, which asks students to memorize and perform already-published poems by established poets. Two students from my class completed in the district competition – they took second and third place. The second place winner, Ryan Titus, is advancing to the state finals in Greensboro in March.

HC: What are some examples of poetry you include?

MS: AP Literature students read the full collection by Clint Smith ("Counting Descent"), RA Villanueva ("Reliquaria"), and Kaveh Akbar ("Portrait of the Alcoholic..."). We also read selected poems spanning from the 1500s to current day so they are prepared for whatever the AP exam may ask them. Creative writing is more student-choice driven, but names that keep popping up as student favorites or as mentor poems are Joshua Bennett, Sarah Kay, Raymond Antrobus and Rebecca Hazelton.

HC: You're able to pick poems that fit your own curriculum. How do you choose?

MS: I offer students choice as much as I possibly can; I want them to read the poems they feel a personal connection with, whoever the poet may be. I have an enormous collection of poetry books (living poets, of course) in my classroom that students are always exploring. For poems we read together as a class, I chose poems that I believe will be impactful and meaningful to students, offer them a new perspective of experience or serve as a window for them to see themselves and that use language in surprising and creative ways.

HC: Why is teaching living poets so important?

MS: #TeachLivingPoets is more than a hashtag; it's a movement of teachers who believe in the importance of teaching modern poetry. I think most students get bored of poems from the same old dead canonical poets. My goal is to show them that poetry is very much alive and happening right now. Through reading living poets, students are exposed to a prism of diverse voices. Poetry helps us to make sense of our world; it can put into words feelings that students may be having, but aren't sure how to express. I believe that poetry absolutely affects societal change, and I hope students will find poetry as ignition to spark advocacy in their own lives.

HC: Poetry is a creative expression. How important is it to foster creativity in your students?

MS: In our education system, there is so much focus on standardized tests. To get into this-or-that college, students need certain test scores. These kids have lost their love of reading because they've been multiple-choiced to death. I believe it is equally important (and I think some college admissions officers would agree with me) to be empathetic, open-minded and able to tell a story. Poetry offers us models of these more personal skills, and can help us become more creative, diverse thinkers. ❑

Courtesy of Melissa Smith

Melissa Smith, 2017 Teacher of the Year at Lake Norman Charter High School, stands, far right, with her students as they use Facetime to talk to a poet during class.

More about Melissa Smith

Melissa Smith is a teacher at Lake Norman Charter High School and teaches AP Literature, honors English and creative writing. She uses poetry in her lessons as often as possible to both educate and inspire her students. Visit her blog at https://teachlivingpoets.com.

Herald Citizen 35

Writing microreviews of poetry collections for literary journals and magazines is also an excellent way to engage with the literary community. (Microreviews could even function as writing assignments that ask students to analyze the readership and editorial preferences of specific literary journals.) Very few poets are agented or have the resources to retain a publicist, which means that reviewing would be a way of promoting good work from emerging writers or collections from small presses. Poets, more so than writers of other genres, depend on the goodwill of readers to share their positive experiences of reading their work. Even writing reviews on websites such as Amazon and Goodreads helps poets reach a larger audience. I learned when my first collection of poems came out that reviews on Goodreads and Amazon make a difference in the way users see your book featured (or not) on those websites. Supporting writers through reviewing is a practical way to give back to the community, almost as much as adopting books for classroom use and buying books.

Finally, and I cannot stress this enough: write to the writers you love. If their email address is available online, it means they don't mind being contacted in this way. Let them know what their words mean to you. Writing is lonely work, and writers are never sure if this thing they spend so much of their time doing really matters. Trust me when I say that your addressee will treasure your words as much as you treasure theirs.

Attend and Present at Professional Conferences

Educators are lifelong learners. We owe it to our students to keep abreast of developments in our profession and to be the best teachers we can be. So much of what I do well in my classroom I attribute to other teachers (which is evident given the many credits to other educators in this book). We don't teach in a vacuum, nor should we. Attending professional conferences is one of the best ways to learn new strategies, ideas, and pedagogy to drive your instruction. And if you are able to attend a conference, consider presenting. No professional development opportunity is too small to present at. While a standing-room-only #TeachLivingPoets presentation at NCTE's Annual Convention was inspiring and affirming, I've also presented to a room of two people on an in-house PD workday. Sharing your experience allows you another avenue for connecting and networking.

Top picture: The #TeachLivingPoets presentation team at the 2018 NCTE Convention: (left to right) Adrian Nester, Karla Hilliard, Susan Barber, Melissa Smith, Sarah Soper, and Jori Krulder. Bottom picture: Melissa Smith gives the keynote speech at NCETA's Spring Symposium Conference.

Join the #TeachLivingPoets Movement

By reading this book, you are already a member of the #TeachLivingPoets community, which we thank you for immensely. We invite you to share your stories, lessons, successes, favorite poems, and pictures on social media using the #TeachLivingPoets hashtag. We also have a website, TeachLivingPoets.com, where we share posts about teaching and poetry reviews by guest authors. If you are interested in writing a guest post or review, please reach out to Melissa Smith (msmith@lncharter.org). We are so grateful for the teachers and poets who already spread the word of #TeachLivingPoets, such as teacher Kelly Herrera and poet Nicole F. Tong; Kelly shares their story below. Melissa is always amazed when someone contacts her to ask if she minds them doing a presentation on or writing an article featuring #TeachLivingPoets. It is exciting to be part of a movement that is rooted in complicating the canon and empowering students through poetry. When other teachers are inspired enough to share their stories on social media or through PD presentations, we are reminded of and inspired by the impact it can have.

Poets Jay Ward and Jericho representing #TeachLivingPoets at the 2019 Middlebury Bread Loaf Writers' Conference.

One Teacher's #TeachLivingPoets Testimony

—Kelly Herrera, Buena High School, Ventura CA

I've been teaching AP Literature and AP Language for most of my twenty-one years in education. I've had consistent results, and I make adjustments each year after I receive my students' scores during the summer. When our community was devastated by the Thomas Fire in December 2017, I knew the scores would be affected. My AP Lit class had more than a dip, and I knew that I needed to make a change.

That's when I found Twitter and Teach Living Poets. I became "friends" with Melissa Smith and read her posts, asked questions about how to get started, and requested recommendations for poetry collections to order. I remember feeling overwhelmed during my first #TeachLivingPoets chat, yet marveling at the process of teachers unpacking contemporary poetry together. Then the poet chimed in and I was speechless.

Once the school year started, I found myself engaging in several Twitter chats per month in addition to building my network: reading articles, following teachers, looking at posts for lessons ideas, then taking what I had learned and channeling it into my classroom. I was busy!

Around the same time, I wrote a grant proposal to our local education partnership—Ventura Education Partnership. I soon found myself with poetry collections by Clint Smith, José Olivarez, Nicole Tong, Elizabeth Acevedo, Victoria Chang—and so many others. I had already started using living poets in AP Literature, and my students were responding. We watched Elizabeth Acevedo's spoken word poem "Hair" and talked about cultural identity; we worked through José Olivarez's "(citizen) (illegal)" and our conversation shifted to immigration.

Poetry became more than literature. In the past as we discussed poets from the literary canon, our conversations focused on the author's use of poetic devices and universal themes, and we always wondered how poets came up with meaning. With living poets there is less wonder. On one assignment for which students had to teach class and present an interpretation, one of my students messaged the author and received a response.

I've seen student engagement increase because many of the topics that living poets write about echo what is going on nationally; these are things students want to discuss. What was new for me was the lack of teacher support materials. I was on new ground, exploring the poems with my students and the #TeachLivingPoets community. I have had to admit when I don't know "the" interpretation (assuming there is one), but that vulnerability and risk has built a community in a classroom of learners.

I started using poetry in my AP Language class for the first time last year. Traditionally a course that focuses on nonfiction, we looked at Clint Smith's "Ode to the Only Black Kid in the Class" and analyzed the rhetoric in his message. We dove deep into the lines and then used Smith's work as a mentor text. How did I not know that poetry could be so powerful in teaching rhetoric? Living poets helped students express their voices, and I knew I was on to something. This became a springboard to similar lessons and has helped students understand the concept of rhetorical situation.

At the end of last year, my AP Literature class had the opportunity to FaceTime with Nicole Tong after we studied her debut poetry collection, *How to Prove a Theory*. Talking with a poet was an inside look at inspiration and stylistic choices. One of my students asked Nicole if her poem "Marathon" was a concrete poem because of its shape on the page, and we learned that Nicole is an avid runner and she composed as she ran. She recorded the lines on her phone, and the length of the lines equaled the intervals between her breaths. These insights, including the dedication to her friend Anna in "Grief Theory" or the background about naming her collection, are not published anywhere.

During the first week of summer, I delivered a TED Talk–style presentation for our community based on the work I had done with my grant money. I shared my journey with #TeachLivingPoets, and in my presentation I shared how I struggled through my mom's passing in 2018. In that struggle, I found the words of Clint Smith and his poem, "This Year Was the First Year I Could Not Remember Your Voice." Smith's words provided the comfort I needed during my first holiday season without her, and I have turned to those lines time and again when I have felt her absence. Poets like Clint Smith and so many others always have the right words.

#TeachLivingPoets has permeated my life and my classroom, and I am excited to see how my students grow as a result.

Conclusion: "Somewhere Other Than a Mirror"

In this book, we've focused on our lived experience of the benefits of teaching living poets for students, but one of the unintended consequences of this work is that the poems work their magic on you, and one day you catch yourself writing down a phrase, maybe a line. Being a writer has nothing to do with being published. Being a writer has everything to do with learning how to cultivate wonder and using words to express that wonder. As teachers, we need this experience, the cardio of putting words to paper, of being practitioners of what we teach, to practice what we preach. All the benefits we see when students read contemporary poetry and write poems extend to teachers when they discover new voices and begin a writing practice: a renewed love of reading, a new appreciation for working writers and artists, and the deep pleasure that comes with creating art.

In the master class workshop with Terrance Hayes at Charlotte Lit (Charlotte Center for Literary Arts).

Here's Melissa describing her experience of being a student in a workshop with Terrance Hayes:

> Being a student in Terrance Hayes's workshop allowed me a rare opportunity to connect to my students in the experience of being on the receiving end of poetry instruction. To close the workshop, Hayes gave us a writing prompt. After about twenty minutes of writing time, we had the opportunity to share our drafts. He was so kind to all who shared. He responded to each of us individually after we read our poem with things that stuck out to him (in a good way) or that he liked. He said some things to me after I read mine, but I'm pretty sure I blacked out for a second due to the fact that he was actually saying words out of his mouth about how he liked a poem I wrote. I remember him mentioning my use of a certain image, but that's about it. And I'm okay with that because I was living in the moment and just so grateful to be in that space. Hayes's kind words of praise in reaction to our poems were a gift to everyone in the room, whether they shared or not. The feelings I experienced are exactly the types of feelings I want my students to have. I want them to feel inspired, maybe even a little daring, and to leave my classroom with an excitement for poetry. #TeachLivingPoets can help you help your students feel this way.

In the introduction, we shared the story of Janais, a student in Melissa's class who had a profound experience with poetry, specifically Kaveh Akbar's work. We'd like to update you on where Janais is now, two years later, as we write this book. And finally, we conclude with one of Janais's poems, which we are honored to share.

COAUTHORS: Where are you now in your educational journey?

JANAIS: I'm currently attending Appalachian State University. I'm majoring in English with a concentration in creative writing. I haven't decided on a minor, but I'm considering double majoring within English so I can add literature studies to my current major.

COAUTHORS: What has been your favorite creative writing class at college and why?

JANAIS: My favorite creative writing class was a poetry class I took with Joseph Bathanti in fall '18. I initially took it to guarantee continued exposure to poetry during college since I hadn't decided to major in English at this point. The class was truly eye-opening for me. It's not every day you get the opportunity to study poetry under the instruction of one of your state's poet laureates! I learned an enormous amount about my own writer's voice and poetry as a craft through Joseph.

COAUTHORS: What does your writing future hold?

JANAIS: I'm not sure what I want out of my future yet. I think an MFA is the best idea of what my future holds. I would definitely love to participate in more slams and readings, mainly to open myself up to the art others have to share. There's nothing more special than the way inspiration brightens the room during a slam.

COAUTHORS: Looking back at your experience with poetry in class your senior year, how would you say it has affected you?

JANAIS: Studying poetry in my senior year changed my entire life. I think poetry was already a lifelong love of mine at that point. I desperately needed an escape from the grief and depression I felt outside of school, so starting each school day studying poetry made me truly happy. I was opened up to studying poetry as a craft rather than just reading it, and that opened me up to my first true academic love.

Back for Poetry Workshop day as an alum! From left to right: Safia Elhillo, Janais Phillips, Kaveh Akbar, R. A. Villanueva.

COAUTHORS: Specifically in regard to Kaveh Akbar, how did reading his work and meeting him impact you?

JANAIS: Reading Kaveh's work helped me see myself somewhere other than [in] a mirror. I couldn't entirely relate to his writing, but I connected to it in a unique way that I can't entirely articulate. His poem was the first thing I felt passionate enough [about] to fully throw myself into for six months since my dad's passing. Meeting him felt like meeting a hero. No one line in his poems told me everything would be okay, but every single one of his poems told me I would make it out okay.

COAUTHORS: Why do you think teachers should teach living poets?

JANAIS: There is no better opportunity for students to connect with the material they study than by teaching living poets. The passion my generation exudes for social justice, mental health, climate change, anything, everything is reflected in poetry from living poets. People like me will take the relevant nature of those poems and run with it, engage with it, and find it easier to love than some older poets. Studying living poets makes the entire discipline of poetry widely accessible to younger students.

COAUTHORS: What was the experience of writing this poem ["High Crime"] like for you?

JANAIS: This poem was difficult to write. It's my *ars poetica*, full of things I hoped I wouldn't have to talk about. I wrote and wrote and rewrote, and it took me three months to reach the final draft. If I'm being honest, the most trouble I had with this poem wasn't being honest enough to write the thing. I had much more trouble finding enough comfort within myself to feel satisfied with where I left it. It was a true challenge to stop myself from changing the whole thing every time I looked at it.

High Crime

after Kaveh Akbar

Dear reader, I wish I could tell you I care.
Words are a delicacy. I am a glutton, and I confess,
I drank poor, poor Merriam's bleeding pages dry.
My guts are bursting with syllables and syntax,
but I'd rather die of excess than feel the roar of want again.

Compulsive desire is a swift summer storm. Fear makes my eyes flash
with gold, with diamonds I stole from the sky.
My hoard of greedy, gluttonous, gilded, gold—
Gild and *guilt* sound too similar to be any less than siblings, no?
Do you find me sensible yet?

Dear reader, I wish I could tell you I'm a trusting person.
No matter how many times I consider opening up about the truth,
Restraint will always ring through my body like a bell striking twelve.
I confess, I have nothing to hide, but hide I will.
I'm not ready to bare my balefire. I'm sorry, my love.

Pity is a scam. Optimism will kill you, snake-eyes blazing.
Validation is the middle ground. *It should be.*
Put me in someone else's shoes. Easy. *It should be.*
I can feign empathy with a "real" smile, "real" sorrow, *real* joy; *I am loved!*
Do you find me practical yet?

Dear reader, I wish I could tell you I made it all up.
My life is full of half-brewed truths and weakly-flavored lies.
When I cast spells with pens and ink, I confess to my crimes wholeheartedly:

My garden grows full of baby's breath, foxglove, and mountain laurels.
This mixture of flowers, a chaos of petals, is the poison on the page.

So, call me divine and hearken to my tale! Call me royalty and bow to my glow!
If I'm sovereign, my crown is always too heavy. *Kneel and watch me wobble.*
If I'm heavenly, my halo is an anchor. Earthly pleasures always outweigh eternity.
I descended with bloody wings and a wine-soaked knife in my right hand.
Do you find me noble yet?

Dear reader, I wish I could tell you that it ends well.
I confess, I'm fortunate to derive satisfaction from my life.
And yet, I lie. I lie. I lie and I won't stop. Why would I?
I will always tear my masterpieces down before they can be seen.
I pray this won't end the same way. I'm sorry, my love.

Dear reader, I confess: Those diamonds in the night sky weren't for the taking.
Regardless, I keep them close, hoping they won't burn holes in my pockets.
I am what I say I am: a poet. I am what I know I am: a criminal.
The *ars poetica* of a thief is an admission of guilt.
I don't have to steal inspiration anymore.
I look at the diamonds and ink spills from my mouth.

How do you find me?

—Janais Phillips

Works Cited

Abdurraqib, Hanif. "I Tend to Think Forgiveness Looks the Way It Does in the Movies." *Wildness*, Issue no. 8, April 2017.

———. *They Can't Kill Us until They Kill Us.* Two Dollar Radio, 2017.

"About Clint Smith." *Clint Smith,* www.clintsmithiii.com/about. Accessed 29 Oct. 2019.

Acevedo, Elizabeth. "In Translation." *The Poet X*, HarperCollins, 2018.

Akbar, Kaveh. *Calling a Wolf a Wolf: Poems*. Alice James Books, 2017.

———. *Portrait of the Alcoholic*. Sibling Rivalry Press, 2017.

———. "The Rumpus Mini-Interview Project #130: Kaveh Akbar." *The Rumpus*, 2018.

Alfaro, Ben, and José Olivarez. *Home Court: Poems*. Red Beard Press, 2014.

Applebee, Arthur N., with Judith A. Langer. *Contexts for Learning to Write: Studies of Secondary School Instruction.* Ablex, 1984.

Aristotle. *The Art of Rhetoric.* Penguin, 1992.

Asghar, Fatimah. "If They Come for Us." *If They Come for Us: Poems*, One World, 2018.

Baca, Jimmy Santiago. "I Am Offering This Poem." *Immigrants in Our Own Land and Selected Early Poems*, New Directions, 1990.

Bayer, Scott, and Joel Garza. *Citizen Illegal by José* Olivarez *Hyperdoc.* docs.google.com/document/d/1KXwTo8eh9UGWR9AEbvAgWmYDpnzFU1Xr1fD2_UwPrYQ/edit.

———. *Counting Descent by Clint Smith Hyperdoc.* docs.google.com/document/d/1WsfkKLmhiqlJOh5t6P2E1Na4vjXMsdXlzETVQf09rXs/edit.

Blake, William. "Introduction." *Songs of Innocence and Experience*, 1789. *The Complete Writings of William Blake*, edited by Geoffrey Keynes, Oxford UP, 1966.

Bransford, John D., et al., editors. *How People Learn: Brain, Mind, Experience, and School.* Expanded ed., National Academy Press, 2004.

Britton, James, et al. *The Development of Writing Abilities (11–18).* Macmillan, 1975.

Brock, Geoffrey. "Homeland Security." *Poetry*, May 2007, https://www.poetryfoundation.org/poetrymagazine/poems/49475/homeland-security.

Brooks, Gwendolyn. "To the Young Who Want to Die." *The Golden Shovel Anthology: New Poems Honoring Gwendolyn Brooks*, Eds. Peter Kahn, Ravi Shanker, and Patricia Smith. U of Arkansas P, 2017.

Brown, Jericho. "A New Way of Living." *Lambda Literary*, 3 Apr. 2018, www.lambdaliterary.org/features/oped/04/03/a-new-way-of-living.

Burt, Stephanie. *Don't Read Poetry: A Book about How to Read Poems.* Basic Books, 2019.

———. *The Poem Is You: 60 Contemporary American Poems and How to Read Them.* Harvard UP, 2016.

Calvert, Laura. "Moving from Compliance to Agency: What Teachers Need to Make Professional Learning Work." Learning Forward and NCTAF, 2016, https://learningforward.org/wp-content/uploads/2017/08/moving-from-compliance-to-agency.pdf.

Calvocoressi, Gabrielle. "Hammond B3 Organ Cistern." *The New Yorker*, 19 Nov. 2018.

Chang, Victoria. "Dear P." *Barbie Chang*, Copper Canyon Press, 2017.

Chatti, Leila. "The Rules." *Poets.org*, 29 May 2019, https://poets.org/poem/rules.

Chen, Chen. *When I Grow Up I Want to Be a List of Further Possibilities.* BOA Editions, 2017.

Christle, Heather. "People Are a Living Structure Like a Coral Reef." *Heliopause*, Wesleyan UP, 2015.

"Citizen Read" *ArtsEmerson*, Jan.–Mar. 2018, artsemerson.org/Online/default.asp?BOparam::WScontent::loadArticle::permalink=Citizen_Read&BOparam::WScontent::loadArticle::context_id=.

Clark, Tiana. "Bear Witness." *Thrush Poetry Journal*, May 2016.

———. "Conversation with Phillis Wheatley #1." *I Can't Talk about the Trees without the Blood*, U of Pittsburgh P, 2018.

"Claudia Rankine: On Whiteness." *YouTube*, 24 Mar. 2017, https://www.youtube.com/watch?v=uCEfUMesedE.

Council of Writing Program Administrators, National Council of Teachers of English, and National Writing Project. *Framework for Success in Postsecondary Writing.* CWPA, NCTE, & NWP, 2011.

Cruz, Cynthia. "Fragment." *The Paris Review*, no. 229, 2019.

Dargan, Kyle. "Call and Response." *Honest Engine: Poems*, U of Georgia P, 2015.

Daye, Tyree. "In His Mouth." *River Hymns*, The American Poetry Review, 2017.

Diaz, Natalie. "Abecedarian Requiring Further Examination of Anglikan Seraphym Subjugation of a Wild Indian Rezervation." *When My Brother Was an Aztec*, Copper Canyon Press, 2012.

Duhamel, Denise. "Reading." *Scald*, U of Pittsburgh P, 2017.

Dungy, Camille T. "Tell It Slant: How to Write a Wise Poem." *Poetry Foundation*, 10 June 2014, https://www.poetryfoundation.org/articles/70128/tell-it-slant.

Ebarvia, Tricia. "Disrupting Texts as a Restorative Practice." *Tricia Ebarvia*, 11 July 2018, triciaebarvia.org/2018/07/11/disrupting-texts-as-a-restorative-practice/. Accessed 15 July 2018.

Effinger, Sandra. "Literary Response Journals." *Ms. Effie's Lifesavers*, 10 Feb. 2017, http://mseffie.com/assignments/poetry/poetrylrj.html.

Elhillo, Safia. *The January Children.* U of Nebraska P, 2017.

Epstein, Andrew. "Ocean Vuong (and Roger Reeves) after Frank O'Hara." *Locus Solus: The New York School of Poets*, 29 Apr. 2015, https://newyorkschoolpoets.wordpress.com/ *2015/04/29/ocean-vuong-and-roger-reeves-after-frank-ohara/.*

Francisco, Rudy. *Helium.* Button Poetry/Exploding Pinecone Press, 2017.

Gabbert, Elisa. "The Moves: Common Maneuvers in Contemporary Poetry." *The Monkey and the Wrench: Essays into Contemporary Poetics*, edited by Mary Biddinger and John Gallaher, U of Akron P, 2011.

Gay, Ross. "Sorrow Is Not My Name." *Bringing the Shovel Down*, U of Pittsburgh P, 2011.

Graff, Gerald, and Cathy Birkenstein. *"They Say/I Say": The Moves That Matter in Academic Writing*. 3rd ed., high school ed., W. W. Norton, 2014.

Haught, Kaylin. "God Says Yes to Me." *The Palm of Your Hand*, Tilbury House, 1995.

Hayes, Terrance. Introduction. *Best American Poetry 2014.* Guest edited by Terrance Hayes, series editor David Lehman, Scribner Poetry, 2014, p. xxv.

Hazelton, Rebecca. "Learning the Poetic Line: How Line Breaks Shape Meaning." *Poetry Foundation*, 8 Sept. 2014, www.poetryfoundation.org/articles/70144/learning-the-poetic-line.

Howe, Marie. "Prayer." *The Kingdom of Ordinary Time*, W.W. Norton, 2008.

Hyde, Lewis. *The Gift: Creativity and the Artist in the Modern World.* Vintage Books, 2007.

"Interview with Jericho Brown." *Lightbox Poetry*, 6 Jan. 2016, lightboxpoetry.com/?p=516.

"Jericho Brown." *Lightbox,* 6 January 2016, http://lightboxpoetry.com/?p=516.

Johnson, Frank. "Reinventing the World: José Olivarez's *Citizen Illegal.*" *The Rumpus*, 13 July 2018, therumpus.net/2018/07/citizen-illegal-by-jose-olivarez/.

Johnson, L. A. *Little Climates: Poems.* Bull City Press, 2017.

Johnson-Eilola, Johndan. "The Database and the Essay: Understanding Composition as Articulation." *Writing New Media: Theory and Applications for Expanding the Teaching of Composition*, edited by Anne Frances Wysocki, et al., Utah State UP, 2004, pp. 199–236.

"José Olivarez Bio." *José Olivarez*, joseolivarez.com/. Accessed 29 Oct. 2019.

@JulianThePoet. "Learn something from the poems you don't enjoy." *Twitter*, 14 Oct. 2019, twitter.com/julianthepoet/status/1183804435593650176?s=21.

Karr, Mary. "Writers on Writing; Negotiating the Darkness, Fortified by Poets' Strength." *The New York Times*, 14 Jan. 2002, www.nytimes.com/2002/01/14/books/writers-on-writing-negotiating-the-darkness-fortified-by-poets-strength.html.

Kaminsky, Ilya. "A Toast." *Dancing in Odessa*, Tupelo Press, 2004.

Kaye, Phil. "Before the Internet." *Button Poetry*, 16 July 2018, https://buttonpoetry.com/phil-kaye-the-big-tree/.

Kelly, Donika. "Love Poem: Centaur." *Bestiary: Poems*, Graywolf Press, 2016.

———. "The moon rose over the bay. I had a lot of feelings." *Poets.org*, 2017.

Killingsworth, M. Jimmie. *Appeals in Modern Rhetoric: An Ordinary-Language Approach*. Southern Illinois UP, 2005.

Kim, Suji Kwock. "Sono." *Best American Poetry 2018*, edited by Dana Gioia and David Lehman, Scribner Poetry, 2018, pp. 50–51.

Kittle, Penny. *Book Love: Developing Depth, Stamina, and Passion in Adolescent Readers*. Heinemann, 2013.

Kooser, Ted. "Abandoned Farmhouse." *Sure Signs: New and Selected Poems*, U of Pittsburgh P, 1980.

León, Concepción de. "3 Writers on the Emotional Toll of Being Undocumented." *The New York Times*, 16 October 2018, https://www.nytimes.com/2018/10/16/books/jose-antonio-vargas-dear-america-undocumented-writers.html.

Lerner, Ben. *The Hatred of Poetry*. Farrar, Straus and Giroux, 2016.

Leszkiewicz, Anna. "Why Are We So Worried about 'Instapoetry'?" *New Statesman America*, 6 Mar. 2019, https://www.newstatesman.com/culture/books/2019/03/instapoetry-rupi-kaur-genre-rm-drake-rh-sin-atticus-hollie-mcnish.

Lewis, Paige. "Hello! This is the poem 'People Are A Living Structure Like a Coral Reef' by Heather Christle @heatherchristle [includes picture of poem]." *Twitter*, 16 Dec. 2018, twitter.com/paige_m_lewis/status/1074490584180645888?s=21.

Limón, Ada. "I had the most immense pleasure of having a meal at Holly Hill Inn in Midway, KY inspired by my poem Carrying. . . . [includes pictures]." *Twitter*, 5 Oct. 2019, twitter.com/adalimon/status/1180655750324113408?s=11.

———. "A New National Anthem." *The Carrying: Poems*, Milkweed Editions, 2018.

———. "The Raincoat." *The Carrying*, Milkweed Editions, 2018.

Lotier, Kristopher M. "Around 1986: The Externalization of Cognition and the Emergence of Postprocess Invention." *College Composition and Communication*, vol. 67, no. 3, 2016, pp. 360–84.

Matejka, Adrian. "Space Is the Place." *Map to the Stars*, Penguin Books, 2017.

McDermott, John J. *Streams of Experience: Reflections on the History and Philosophy of American Culture*. U of Massachusetts P, 1986.

Melzer, Dan. *Assignments across the Curriculum: A National Study of College Writing*. Utah State UP, 2014.

Miller, Donalyn. *The Book Whisperer: Awakening the Inner Reader in Every Child*. Jossey-Bass, 2009.

Mishler, Peter. "Clint Smith on Protest, Art, and Protest-Art." *Literary Hub*, 9 Feb. 2017, lithub.com/clint-smith-on-protest-art-and-protest-art/.

Mishra, Pankaj. "'Open the doors and let these books in'—What Would a Truly Diverse Reading List Look Like?" *The Guardian*, 11 Nov. 2017, www.theguardian.com/books/2017/nov/11/black-and-minority-ethnic-books-authors-on-decolonising-the-canon-university-english-literature-syllabus. Accessed 15 July 2018.

O'Hara, Frank. "Katy." *The Collected Poems of Frank O'Hara*, edited by Don Allen, rev. ed., U of California P, 1995.

Olivarez, José. *Citizen Illegal: Poems*. Haymarket Books, 2018.

———. "I love talking to students about poems. . . ." *Twitter*, 4 Apr. 2019, twitter.com/_joseolivarez/status/1113879228746014720?s=21.

———. "José Olivarez: How I Wrote 'A Mexican Dreams of Heaven.'" *The Adroit Journal*, 27 February 2019, theadroitjournal.org/2019/02/27/jose-olivarez-how-i-wrote-a-mexican-dreams-of-heaven/.

———. "Remix Poems: National Poetry Month Writing Prompt 11/30." *YCA Blog*, youngchicagoauthors.org/blog/national-poetry-month-writing-prompt-11-30.

———. "Say My Name: National Poetry Month Writing Prompt 12/30." *YCA Blog*, youngchicagoauthors.org/blog/national-poetry-month-writing-prompt-12-30.

Oliver, Mary. "Wild Geese." *Dream Work*, The Atlantic Monthly Press, 1986, p. 21.

Partridge, Kate. "Say When." *RHINO*, The Poetry Forum, 2014.

———. *Ends of the Earth: Poems*. U of Alaska P, 2017.

Payton, John, et al. "The Positive Impact of Social and Emotional Learning for Kindergarten to Eighth-Grade Students." CASEL, 2008, www.casel.org/wp-content/uploads/2016/08/PDF-4-the-positive-impact-of-social-and-emotional-learning-for-kindergarten-to-eighth-grade-students-executive-summary.pdf.

Phillips, Emilia. "The Poetics of Bewilderment." *Ploughshares*, 16 Dec. 2017, blog.pshares.org/index.php/the-poetics-of-bewilderment/.

———. "The Poetics of Body Positivity." *Ploughshares*, 27 Mar. 2018, http://blog.pshares.org/index.php/the-poetics-of-body-positivity/.

Plato. *Ion*. *The Internet Classics Archive*, n.d., http://classics.mit.edu/Plato/ion.html.

"The Quarry: A Social Justice Poetry Database." *Split This Rock*, 2013, www.splitthisrock.org/poetry-database.

Rader, Dean. "Cartography; or American Allegory I." *Self-Portrait as a Wikipedia Entry*, Copper Canyon Press, 2017.

Rankine, Claudia. *Citizen: An American Lyric*. Graywolf Press, 2014.

Reiff, Mary Jo, and Anis Bawarshi. "Tracing Discursive Resources: How Students Use Prior Genre Knowledge to Negotiate New Writing Contexts in First-Year Composition." *Written Communication*, vol. 28, no. 3, pp. 312–37, 2011, english.utk.edu/wp-content/uploads/2017/06/Reiff-and-Bawarshi-Prior-Genre-Knowledge.pdf.

Rosal, Patrick. "If All My Relationships Fail and I Have No Children Do I Even Know What Love Is." *Academy of American Poets*, 23 April 2018, https://poets.org/poem/if-all-my-relationships-fail-and-i-have-no-children-do-i-even-know-what-love.

Rottmann, Amy. "Blind Date Poetry: Introducing Poetry to Today's High School Students." *Journal of Educational Research and Practice*, vol. 8, no. 1, 2018, pp. 31–40. Walden University Publishing, https://scholarworks.waldenu.edu/cgi/viewcontent.cgi?article=1260&context=jerap.

Rowlands, Kathleen Dudden. "Slay the Monster! Replacing Form-First Pedagogy with Effective Writing Instruction." *English Journal*, vol. 105, no. 6, 2016, pp. 52–58.

Ryan, Kay. "Party Ship." *Poetry*, May 2013, https://www.poetryfoundation.org/poetrymagazine/poems/56245/party-ship.

Salter, James. *Light Years*. Knopf Doubleday Publishing Group, 1975.

Santos, Greg. "Hulk Smash!" *The Best American Poetry*, 15 Apr. 2009, blog.bestamericanpoetry.com/the_best_american_poetry/2009/04/hulk-smash-by-greg-santos.html.

Serravallo, Jennifer. *Independent Reading Assessment: Grade 3, Fiction*. Scholastic, 2012.

———. *Independent Reading Assessment: Grade 4, Fiction*. Scholastic, 2012.

———. *Independent Reading Assessment: Grade 5, Fiction*. Scholastic, 2012.

Share, Don. "Introduction: The Golden Shovel." *Poetry Foundation*, 1 Feb. 2017, www.poetryfoundation.org/poetrymagazine/articles/92023/introduction-586e948ad9af8.

Smith, Clint. *Counting Descent*. Write Bloody Publishing, 2016.

———. "The Danger of Silence." *Ted.com*, July 2014, https://www.ted.com/talks/clint_smith_the_danger_of_silence?referrer=playlist-10_great_talks_to_celebrate_bl

Smith, Maggie. "Good Bones." *Good Bones*, Tupelo Press, 2017.

Soliday, Mary. *Everyday Genres: Writing Assignments Across the Disciplines*. Southern Illinois UP, 2011.

Sontag, Susan. *Regarding the Pain of Others*. Penguin, 2013.

Stevens, Wallace. *The Necessary Angel: Essays on Reality and the Imagination*. Vintage, 1965.

Stewart, Melissa. "Teaching Poetry Collections: 3 Engaging Activity Ideas to Get Your Students Thinking." *TeachLivingPoets.com*, 23 August 2018, https://teachlivingpoets.com/2018/08/23/teaching-poetry-collections-3-engaging-activity-ideas-to-get-your-students-thinking/.

Swales, John M. *Genre Analysis: English in Academic and Research Settings*. Cambridge UP, 1990.

Tamás, Rebecca. "Interview with Ariana Reines." *The White Review*, July 2019, www.thewhitereview.org/feature/interview-ariana-reines/.

Tong, Nicole. *How to Prove a Theory*. Washington Writers' Publishing House, 2017.

Villanueva, R. A. *Reliquaria*. U of Nebraska P, 2014.

Voight, Ellen Bryant. *The Art of Syntax: Rhythm of Thought, Rhythm of Song*. Graywolf Press, 2009.

Vuong, Ocean. "Someday I'll Love Ocean Vuong." *The New Yorker*, 27 Apr. 2015.

Ward, Junious. *Sing Me a Lesser Wound*. Bull City Press, 2020.

Williams, William Carlos. "Introduction to *The Wedge*." *Poetry Foundation*, 13 Oct. 2009, www.poetryfoundation.org/articles/69410/introduction-to-the-wedge.

Yancey, Kathleen Blake. "Writing in the 21st Century." NCTE Report, Feb. 2009, www.ncte.org/library/NCTEFiles/Press/Yancey_final.pdf.

Young, Dean. *The Art of Recklessness: Poetry as Assertive Force and Contradiction.* Graywolf Press, 2010, p. 14.

Zagajewski, Adam. "Try to Praise the Mutilated World." *Without End: New and Selected Poems,* Farrar, Straus and Giroux, 2002.

Zapruder, Matthew. *Why Poetry.* HarperCollins, 2017.

Zucker, Rachel. "Episode 4: Claudia Rankine." *Commonplace Podcast: Conversations with Poets (and Other People)*, 15 July 2016, www.commonpodcast.com/home/2016/7/15/episode-4-claudia-rankine.

Index

Note: An *f* following a page number indicates a figure.

Permission Acknowledgments

Selected poem from *The Poet X* by Elizabeth Acevedo. Text Copyright © 2018 by Elizabeth Acevedo. Used by permission of HarperCollins Publishers.

Excerpt from Gabrielle Calvocoressi's "Hammond B3 Organ Cistern" reprinted with permission of the author.

Victoria Chang, "Dear P" from *Barbie Chang*. Copyright © 2017 by Victoria Chang. Reprinted with the permission of The Permissions Company, LLC on behalf of Copper Canyon Press, www.coppercanyonpress.org.

Leila Chatti, "The Rules," originally published in Poem-a-Day on May 29, 2019, by the Academy of American Poets.

"When I Grow Up I Want to Be a List of Further Possibilities" from *When I Grow Up I Want to Be a List of Further Possibilities*. Copyright © 2017 by Chen Chen. Reprinted with the permission of The Permissions Company, LLC on behalf of BOA Editions, Ltd., boaeditions.org.

"People Are a Living Structure Like a Coral Reef" from What is Amazing © 2012 by Heather Christle. Published by Wesleyan University Press and reprinted with permission.

"Conversation with Phillis Wheatley #1" from *I Can't Talk about the Trees without the Blood* by Tiana Clark, ©2018. Reprinted by permission of the University of Pittsburgh Press.

"Fragment" from *How the End Begins* © 2016 by Cynthia Cruz. Appears with permission of Four Way Books. All rights reserved.

"Reading" from *Scald* by Denise Duhamel, © 2017. Reprinted by permission of the University of Pittsburgh Press.

"Sorrow Is Not My Name" from *Bringing the Shovel Down* by Ross Gay, ©2001. Reprinted by permission of the University of Pittsburgh Press.

"Love Poem: centaur" from *Bestiary*. Copyright © 2016 by Donika Kelly. Reprinted with the permission of The Permissions Company, LLC on behalf of Graywolf Press, Minneapolis, Minnesota, graywolfpress.org.

Donika Kelly, "The moon rose over the bay. I had a lot of feelings." Originally published in Poem-a-Day on November 20, 2017, by the Academy of American Poets.

"A New National Anthem" from *The Carrying* by Ada Limón (Minneapolis: Milkweed Editions, 2018). Copyright © 2018 by Ada Limón. Reprinted with permission from Milkweed Editions.

"Space Is the Place" from MAP TO THE STARS by Adrian Matejka, copyright © 2017 by Adrian Matejka. Used by permission of Penguin Books, an imprint of Penguin Publishing Group, a division of Penguin Random House LLC. All rights reserved.

"Say When" by Kate Partridge. *RHINO,* The Poetry Forum, © 2014. Reprinted with permission of the author.

Authors

Lindsay Illich received her PhD in English from Texas A&M University. She teaches writing at Curry College and serves as the director of Writing Programs. Illich is the author of three books of poetry, *Heteroglossia* (2016); *Rile & Heave,* winner of the Texas Review Press Breakthrough Prize in Poetry (2017); and *Fingerspell* (2020). Her scholarly work focuses on creativity, invention, and collaboration. She lives with her family in Milton, Massachusetts.

Melissa Alter Smith teaches high school English in Huntersville, North Carolina. She is 2017 District Teacher of the Year, an AP Reader, an NCETA Executive Board member, and a National Board Certified Teacher. She has presented at NCTIES, WVELA, NCETA, NCTE-WLU Summer Institute, NCTE, AWP, and the AP Annual Conference. Smith is also a coauthor of the Instructor's Manual and AP Correlation Guide for the 13th high school edition of *The Norton Introduction to Literature*. A runner-up for NCTE and Penguin Random House's Maya Angelou Teacher of Poetry Award, Smith is also a contributing author for aplithelp.com and the NCTE Verse project. She is the creator of the #TeachLivingPoets hashtag, and the manager and editor of teachlivingpoets.com. She has been featured on LitHub .com, in NEATE News, in NCTE's *Council Chronicle*, in ASCD's *Education Update*, at Prestwick House, at The Poetry Question, and on Education Talk Radio. Her work is focused on complicating the canon, supporting teachers, and empowering students through poetry. She lives with her family in Charlotte, North Carolina. You can follow her on Twitter and Instagram @MelAlterSmith.

This book was typeset in TheMix and Palatino by Barbara Frazier.

Typefaces used on the cover include SuperFly One and Akzidenz-Grotesk.

The book was printed on 50-lb. White Offset paper by Seaway Printing Company, Inc.